BERLITZ®

NORWEGIAN
for travellers

By the staff of Berlitz Guides

How best to use this phrase book

● We suggest that you start with the **Guide to pronunciation** (pp. 6–9), then go on to **Some basic expressions** (pp. 10–15). This gives you not only a minimum vocabulary, but also helps you get used to pronouncing the language. The phonetic transcription throughout the book enables you to pronounce every word correctly.

● Consult the **Contents** pages (3–5) for the section you need. In each chapter you'll find travel facts, hints and useful information. Simple phrases are followed by a list of words applicable to the situation.

● Separate, detailed contents lists are included at the beginning of the extensive **Eating out** and **Shopping guide** sections (Menus, p. 39, Shops and services, p. 97).

● If you want to find out how to say something in Norwegian, your fastest look-up is via the **Dictionary** section (pp. 164–189). This not only gives you the word, but is also cross-referenced to its use in a phrase on a specific page.

● If you wish to learn more about constructing sentences, check the **Basic grammar** (pp. 159–163).

● Note the **colour margins** are indexed in Norwegian and English to help both listener and speaker. Additionally, there is an **index in Norwegian** for the use of your listener.

● Throughout the book, this symbol ☛ suggests phrases your listener can use to answer you. If you still can't understand, hand this phrase book to the Norwegian-speaker to encourage pointing to an appropriate answer. The English translation for you is just alongside the Norwegian.

Second revised edition—2nd printing 1990
Printed in Switzerland

Contents

Travelling around 65

Sightseeing 80

Relaxing 86

Making friends 92

Shopping guide 97

Acknowledgments
We are particularly grateful to Dr. T.J.A. Bennett who devised the phonetic transcription of this book.

Guide to pronunciation

You'll find the pronunciation of Norwegian letters and sounds—based on the Oslo accent—explained below, as well as the symbols we use in the transcriptions. The imitated pronunciation should be read as if it were English, with exceptions as indicated below. It is based on Standard British pronunciation, though we have tried to take into account General American pronunciation as well. If you follow the instructions carefully, you'll have no difficulty in reading our transcriptions so as to make yourself understood.

In the phonetic transcription, some letters are placed in parentheses, e.g. meh(d). In daily conversation, these are rarely pronounced, although it is certainly not incorrect to do so. A bar over a vowel symbol indicates a long sound, usually a pure vowel, not a diphthong (see explanations below). Syllables printed in **bold type** should be stressed.

Consonants

Letter	Approximate pronunciation	Symbol	Example	
b, c, d, f, h, l, m, n, p, q, t, v, x	as in English			
g	1) before **ei**, **i** and **y**, generally like **y** in **y**es	y	**gi**	yee
	2) before **e** and **i** in some words of French origin, like **sh** in **sh**ut	sh	**geni**	sheh**nee**
	3) elsewhere, like **g** in **g**o	g	**gått**	got
gj	like **y** in **y**es	y	**gjest**	yehst
j	like **y** in **y**es	y	**ja**	yaa
k	1) before **i**, and **y**, generally like **ch** in German i**ch** (quite like **h** in **h**uge, but with the tongue raised a little higher)	kh	**kino**	**khee**noo
	2) elsewhere, like **k** in **k**it	k	**kaffe**	**kah**fer

kj	like **ch** in German **ich** (quite like **h** in **h**uge, but with the tongue raised a little higher)	kh	**kjøre**	**khū**rrer
r	rolled near the front of the mouth (except in south-western Norway, where it's pronounced in the back of the mouth, like in French)	r	**rare**	raarer
rs	like **sh** in **sh**ut	sh	**norsk**	noshk
s	like **s** in **s**it	s/ss	**spise**	sp**ee**sser
sj	generally like **sh** in **sh**ut	sh	**stasjon**	stah**shōōn**
sk	1) before **i, y** and **ø**, generally like **sh** in **sh**ut	sh	**ski**	shee
	2) elsewhere, like **sk** in **sk**ate	sk	**skole**	**skōō**ler
skj	like **sh** in **sh**ut	sh	**skje**	shāy
w	like **v** in **v**ice	v	**whisky**	viski
z	like **s** in **s**it	s	**zoom**	sōōm

If preceded by **r**, the consonants **l, n** and **t** (and sometimes **d**) are pronounced with the tip of the tongue turned up well behind the front teeth. The **r** then ceases to be pronounced, but influences the tone of the following consonant. We indicate this pronunciation by printing a small **r** above the line (e.g. pah^{r}t). (This "retroflex" pronunciation also occurs in words ending with an **r** if the following word begins with a **d**, **l**, **n**, **s** or **t**.)

Silent consonants

1. The letter **d** is generally silent after **l, n** or **r** (e.g. ho**ld**e, la**nd**, gå**rd**).
2. The letter **g** is silent in the endings **-lig** and **-ig**.
3. The letter **h** is silent when followed by a consonant (e.g. **h**jem, **h**va).
4. The letter **t** is silent in the definite form ("the") of neuter nouns (e.g. eple**t**) and in the pronoun **det**.
5. The letter **v** is silent in certain words (e.g. sel**v**, tol**v**, hal**v**).

Vowels

In Norwegian, a vowel is generally long in stressed syllables when it's the final letter or followed by one consonant only, and short if followed by two or more consonants.

a	1) when long, like **a** in car	aa	**dag**	daag
	2) when short, between **a** in cat and **u** in cut	ah	**takk**	tahk
e	1) when long, like **ay** in say, but a pure vowel, not a diphthong	a̅y̅	**sent**	sa̅y̅nt
	2) when followed by **r**, often like **a** in man (long or short)	æ̅	**her**	hæ̅r
		æ	**herre**	**hæ**rer
	3) when short, like **e** in get	eh	**penn**	pehn
	4) when unstressed, like **a** in about	er *	**betale**	ber**taa**ler
i	1) when long, like **ee** in bee	ee	**hit**	heet
	2) when short, like **i** in sit	i	**sitt**	sit
o	1) when long, often like **oo** in soon, but with the lips more tightly rounded	o̅o̅	**ord**	o̅o̅r
	2) the same sound can be short, like **oo** in foot	oo	**ost**	oost
	3) when long, sometimes like **aw** in saw	aw	**tog**	tawg
	4) when short, sometimes like **o** in got (British pronunciation)	o	**stoppe**	**stop**per
u	1) something like **ew** in few, or Scottish **oo** in good (long or short); since it is very close to the Norwegian **y**-sound, we use the same symbol for both	e̅w̅	**mur**	me̅w̅r
		ew	**busk**	bewsk
	2) occasionally like **oo** in foot	oo	**nummer**	**noom**merr
y	very much like the sound described under **u** (1) above (long or short); put your tongue in the position for the **ee** in bee, and then round your lips as for the **oo** in pool	e̅w̅	**by**	be̅w̅
		ew	**bygge**	**bew**ger

* The **r** should not be pronounced when reading this transcription.

æ	like **a** in **act** (long or short)	ǣ æ	**lære** **færre**	lǣrer færer
ø	like **ur** in **fur**, but with the lips rounded (long or short)	ūr̄ * ur *	**dør** **sønn**	dūr̄r surn
å	1) when long, like **aw** in **saw** 2) when short, like **o** in **got** (British pronunciation)	aw o	**såpe** **sånn**	**saw**per son

Diphthongs

au	rather like **ou** in **loud**, though the first part is the Norwegian æ-sound	ou	**sau**	sou
ei, eg, egn	like **ai** in **wait**, though the first part is the Norwegian æ-sound	æi	**geit** **jeg** **tegne**	yæit yæi **tæi**ner
øy	rather like **oy** in **boy**, though the first part is the Norwegian ø-sound	oy	**gøy**	goy

Intonation

Norwegian uses intonation (tones) to distinguish between certain words. Since no one expects a foreigner to master such subtleties, these tones are not shown in our transcriptions.

Pronunciation of the Norwegian alphabet

A	aa	**I**	ee	**Q**	kēw̄	**X**	ehkss
B	bāȳ	**J**	yod	**R**	ær	**Y**	ēw̄
C	sāȳ	**K**	kaw	**S**	ehss	**Z**	seht
D	dāȳ	**L**	ehl	**T**	tāȳ	**Æ**	ǣ
E	āȳ	**M**	ehm	**U**	ēw̄	**Ø**	ūr̄
F	ehf	**N**	ehn	**V**	vāȳ	**Å**	aw
G	gāȳ	**O**	ōō	**W**	**dob**berlt-vāȳ		
H	haw	**P**	pāȳ				

* The r should not be pronounced when reading this transcription.

Some basic expressions

Yes.	**Ja.**	yaa
No.	**Nei.**	næi
Please.	**Vær (så) snill å … / …, takk.**	vǣr (saw) snil aw/ … tahk
Thank you.	**Takk.**	tahk
Thank you very much.	**Mange takk.**	**mahng**er tahk
That's all right/ You're welcome.	**Ingen årsak.**	**ing**ern **aw**shaak

Greetings *Hilsning*

Good morning.	**God morgen.**	goo**mawer**^{r}n
Good afternoon.	**God dag.**	goo**daag**
Good evening.	**God aften/God kveld.**	goo(d)**ahf**tern/goo**kvehl**
Good night.	**God natt.**	goo**naht**
Goodbye.	**Adjø.**	ah**dyūr**
See you later.	**På gjensyn/Vi ses.**	paw **yehn**sēwn/vee sāyss
Hello/Hi!	**Hallo/Hei!**	hah**lōō**/hæi
How do you do? (Pleased to meet you.)	**God dag.**	goo**daag**
How are you?	**Hvordan står det til?**	**voo**^{r}dahn stawr deh til
Very well, thanks. And you?	**Bare bra, takk. Og med deg?**	**baa**rer braa tahk. o(g) meh(d) dæi
Fine.	**Bra, takk.**	braa tahk
I beg your pardon?	**Unnskyld?**	**ewn**shewl
Excuse me. (May I get past?)	**Unnskyld.**	**ewn**shewl
Sorry!	**Beklager!**	ber**klaa**gerr

INTRODUCTIONS, see page 92

Questions *Spørsmål*

Where?	**Hvor?**	voor
How?	**Hvordan/Hvor?**	**voo**[r]dahn/voor
When?	**Når?**	nor
What?	**Hva?**	vaa
Why?	**Hvorfor?**	**voor**for
Who?	**Hvem?**	vehm
Which?	**Hvilken*?**	**vil**kern
Where is ...?	**Hvor er ...?**	voor ær
Where are ...?	**Hvor er ...?**	voor ær
Where can I find ...?	**Hvor finner jeg ...?**	voor **fin**nerr yæi
Where can I get ...?	**Hvor kan jeg få tak i ...?**	voor kahn yæi faw taak ee
How far?	**Hvor langt?**	voor lahngt
How long?	**Hvor lenge?**	voor **leh**nger
How much?	**Hvor mye?**	voor **mew**er
How many?	**Hvor mange?**	voor **mah**nger
How much does this cost?	**Hvor mye koster dette**?**	voor **mew**er **kos**terr **deh**ter
How do I get to ...?	**Hvordan kommer jeg til ...?**	**voo**[r]dahn **kom**merr yæi til
When does ... open/close?	**Når åpner/ stenger ...?**	nor **awp**nerr/ **stehng**err
What do you call this/that in Norwegian?	**Hva heter dette/ det på norsk?**	vaa **hay**terr **deh**ter/ deh paw noshk
What does this/ that mean?	**Hva betyr dette/ det?**	vaa ber**tewr** **deh**ter/deh
Who's that?	**Hvem er det?**	vehm ær deh
Which bus goes to ...?	**Hvilken buss går til ...?**	**vil**kern bewss gawr til

* Common gender; neuter = *hvilket*; plural = *hvilke*.
** Neuter; common gender = *denne*; plural = *disse* (see also grammar section, page 161).

Do you speak ...? *Snakker du ...?*

Do you speak English?	**Snakker du engelsk?**	**snah**kerr dew **ehng**erlsk
Does anyone here speak English?	**Er det noen her som snakker engelsk?**	ær deh **no̅o̅**ern hæ̅r som **snah**kerr **ehng**erlsk
I don't speak (much) Norwegian.	**Jeg snakker ikke (så bra) norsk.**	yæi **snah**kerr **ik**ker (saw braa) noshk
Could you speak more slowly?	**Kan du snakke litt langsommere?**	kahn dew **snah**ker lit **lahng**sommerer
Could you repeat that?	**Kan du gjenta det?**	kahn dew **yehn**tah deh
Could you spell it?	**Kan du stave det?**	kahn dew **staa**ver deh
How do you pronounce this?	**Hvordan uttaler du dette?**	**voo**[r]dahn **e̅w̅**tahlerr dew **deh**ter
Could you write it down, please?	**Kan du skrive det ned, er du snill?**	kahn dew **skree**ver deh na̅y̅(d) ær dew snil
Can you translate this for me/us?	**Kan du oversette dette for meg/oss?**	kahn dew **aw**vershehter **deh**ter for mæi/oss
Could you point to the ... in the book?	**Kan du peke på ... i boken?**	kahn dew **pa̅y̅**ker paw ... ee **bo̅o̅**kern
phrase	**uttrykket***	**e̅w̅**trewker
sentence	**setningen**	**seht**ningern
word	**ordet**	**o̅o̅**rer
Just a moment.	**Et øyeblikk.**	eht **oy**erblik
I'll see if I can find it in this book.	**Jeg skal se om jeg kan finne det i denne boken.**	yæi skahl sa̅y̅ om yæi kahn **fin**ner deh ee **deh**ner **bo̅o̅**kern
I understand.	**Jeg forstår.**	yæi fo**shtawr**
I don't understand.	**Jeg forstår ikke.**	yæi fo**shtawr ik**ker
Do you understand?	**Forstår du?**	fo**shtawr** dew

Can/May ...? *Kan ...?*

Can I have ...?	**Kan jeg få ...?**	kahn yæi faw
Can we have ...?	**Kan vi få ...?**	kahn vee faw

* For information on the definite article, see grammar section, page 159.

Can you show me ...?	**Kan du vise meg ...?**	kahn dew **veesser** mæi
I can't.	**Jeg kan ikke.**	yæi kahn **ikker**
Can you tell me ...?	**Kan du si meg ...?**	kahn dew see mæi
Can you help me?	**Kan du hjelpe meg?**	kahn dew **yehl**per mæi
Can I help you?	**Kan jeg hjelpe deg?**	kahn yæi **yehl**per dæi
Can you direct me to ...?	**Kan du vise meg veien til ...?**	kahn dew **veesser** mæi **væiern** til

Do you want ...? *Ønsker du ...?*

I'd like to ...	**Jeg vil gjerne ...**	yæi vil **yǣʳner**
We'd like to ...	**Vi vil gjerne ...**	vee vil **yǣʳner**
I'd like a ...	**Jeg vil gjerne ha en/et ...**	yæi vil **yǣʳner** haa ehn/eht
Could you bring/ give me ...?	**Kan du gi meg ...?**	kahn dew yee mæi
Could you show me ...?	**Kan du vise meg ...?**	kahn dew **veesser** mæi
I'm looking for ...	**Jeg ser etter ...**	yæi sa̅y̅r **ehterr**
I'm searching for ...	**Jeg leter etter ...**	yæi **la̅y̅**terr **ehterr**
I'm hungry.	**Jeg er sulten.**	yæi ær **sewl**tern
I'm thirsty.	**Jeg er tørst.**	yæi ær tursht
I'm tired.	**Jeg er trett.**	yæi ær treht
I'm lost.	**Jeg hat gått meg bort.**	yæi haar got mæi booʳt
It's important.	**Det er viktig.**	deh ær **vikti**
It's urgent.	**Det haster.**	deh **hah**sterr

It is/There is ... *Det er ...*

It is ...	**Det er ...**	deh ær
Is it ...?	**Er det ...?**	ær deh
It isn't ...	**Det er ikke ...**	deh ær **ikker**
Here it is.	**Her er det/den.**	hǣr ær deh/dehn
Here they are.	**Her er de.**	hǣr ær dee

There it is.	**Der er det.**	dǣr ær deh
There they are.	**Der er de.**	dǣr ær dee
There is/are ...	**Det er ...**	deh ær
Is/Are there ...?	**Er det ...?**	ær deh
There isn't/aren't ...	**Det er ikke ...**	deh ær **ik**ker
There isn't any.	**Det er ikke noe.**	deh ær **ik**ker **nōō**er
There aren't any.	**Det er ikke noen.**	deh ær **ik**ker **nōō**ern

Opposites *Motsetninger*

beautiful/ugly	**pen/stygg***	pāyn/stewg
better/worse	**bedre/verre**	**bāy**drer/**væ**rer
big/small	**stor/liten**	stōōr/**lee**tern
cheap/expensive	**billig/dyr**	**bil**li/dēwr
early/late	**tidlig/sen**	**tee**li/sāyn
easy/difficult	**lett/vanskelig**	leht/**vahn**skerli
free (vacant)/ occupied	**ledig/opptatt**	**lāy**di/**op**taht
full/empty	**full/tom**	fewl/tom
good/bad	**bra/dårlig**	braa/**daw**^{r}li
heavy/light	**tung/lett**	toong/leht
here/there	**her/der**	hǣr/dǣr
hot/cold	**varm/kald**	vahrm/kahl
near/far	**nær/fjern**	nǣr/fyǣ^{r}n
next/last	**neste/siste**	**neh**ster/**sis**ter
old/new	**gammel/ny**	**gah**merl/nēw
old/young	**gammel/ung**	**gah**merl/oong
open/shut	**åpen/stengt**	**aw**pern/stehngt
quick/slow	**rask/sakte**	rahsk/**sahk**ter
right/wrong	**riktig/feil**	**rik**ti/fæil

Quantities *Mengde*

a little/a lot	**lite/mye**	**lee**ter/**mēw**er
few/a few	**få/noen (få)**	faw/**nōō**ern (faw)
much/many	**mye/mange**	**mēw**er/**mahng**er
more/less	**mer/mindre**	māyr/**min**drer
more than/less than	**mer enn/mindre enn**	māyr ehn/**min**drer ehn

* For neuter and plural forms, see grammar section, page 160 (adjectives).

enough/too much	**nok/for mye**	nok/for **mewer**
some/any	**litt, noe(n)/noe(n)**	lit, **noo**er(n)/**noo**er(n)

A few more useful words *Noen flere nyttige ord*

above	**over**	**aw**verr
after	**etter**	**eh**terr
and	**og**	o(g)
at	**ved**	veh(d)
before	**før**	furr
behind	**bak**	baak
below	**under**	**ew**nerr
between	**mellom**	**meh**lom
but	**men**	mehn
down/downstairs	**ned/nede**	nay(d)/**nay**der
during	**i løpet av**	ee **lur**per(t) ahv
for	**for**	for
from	**fra**	fraa
in	**i**	ee
inside	**inne**	**in**ner
never	**aldri**	**ahl**dri
next to	**ved siden av**	veh(d) **see**dern ahv
none	**ingen**	**ing**ern
not	**ikke**	**ik**ker
nothing	**ingenting, ikke noe**	**ing**ernting, **ik**ker **noo**er
now	**nå**	naw
on	**på**	paw
only	**bare**	**baa**rer
or	**eller**	**eh**lerr
outside	**ute**	**ew**ter
perhaps	**kanskje**	**kahn**sher
since	**siden**	**see**dern
soon	**snart**	snaa[r]t
then	**da**	dah/daa
through	**gjennom**	**yeh**nom
to	**til**	til
too (also)	**også**	**os**so
towards	**mot**	moot
under	**under**	**ew**nerr
until	**til**	til
up/upstairs	**opp/oppe**	op/**op**per
very	**meget**	**may**gert
with	**med**	meh(d)
without	**uten**	**ew**tern
yet	**ennå**	**eh**naw

Arrival

Passport control *Passkontroll*

Here's my passport.	**Her er passet mitt.**	hæ̅r ær **pah**sser mit
I'll be staying ...	**Jeg kommer til å bli ...**	yæi **kom**merr til aw blee
a few days a week a month	**noen dager** **en uke** **en måned**	**noo**ern **daa**gerr ehn **ew**ker ehn **maw**nerd
I don't know yet.	**Jeg vet ikke ennå.**	yæi vāyt **ik**ker **eh**naw
I'm here on holiday (vacation).	**Jeg er her på ferie.**	yæi ær hæ̅r paw **fāy**ryer
I'm here on business.	**Jeg er her i forretninger.**	yæi ær hæ̅r ee forr**eht**ningerr
I'm just passing through.	**Jeg er bare på gjennomreise.**	yæi ær **baa**rer paw **yeh**nomræisser

If things become difficult:

I'm sorry, I don't understand.	**Jeg beklager, men jeg forstår ikke.**	yæi ber**klaa**gerr mehn yæi fo**shtawr ik**ker
Does anyone here speak English?	**Er det noen her som snakker engelsk?**	ær deh **noo**ern hæ̅r som **snah**kerr **ehng**erlsk

TOLL
CUSTOMS

After collecting your baggage at the airport (*flyplassen*—**flew**plahssern), you have a choice: use the green exit if you have nothing to declare, or leave via the red exit if you have items to declare.

varer å fortolle goods to declare	**ingenting å fortolle** nothing to declare

The chart below shows what you can bring in duty (tax) free (the allowances in parentheses are for non-European residents).*

Cigarettes		Cigars		Tobacco	Spirits		Wine
200 (400)	or	250 g. (500 g.)	or	250 g. (500 g.)	1 l. (1 l.	and and	1 l. 1 l.)

I have nothing to declare.	**Jeg har ikke noe å fortolle.**	yæi haar **ikker nooer** aw fo^r**toller**
I have ...	**Jeg har ...**	yæi haar
a carton of cigarettes	**en kartong sigaretter**	ehn kah^r**tong** siggahr**reh**terr
a bottle of whisky	**en flaske whisky**	ehn **flahs**ker **vis**ki
That's for my personal use.	**Det er til personlig bruk.**	deh ær til pæ**shoon**li brewk
This is a gift.	**Dette er en gave.**	**deh**ter ær ehn **gaa**ver

Passet, takk.	Your passport, please.
Har du noe å fortolle?	Do you have anything to declare?
Vær snill å åpne denne bagen.	Please open this bag.
Du må betale toll for dette.	You'll have to pay duty (tax) on this.
Har du mer bagasje?	Do you have any more luggage?

* All allowances are subject to change.

Baggage—Porter *Bagasje – Bærer*

Where are the luggage trolleys (carts)?	**Hvor er bagasje-trallene?**	voor ær bah**gaa**sher-trahlerner
Porter!	**Bærer!**	**bǣ**rerr
Please take this luggage.	**Vær så snill å ta denne bagasjen.**	vǣr saw snil aw taa **deh**ner bah**gaa**shern
That's my suitcase/ bag.	**Det er min koffert/ bag.**	deh ær meen **kooffer**^{r}t/ "bag"
That one is mine.	**Den der er min.**	dehn dǣr ær meen
Please take this to the ...	**Vær så snill å ta dette til ...**	vǣr saw snil aw taa **deh**ter til
bus	**bussen**	**bews**sern
information desk	**informasjons-skranken**	informah**shōōns**-skrahngkern
luggage lockers	**oppbevarings-boksene**	**op**bervaaringsbokserner
taxi	**drosjen**	**dro**shern
How much is that?	**Hvor mye blir det?**	voor **mew**er bleer deh
There's one suit-case missing.	**Det mangler en koffert.**	deh **mahng**lerr ehn **kooffer**^{r}t

Changing money *Valutaveksling*

Where's the currency exchange office?	**Hvor er vekslings-kontoret?**	voor ær **vehk**shlings-koon**tōō**rer
Can you change these traveller's cheques (checks)?	**Kan du veksle disse reisesjekkene?**	kahn dew **vehk**shler **dis**ser **ræi**ssershehkerner
I'd like to change some ...	**Jeg vil gjerne veksle noen ...**	yæi vil **yæ**^{r}ner **vehk**shler **nōō**ern
dollars	**dollar**	**dol**lahr
pounds	**pund**	pewn
Can you change this into Norwegian kroner?	**Kan du veksle dette til norske kroner?**	kahn dew **vehk**shler **deh**ter til **nosh**ker **krōō**nerr
What's the ex-change rate?	**Hva er vekslings-kursen?**	vaa ær **vehk**shlings-kewshern

BANK—CURRENCY, see page 129

Where ...? *Hvor ...?*

Where is the ...?	**Hvor er ...?**	voor ær
booking office	**billettkontoret**	bil**leht**koontoorer
duty (tax)-free shop	**tax-free-butikken**	**tahks**-free-bewtikkern
newsstand	**aviskiosken**	ah**vees**khyoskern
restaurant	**restauranten**	rehstew**rahng**ern
Where can I hire (rent) a car?	**Hvor kan jeg leie en bil?**	voor kahn yæi **læi**er ehn beel
Where can I get a taxi?	**Hvor kan jeg få tak i en drosje?**	voor kahn yæi faw taak ee ehn **dro**sher
How do I get to ...?	**Hvordan kommer jeg til ...?**	**voo**^{r}dahn **kom**merr yæi til
Is there a bus into town?	**Går det en buss inn til byen?**	gawr deh ehn bewss in til **bew**ern

Hotel reservation *Værelsesbestilling*

Do you have a hotel guide (directory)?	**Har du en hotell-fortegnelse?**	haar dew ehn hoo**tehl**-fo^{r}tæinerlser
Could you reserve a room for me?	**Kan du bestille et rom til meg?**	kahn dew ber**stil**ler eht room til mæi
in the centre	**i sentrum**	ee **sehn**trewm
near the airport	**i nærheten av flyplassen**	ee **nær**hehtern ahv **flew**plahssern
near the railway station	**i nærheten av jernbanestasjonen**	ee **nær**hehtern ahv **yæ^{r}n**baanerstah-shoonern
a single room	**et enkeltrom**	eht **ehng**kerltroom
a double room	**et dobbeltrom**	eht **dob**berltroom
not too expensive	**ikke for dyrt**	**ik**ker for dew^{r}t
I'll be staying from ... to ...	**Jeg kommer til å bli fra ... til ...**	yæi **kom**merr til aw blee fraa ... til
Where is the hotel?	**Hvor er hotellet?**	voor ær hoo**teh**ler
Can you recommend a guesthouse?	**Kan du anbefale et pensjonat?**	kahn dew **ahn**berfahler eht pahngshoo**naat**
Are there any flats (apartments) vacant?	**Fins det noen ledige leiligheter?**	finss deh **noo**ern **lay**-deeyer **læi**lihehterr
Do you have a street map?	**Har du et kart over byen?**	haar dew eht kah^{r}t **aw**verr **bew**ern

HOTEL/ACCOMMODATION, see page 22

Car hire (rental) *Bilutleie*

To hire a car you must produce a valid driving licence, that you have held for at least one year, and your passport. Some firms set a minimum age of 21, others 23, 25 or 30 depending on the vehicle's engine size. Most companies require a deposit, but this is waived if you present a recognized credit card.

I'd like to hire (rent) a car.	**Jeg vil gjerne leie en bil.**	yæi vil **yæ**^{r}ner **læi**er ehn beel
small	**liten**	**lee**tern
medium-sized	**mellomstor**	**meh**lomsto̅o̅r
large	**stor**	sto̅o̅r
automatic	**med automatgir**	meh(d) outoo**maat**geer
I'd like it for ...	**Jeg vil ha den ...**	yæi vil haa dehn
a day	**en dag**	ehn daag
a week	**en uke**	ehn **e̅w̅**ker
Are there any weekend arrangements?	**Fins det noen weekend-tilbud?**	finss deh **no̅o̅**ern **veek**ehnd-tilbe̅w̅d
Do you have any special rates?	**Har dere noen spesialpriser?**	haar **da̅y̅**rer **no̅o̅**ern spehsseе**aal**preesserr
What's the charge ...?	**Hvor mye koster det ...?**	voor **me̅w̅**er **kos**terr deh
per day	**pr. dag**	pær daag
per week	**pr. uke**	pær **e̅w̅**ker
Is mileage included?	**Er kjørelengden inkludert?**	ær **khu̅r̅**rerlehngdern inklew**day**^{r}**t**
What's the charge per kilometre?	**Hvor mye koster det pr. kilometer?**	voor **me̅w̅**er **kos**terr deh pær **khil**loomayterr
I'd like to leave the car in ...	**Jeg vil gjerne levere bilen tilbake i ...**	yæi vil **yæ**^{r}ner leh**va̅y̅**rer **bee**lern til**baa**ker ee
I'd like full insurance.	**Jeg vil ha full forsikring.**	yæi vil haa fewl fo**shik**ring
How much is the deposit?	**Hvor mye må jeg betale i depositum?**	voor **me̅w̅**er maw yæi ber**taa**ler ee deh**po̅o̅**-ssitewm
I have a credit card.	**Jeg har kredittkort.**	yæi haar kreh**dit**ko^{r}t
Here's my driving licence.	**Her er førerkortet mitt.**	hær ær **fu̅r̅**rerrko^{r}ter mit

CAR, see page 75

Taxi *Drosje/Taxi*

All taxis are metered. When they are free, the "Taxi" sign on the roof is illuminated. Drivers rarely cruise for passengers and are not allowed to pick up customers within 100 metres of a taxi rank (those waiting at the rank have priority).

Where can I get a taxi?	**Hvor kan jeg få tak i en drosje?**	voor kahn yæi faw taak ee ehn **dro**sher
Where is the taxi rank (stand)?	**Hvor er drosje-holdeplassen?**	voor ær **dro**sher-hollerplahssern
Could you get me a taxi?	**Kan du skaffe meg en drosje?**	kahn dew **skah**fer mæi ehn **dro**sher
What's the fare to ...?	**Hva koster det til ...?**	vaa **kos**terr deh til
How far is it to ...?	**Hvor langt er det til ...?**	voor lahngt ær deh til
Take me to ...	**Kjør meg til ...**	khu̅r̅r mæi til
this address	**denne adressen**	**deh**ner ah**drehs**sern
the airport	**flyplassen**	**fle̅w̅**plahssern
the town centre	**sentrum**	**sehn**trewm
the ... Hotel	**... hotell**	... hoo**tehl**
the railway station	**jernbanestasjonen**	**yæ^{r}n**baanerstahsho̅o̅nern
Turn ... at the next corner.	**Sving til ... ved neste gatehjørne.**	sving til ... veh(d) **neh**ster **gaa**teryu̅r̅^{r}ner
right/left	**høyre/venstre**	**hoy**rer/**vehn**strer
Go straight ahead.	**Kjør rett frem.**	khu̅r̅r reht frehm
Please stop here.	**Stans her.**	stahnss hæ̅r̅
I'm in a hurry.	**Jeg har det travelt.**	yæi haar deh **traa**verlt
Could you drive more slowly?	**Kan du kjøre litt saktere?**	kahn dew khu̅r̅rer lit **sahk**terrer
Could you help me carry my luggage?	**Kan du hjelpe meg å bære bagasjen?**	kahn dew **yehl**per mæi aw **bæ̅r̅**er bah**gaa**shern
Could you wait for me?	**Kan du vente på meg?**	kahn dew **vehn**ter paw mæi
I'll be back in 10 minutes.	**Jeg er tilbake om 10 minutter.**	yæi ær til**baa**ker om 10 min**new**ter
How much do I owe you?	**Hvor mye skylder jeg?**	voor **me̅w̅**er **shew**lerr yæi?

TIPPING, see inside back cover

Hotel—Other accommodation

Early reservation and confirmation are essential in most major tourist centres during high season. Most towns and arrival points have a tourist information office (*turistkontor*—tew**rist**koontoor) with an accommodation service (*innkvarterings-service*—**in**kvah^{r}tayrings-surrviss); that's the place to go to if you're stuck for a room.

Although there is no official rating system, there are different classes of accommodation.

Hotell (hoo**tehl**) — Hotel; simple or deluxe, your room will be spotless. Facilities—and prices—vary across a wide range. Breakfast is usually included; half- and full-board accommodation is also available.

Turisthotell (tew**rist**hootehl) — Tourist hotel; high-standard resort establishments mostly located in the fjord country. Most offer only half- or full-board accommodation.

Hytte (**hew**ter) — Hut/Chalet; self-catering accommodation that can be hired by the week.

Høyfjellshotell (**hoy**fyehls-hootehl) — Mountain hotel; first-class or deluxe establishments in winter-sports resorts. Most offer only full-board accommodation.

Fjellstue (**fyehl**stewer) — Mountain inn; unpretentious but scrupulously clean establishments. Most offer only full-board accommodation, serving wholesome food.

Pensjonat (pahngshoo**naat**) — Guesthouse; offers full- or half-board accommodation.

Turisthytte (tew**rist**hewter) — Tourist hut; simple hostels, some with a café in the grounds. Most bedrooms are for four to six people.

Vandrerhjem (**vahn**drerryehm) — Youth and family hostel; for the backpack brigade. Sleeping arrangements may be in dormitories.

Checking in—Reception *Ankomst – Resepsjon*

My name is ...	**Mitt navn er ...**	mit nahvn ær
I have a reservation.	**Jeg har bestilt rom.**	yæi haar ber**stilt** room
We've reserved 2 rooms.	**Vi har bestilt 2 rom.**	vee haar ber**stilt** 2 room
Here's the confirmation.	**Her er bekreftelsen.**	hæ̅r ær ber**krehf**terlsern
Do you have any vacancies?	**Har dere noen ledige rom?**	haar **da̅y̅**rer **no̅o̅**ern **la̅y̅**deeyer room
I'd like a ...	**Jeg vil gjerne ha et ...**	yæi vil **yæ^{r}**ner haa eht
single room	**enkeltrom**	**ehng**kerltroom
double room	**dobbeltrom**	**dob**berltroom
We'd like a room ...	**Vi vil gjerne ha et rom ...**	vee vil **yæ^{r}**ner haa eht room
with twin beds	**med to senger**	meh(d) to̅o̅ **sehng**err
with a double bed	**med dobbeltseng**	meh(d) **dob**berltsehng
with a bath	**med bad**	meh(d) baad
with a shower	**med dusj**	meh(d) dewsh
with a balcony	**med balkong**	meh(d) bahl**kong**
with a view	**med utsikt**	meh(d) **e̅w̅**tsikt
at the front	**på forsiden**	paw **fo**sheedern
at the back	**på baksiden**	paw **baak**seedern
It must be quiet.	**Det må være rolig.**	deh maw **væ̅**rer **ro̅o̅**li
What floor is it on?	**I hvilken etasje er det?**	ee **vil**kern eh**taa**sher ær deh
Is there ...?	**Fins det ...?**	finss deh
air conditioning	**air-conditioning**	**a̅y̅r**-kondisherning
a conference room	**konferanserom**	koonferr**ahng**serroom
a gymnasium	**trimrom**	**trim**room
heating	**varme**	**vahr**mer
hot water	**varmt vann**	vahrmt vahn
a laundry service	**vaskeri-service**	vahskerr**ee**-su̅rrviss
a radio/television in the room	**radio/TV på rommet**	**raa**dyoo/**ta̅y̅**veh paw **room**mer
running water	**rennende vann**	**reh**nerner vahn
a sauna	**badstue/sauna**	**bah**stew/**sou**nah
a swimming pool	**badebasseng**	**baa**derbahssehng
a private toilet	**toalett på rommet**	tooah**leht** paw **room**mer

CHECKING OUT, see page 31

Could you put an extra bed/a cot in the room?	**Kan du sette inn en ekstra seng/barne-seng på rommet?**	kahn dew **seh**ter in ehn **ehks**trah sehng/**baa^{r}**ner-sehng paw **room**mer

How much? *Hvor mye?*

How much does it cost ...?	**Hvor mye koster det ...?**	voor **mew**er **kos**terr deh
per night	**pr. natt**	pær naht
per week	**pr. uke**	pær **ew**ker
for bed and breakfast	**for rom med frokost**	for room meh(d) **froo**kost
excluding meals	**uten måltider**	**ew**tern **mawl**teederr
for full board (A.P.)	**for helpensjon**	for **hay**lpahngshoon
for half board (M.A.P.)	**for halvpensjon**	for **hahl**pahngshoon
Is ... included?	**Er ... inkludert?**	ær ... inklew**day^{r}t**
breakfast	**frokost**	**froo**kost
value-added tax (sales tax)	**moms**	moomss
Do you have reduced rates for the weekend?	**Er det lavere pris i helgen?**	ær deh **laa**verrer preess ee **hehl**gern
Is there any reduction for children?	**Er det reduksjon for barn?**	ær deh rehdewk**shoon** for baa^{r}n
Do you charge for the baby?	**Koster det noe for babyen?**	**kos**terr deh **noo**er for **bay**byern
That's too expensive.	**Det er for dyrt.**	deh ær for dew^{r}t
Do you have anything cheaper?	**Har dere noe rimeligere?**	haar **day**rer **noo**er **ree**merleeyerrer

How long? *Hvor lenge?*

We'll be staying ...	**Vi blir ...**	vee bleer
overnight only	**bare natten over**	**baa**rer **nah**tern **aw**verr
a few days	**et par dager**	eht pahr **daa**gerr
until Sunday morning	**til søndag morgen**	til **surn**dah(g) **mawer^{r}n**
a week (at least)	**en uke (minst)**	ehn **ew**ker (minst)
I don't know yet.	**Jeg vet ikke ennå.**	yæi vayt **ik**ker **eh**naw

NUMBERS, see page 147/DAYS OF THE WEEK, see page 150

Decision *Beslutning*

May I see the room?	**Kan jeg få se rommet?**	kahn yæi faw sa̅y̅ **room**mer
That's fine. I'll take it.	**Det er bra. Jeg tar det.**	deh ær braa. yæi taar deh
No. I don't like it.	**Nei. Jeg liker det ikke.**	næi. yæi **lee**kerr deh **ikk**er
It's too ...	**Det er for ...**	deh ær for
cold/hot dark/small/noisy	**kaldt/varmt** **mørkt/lite/støyende**	kahlt/vahrmt murrkt/**lee**ter/**stoy**erner
I asked for a room with a bath.	**Jeg ba om et rom med bad.**	yæi baa om eht room meh(d) baad
Do you have anything ...?	**Har dere noe ...?**	haar **da̅y̅**rer **no̅o̅**er
better bigger cheaper quieter	**bedre** **større** **rimeligere** **roligere**	**ba̅y̅d**rer **stu̅r̅**rer **ree**merleeyerrer **ro̅o̅**leeyerrer
Do you have a room with a (better) view?	**Har dere et rom med (bedre) utsikt?**	haar **da̅y̅**rer eht room meh(d) (**ba̅y̅d**rer) **e̅w̅**tsikt

Registration *Innskriving*

Upon arrival at a hotel or guesthouse you'll be asked to fill in a registration form (*meldeskjema*—**meh**lersha̅y̅mah).

Etternavn/Fornavn	Surname/First name
Fødselsdato/Fødested	Date of birth/Place of birth
Yrke	Occupation
Hjemsted	Home town
Nasjonalitet	Nationality
Passnummer	Passport No.
Passutstedende myndighet	Issuing passport authority
Dato for ankomst til Skandinavia/Norge	Date of arrival in Scandinavia/Norway
Hensikt med oppholdet	Reason for visit
Underskrift	Signature

What does this mean?	**Hva betyr dette?**	vaa bert**ēwr deh**ter

Kan jeg få se passet, takk?	May I see your passport, please?
Kan du fylle ut dette skjemæt?	Would you mind filling in this form?
Undertegn her.	Please sign here.
Hvor lenge kommer du til å bli?	How long will you be staying?

What's my room number?	**Hvilket romnummer har jeg?**	**vil**kert **room**noommerr haar yæi
Will you have our luggage sent up?	**Kan jeg få brakt opp bagasjen?**	kahn yæi faw brahkt op bah**gaa**shern
Where can I park my car?	**Hvor kan jeg parkere bilen?**	voor kahn yæi pahr**kāy**rer **bee**lern
Does the hotel have a garage?	**Har hotellet egen garasje?**	haar hoo**teh**lert **āy**gern gah**raa**sher
I'd like to leave this in the hotel safe.	**Jeg vil gjerne deponere dette i hotellets safe.**	yæi vil **yæ**ʳner dehpoo**nāy**rer **deh**ter ee hoo**teh**lerss "safe"

Hotel staff *Hotellpersonale*

hall porter (bell captain)	**portier**	pooʳ**tyāy**
maid	**værelsespike**	**vær**erlserspeeker
manager	**direktør**	dirrehk**tūrr**
porter (bellman)	**bærer**	**bær**err
receptionist	**resepsjonist**	rehsehpshoo**nist**
switchboard operator	**sentralbord-betjent**	sehn**traal**bōōr-bertyāynt
waiter	**kelner/servitør**	**kehl**nerr/særvee**tūrr**
waitress	**serveringsdame/servitør**	sær**vāy**ringsdaamer/særvee**tūrr**

To attract the attention of staff members say "Excuse me" —*Unnskyld* (**ewn**shewl).

TELLING THE TIME, see page 153

General requirements *Allmenne forespørsler*

The key to room ..., please.	**Nøkkelen til rom ..., takk.**	**nur**kerlern til room ... tahk
Could you wake me at ..., please?	**Kan du vekke meg kl. ...?**	kahn dew **veh**ker mæi **klok**kern
When is breakfast/ lunch/dinner served?	**Når serveres det frokost/lunsj/middag?**	nor sær**vay**rerss deh **froo**kost/lurnsh/**mid**dah(g)
May we have breakfast in our room, please?	**Kan vi få frokosten servert på rommet?**	kahn vee faw **froo**kostern sær**vay**^{r}**t** paw **room**mer
Is there a bath on this floor?	**Fins det bad i denne etasjen?**	finss deh baad ee **deh**ner ehtaashern
Where's the shaver socket (outlet)?	**Hvor er stikkontakten for barbermaskinen?**	voor ær **stikk**koontahktern for bahr**bayr**mahsheenern
Can you find me a ...?	**Kan du skaffe meg en ...?**	kahn dew **skah**fer mæi ehn
babysitter	**barnevakt**	**baa**^{r}nervahkt
secretary	**sekretær**	sehkrer**tær**
typewriter	**skrivemaskin**	**skree**vermahsheen
May I have a/an/ some ...?	**Kan jeg få ...?**	kahn yæi faw
bath towel	**et badehåndkle**	eht **baa**derhongkler
(extra) blanket	**et (ekstra) ullteppe**	eht (**ehk**strah) **ewl**tehper
hangers	**noen hengere**	**noo**ern **heng**errer
hot-water bottle	**en varmeflaske**	ehn **vahr**merflahsker
ice cubes	**noen isbiter**	**noo**ern **ees**beeterr
needle and thread	**nål og tråd**	nawl o(g) traw
(extra) pillow	**en (ekstra) pute**	ehn (**ehk**strah) **pew**ter
(extra) quilt	**en (ekstra) dyne**	ehn (**ehk**strah) **dew**ner
reading lamp	**en leselampe**	ehn **lay**sserlahmper
soap	**en såpe**	ehn **saw**per
Where's the ...?	**Hvor er ...?**	voor ær
bathroom	**badet**	**baa**der
dining room	**spisesalen**	**spee**sserssaalern
emergency exit	**nødutgangen**	**nur**dewtgahngern
hairdresser	**frisørsalongen**	fris**sur**shahlongern
lift (elevator)	**heisen**	**hæi**ssern
telephone	**telefonen**	tehler**foo**nern
Where are the toilets?	**Hvor er toalettet?**	voor ær tooah**leh**ter

BREAKFAST, see page 38

Telephone—Post (Mail) *Telefon – Post*

Can you get me Tromsø 123456?	**Kan jeg få Tromsø 123456?**	kahn yæi faw **troom**sur 123456
Do you have any stamps?	**Har du frimerker?**	haar dew **free**mærkerr
Would you post (mail) this for me, please?	**Kan du poste dette for meg?**	kahn dew **pos**ter **deh**ter for mæi
Are there any letters for me?	**Er det noen brev til meg?**	ær deh **noo**ern brayv til mæi
Are there any messages for me?	**Er det noen beskjed til meg?**	ær deh **noo**ern ber**shay** til mæi
How much is my telephone bill?	**Hvor stor er telefon-regningen min?**	voor stoor ær tehler**foon**-ræiningern meen

Difficulties *Vanskeligheter*

The ... doesn't work.	**... virker ikke.**	... **vir**kerr **ik**ker
air conditioning	**air-conditioningen**	**ayr**-kondisherningern
bidet	**bidetet**	bee**day**er
heating	**varmen**	**vahr**mern
light	**lyset**	**lew**sser
radio	**radioen**	**raad**yooern
refrigerator	**kjøleskapet**	**khur**lerskaaper
television	**TV'en**	**tay**vehern
The tap (faucet) is dripping.	**Kranen drypper.**	**kraa**nern **drew**perr
There's no hot water.	**Det er ikke noe varmt vann.**	deh ær **ik**ker **noo**er vahrmt vahn
The washbasin (sink) is blocked.	**Vasken er tett.**	**vahs**kern ær teht
The window is jammed.	**Vinduet sitter fast.**	**vin**dewer **sit**terr fahst
The curtains are stuck.	**Gardinene henger fast.**	gah[r]**dee**nerner **hehng**err fahst
The bulb is burned out.	**Lyspæren har gått.**	**lews**pærern haar got
My bed hasn't been made up.	**Sengen min er ikke blitt redd opp.**	**sehng**ern meen ær **ik**ker blit rehd op

POST OFFICE AND TELEPHONE, see page 132

The ... is/are broken.	**... er i stykker.**	... ær ee **stew**kerr
blind	**rullegardinen**	**rew**lergah^{r}deenern
lamp	**lampen**	**lahm**pern
plug	**støpslet**	**sturp**shler
switch	**bryteren**	**brew**terrern
venetian blinds	**persiennen**	pæsh**yeh**nern
Can you get it repaired?	**Kan du få det reparert?**	kahn dew faw deh rehpah**ray^{r}t**

Laundry—Dry cleaner's *Vask – Rens*

I'd like these clothes ...	**Jeg vil gjerne ha disse klærne ...**	yæi vil **yæ^{r}**ner haa disser **klæ^{r}**ner
dry-cleaned	**renset**	**rehn**sert
ironed	**strøket**	**strur**kert
pressed	**presset**	**prehs**sert
washed	**vasket**	**vahs**kert
I need them ...	**Jeg trenger dem ...**	yæi **trehng**err dehm
today	**i dag**	ee daag
tonight	**i kveld**	ee kvehl
tomorrow	**i morgen**	ee **mawer^{r}**n
before Friday	**før fredag**	furr **fray**dah(g)
Can you ... this?	**Kan du ... dette?**	kahn dew ... **deh**ter
mend/stitch	**lappe/sy sammen**	**lah**per/sew **sah**mern
Can you sew on this button?	**Kan du sy i denne knappen?**	kahn dew sew ee **deh**ner **knah**pern
Can this be invisibly mended?	**Kan du kunststoppe dette?**	kahn dew **kewnst**stopper **deh**ter
Can you get this stain out?	**Kan du få bort denne flekken?**	kahn dew faw boo^{r}t **deh**ner **fleh**kern
Is my laundry ready?	**Er vasken min klar?**	ær **vah**skern meen klaar
This isn't mine.	**Dette er ikke mitt.**	**deh**ter ær **ik**ker mit
There's something missing.	**Det er noe som mangler.**	deh ær **noo**er som **mahng**lerr
There's one item missing.	**Det mangler et plagg.**	deh **mahng**lerr eht plahg
There's a hole in this.	**Det er gått hull i dette.**	deh ær got hewl ee **deh**ter

Hairdresser—Barber *Damefrisør – Herrefrisør*

Is there a ... in the hotel?	**Fins det en ... på hotellet?**	finss deh ehn ... paw hoot**eh**ler
hairdresser	**frisørsalong**	fri**ssūr**shahlong
beauty salon	**skjønnhetssalong**	**shurn**hehtssahlong
Can I make an appointment for Thursday?	**Kan jeg få time på torsdag?**	kahn yæi faw **tee**mer paw **tawsh**dah(g)
Could you ... my hair, please?	**Kan du ... håret mitt?**	kah dew ... **haw**rer mit
blow-dry	**føne**	**fūr**ner
cut	**klippe**	**klip**per
dye	**farge**	**fahr**gger
tint	**tone**	**tōō**ner
with a fringe (bangs)	**med lugg**	meh(d) lewg
I'd like a/some ...	**Jeg vil gjerne ha ...**	yæi vil **yæ^{r}**ner haa
colour rinse	**fargeskylling**	**fahr**ggershewling
face massage	**ansiktsmassasje**	**ahn**siktsmahsaasher
face pack	**ansiktsmaske**	**ahn**siktsmahsker
manicure	**manikyr**	mahni**kēwr**
permanent wave	**permanent**	pærmah**nehnt**
setting lotion	**leggevann**	**leh**gervahn
shampoo and set	**vask og legg**	vahsk o(g) lehg
I'd like a shampoo for ... hair.	**Jeg vil ha en sjampo for ... hår.**	yæi vil haa en **sham**poo for ... hawr
normal	**normalt**	noor**maalt**
dry	**tørt**	tur^{r}t
greasy (oily)	**fett**	feht
Do you have a colour chart?	**Har du et farge-kart?**	haar dew eht **fahr**gger-kah^{r}t
I don't want any hair spray.	**Jeg vil ikke ha hårlakk.**	yæi vil **ik**ker haa **haw^{r}**lahk
I'd like a haircut. please.	**Klipping, takk.**	**klip**ping tahk
Don't cut it too short.	**Klipp det ikke for kort.**	klip deh **ik**ker for ko^{r}t
A little more off the ...	**Ta litt mer ...**	taa lit māyr
back	**bak**	baak

DAYS OF THE WEEK, see page 150

top	**på issen**	paw **iss**ern
neck	**i nakken**	ee **nah**kern
sides	**på sidene**	paw seederner
I'd like a shave.	**Barbering, takk.**	bahr**b̅a̅y̅**ring tahk
Would you trim my ..., please?	**Kan du stusse ...?**	kahn dew **stew**sser
beard	**skjegget**	**sheh**ger
moustache	**barten**	**bah^{r}**tern
sideboards (sideburns)	**kinnskjegget**	**khin**shehger

Checking out *Avreise*

May I have my bill, please?	**Kan jeg få regningen?**	kahn yæi faw **ræi**ningern
I'm leaving early in the morning.	**Jeg reiser i morgen tidlig.**	yæi **ræi**sserr ee **mawer^{r}n teel**i
Please have my bill ready.	**Kan du ha regningen klar?**	kahn dew haa **ræi**ningern klaar
We'll be checking out around noon.	**Vi reiser ved tolvtiden.**	vee **ræi**sserr veh(d) **tol**teedern
I must leave at once.	**Jeg må reise med én gang.**	yæi maw **ræi**sser meh(d) a̅y̅n gahng
Can I pay by credit card?	**Kan jeg betale med kredittkort?**	kahn yæi ber**taa**ler meh(d) kreh**dit**ko^{r}t
I think there's a mistake in the bill.	**Jeg tror det er en feil på regningen.**	yæi tro̅o̅r deh ær ehn fæil paw **ræi**ningern
Can you get us a taxi?	**Kan du skaffe oss en drosje?**	kahn dew **skah**fer oss ehn **dro**sher
Could you have our luggage brought down?	**Kan vi få båret ned bagasjen?**	kahn vee faw **baw**rert na̅y̅(d) bah**gaa**shern
Here's the forwarding address.	**Her er ettersendingsadressen.**	hæ̅r ær **eh**terrsehningsahdrehssern
You have my home address.	**Du har min hjemstedsadresse.**	dew haar meen **yehm**sta̅y̅dsahdrehsser
It's been a very enjoyable stay.	**Det har vært et meget hyggelig opphold.**	deh haar væ^{r}t eht **m̅a̅y̅**gert **hew**gerli **op**hol

TIPPING, see inside back cover

Camping *Camping*

Norway has some 1,500 registered camp sites, classified by one, two or three stars according to facilities offered. Many have cabins for rent. The camping season is normally from mid-May or early June to the end of August. Camping outside organized sites is permitted, but you will have to ask permission from the landowner or tenant.

Is there a camp site nearby?	**Er det en campingplass i nærheten?**	ær deh ehn **kæm**ping-plahss ee **nǣr**hehtern
Can we camp here?	**Kan vi campe her?**	kahn vee **kæm**per hǣr
Do you have room for a ...?	**Har dere plass til ...?**	haar **dāy**rer plahss til
tent	**et telt**	eht tehlt
caravan (trailer)	**en campingvogn**	ehn **kæm**pingvongn
What's the charge ...?	**Hva koster det ...?**	vaa **kos**terr deh
per day	**pr. dag**	pær daag
per person	**pr. person**	pær pæ**shōōn**
for a car	**for en bil**	for ehn beel
for a tent	**for et telt**	for eht tehlt
for a caravan	**for en campingvogn**	for ehn **kæm**pingvongn
Is there/Are there (a) ...?	**Fins det ...?**	finss deh
cabins	**hytter**	**hew**terr
cafeteria	**kafeteria**	kahfer**tāy**reeah
cooking facilities	**kokemuligheter**	**kōō**kermewlihehterr
drinking water	**drikkevann**	**drik**kervahn
electricity	**elektrisitet**	ehlehktrissi**tāyt**
playground	**lekeplass**	**lāy**kerplahss
restaurant	**restaurant**	rehstew**rahng**
shopping facilities	**shoppingmuligheter**	**shop**pingmewlihehterr
sauna	**badstue/sauna**	**bah**stew/**sou**nah
swimming pool	**badebasseng**	**baa**derbahssehng
Where are the showers/toilets?	**Hvor er dusjene/toalettet?**	voor ær **dew**sherner/tooah**leh**ter
Where can I get butane gas?	**Hvor kan jeg få tak i butangass?**	voor kahn yæi faw taak ee bew**taan**gahss
Is there a youth hostel nearby?	**Er det et vandrerhjem i nærheten?**	ær deh eht **vahn**drerr-yehm ee **nǣr**hehtern

CAMPING EQUIPMENT, see page 106

Eating out

The following rundown of places to eat will help you decide what to look for.

Bar (baar) — Only found in hotels in large towns.

Bistro (**bis**troo) — Small, informal restaurant.

Brasserie (brahsser**ree**) — Normally a simple but welcoming medium-priced establishment.

Fiskerestaurant (**fis**kerrehstewrahng) — Fish and seafood specialities.

Gatekjøkken (**gaa**terkhurkern) — "Kitchen on the street". Serves fast food like sausages and hamburgers with mashed potatoes or chips (French fries); *pølse med lompe*, frankfurter (wienerwurst) in a small potato pancake; ice cream and soft drinks.

Kafé (kah**fay**) — Café, also called *kaffebar* (**kah**ferbaar); serves pastries and open sandwiches, coffee, tea and soft drinks.

Kafeteria (kahfer**tay**reeah) — Cafeteria.

Konditori (koondittoo**ree**) — Teashop (coffee shop); often a bakery, serving pastries, ice cream and sandwiches.

Kro (kroo) — Usually a road-side diner; mostly self service.

Lunsjbar (**lurnsh**baar) — Lunch bar; usually self service.

Pizzapub/-bar (**pit**sah"pub"/-baar) — Pizzas in different sizes or by the slice.

Pølsebod (**purl**serbood) — Hot-dog stand.

Restaurant (rehstew**rahng**) — Up-market establishment serving Norwegian and international food with all the trimmings.

Rotisserie (rotisser**ree**) — Specializes in grilled meat; can be expensive.

Salatbar (sah**laat**baar) — Salad bar.

Vertshus (væ'tshēwss) — Normally a small and informal neighbourhood restaurant.

Eating habits *Spisevaner*

Most Norwegians start the day with a meal that is somewhat more substantial than the typical continental breakfast—coffee or tea and open sandwiches (*smørbrød*). Country hotels and some places in the city offer breakfast buffets. Lunch is usually a fast-food snack, but many hotels and restaurants serve hot meals, and some feature a smorgasbord (*koldtbord*). Dinner is the main meal of the day.

Norwegians often drink plain tap water with their meals. Most restaurants are licensed to serve beer, and many offer wine, too; only the more elegant ones have a licence to serve spirits (liquor).

Meal times *Spisetider*

Breakfast (*frokost*—**froo**kost) is usually served from 7 or 8 to 10 a.m. and is often included in the hotel arrangement.

Lunch (*lunsj*—lurnsh) is normally served from 11 a.m. and dinner (*middag*—**mid**dah[g]) from around 6 p.m. (much earlier in smaller establishments).

Norwegian cuisine *Det norske kjøkken*

Some of the best food in Norway comes from the sea, which is to be expected in one of the world's leading fishing nations. You can dine on lobster or salmon in elegant surroundings, or go down to the waterfront and buy a picnic lunch of prawns (shrimp) right off the trawler. But you'll also find beef, pork, mutton and game dishes.

Norwegians go berserk over berries. They love scouring the countryside in search of wild berries, to eat them fresh or in jams. The supreme delicacy is *multer med krem*, arctic cloudberries with cream.

For those who enjoy a slice of bread with their meal, Norway offers a wide variety ranging from white, black, unleavened and wholemeal to crispy crackers and delicate wafers in all shapes and sizes. You'll probably see the full range at breakfast or when having *koldtbord*—the traditional self-service buffet.

Hva skal det være?	What would you like?
Jeg kan anbefale dette.	I recommend this.
Hva vil du/dere* ha å drikke?	What would you like to drink?
Vi har ikke ...	We don't have ...
Vil du ha ...?	Would you like ...?

Hungry? *Sulten?*

I'm hungry/I'm thirsty.	**Jeg er sulten/ Jeg er tørst.**	yæi ær **sewl**tern/ yæi ær tursht
Can you recommend a good restaurant?	**Kan du anbefale en bra restaurant?**	kahn dew **ahn**berfaaler ehn braa rehstew**rahng**
Are there any inexpensive restaurants around here?	**Fins det noen rimelige restauranter i nærheten?**	finss deh **nōō**ern **ree**merleeyer rehstew**rahng**err ee **nǣr**hehtern

If you want to be sure of getting a table in a popular restaurant, it's better to book in advance.

I'd like to reserve a table for 4.	**Jeg vil gjerne bestille et bord til 4.**	yæi vil **yǣ[r]**ner ber**stil**ler eht bōōr til 4
We'll come at 8.	**Vi kommer kl. 8.**	vee **kom**merr **klok**kern 8

* *du* = singular, *dere* = plural

Could we have a ...?	**Kan vi få et ...?**	kahn vee faw eht
table in the corner	**hjørnebord**	**yur**^{r}nerboor
table by the window	**vindusbord**	**vin**dewsboor
table outside	**bord ute**	boor **ew**ter
Could we have a table in a ...?	**Kan vi få et bord ...?**	kahn vee faw eht boor
non-smoking area	**for ikke-røykere**	for **ik**ker-roykerrer
smoking area	**for røykere**	for **roy**kerrer

Asking and ordering *Spørsmål og bestilling*

Waiter/Waitress!	**Unnskyld!** *	**ewn**shewl
We'd like to eat.	**Vi vil gjerne spise.**	vee vil **yæ**^{r}ner **spee**sser
I'd like something to eat/drink.	**Jeg vil gjerne ha noe å spise/drikke.**	yæi vil **yæ**^{r}ner haa **noo**er aw **spee**sser/**drik**ker
May I have the menu, please?	**Kan jeg få se spisekartet?**	kahn yæi faw say **spee**sserkah^{r}ter
Do you have a ...?	**Har dere en ...?**	haar **day**rer ehn
set menu	**meny**	meh**new**
children's menu	**barnemeny**	**baa**^{r}nermehnew
local speciality	**lokal spesialitet**	loo**kaal** spehsseeahli**tayt**
What do you recommend?	**Hva kan du anbefale?**	vaa kahn dew **ahn**berfaaler
Could we have a/an ..., please?	**Kan vi få ...?**	kahn vee faw
ashtray	**et askebeger**	eht **ahs**kerbaygerr
cup	**en kopp**	ehn kop
extra chair	**en stol til**	ehn stool til
fork	**en gaffel**	ehn **gah**ferl
glass	**et glass**	eht glass
knife	**en kniv**	ehn kneev
napkin (serviette)	**en serviett**	ehn sehrv**yeht**
plate	**en tallerken**	ehn tah**lær**kern
spoon	**en skje**	ehn shay
May I have some ...?	**Kan jeg få litt ...?**	kahn yæi faw lit
bread	**brød**	brur
butter	**smør**	smurr

* *Unnskyld*: Excuse me

NUMBERS, see page 147

oil/vinegar	**olje/eddik**	olyer/**eh**dik
salt/pepper	**salt/pepper**	sahlt/**peh**perr
seasoning	**krydder**	**krew**derr
sugar	**sukker**	**sook**kerr

Some useful expressions for those with special requirements:

I'm on a special diet.	**Jeg holder diett.**	yæi **hol**lerr dee**yeht**
I mustn't eat food containing ...	**Jeg kan ikke spise mat som inneholder ...**	yæi kahn **ik**ker **spees**ser maat som **in**nerhollerr
fat/flour	**fett/mel**	feht/māyl
salt/sugar	**salt/sukker**	sahlt/**sook**kerr
Do you have any ... dishes?	**Har dere retter med ...?**	haar **dāy**rer **reh**terr meh(d)
low-fat	**lavt fettinnhold**	laavt **feht**inhol
low-cholesterol	**lavt kolesterolinnhold**	laavt koolehsterr**ōō**linhol
Is there alcohol in it?	**Er det alkohol i det?**	ær deh ahlkoo**hōōl** ee deh
Do you have ... for diabetics?	**Har dere ... for diabetikere?**	haar **dāy**rer ... for deeah**bāy**tikkerrer
cakes	**kaker**	**kaa**kerr
a fruit juice	**en juice**	ehn **yēw**ss
a special menu	**en spesialmeny**	ehn spehssee**aal**meh**nēw**
Do you have any vegetarian dishes?	**Har dere noen vegetariske retter?**	haar **dāy**rer **nōō**ern vehger**taa**risker **reh**terr
Could I have ... instead of dessert?	**Kan jeg få ... i stedet for dessert?**	kahn yæi faw ... ee **stāy**der for deh**ssær**
Can I have an artificial sweetener?	**Kan jeg få et søtningsmiddel?**	kahn yæi faw eht **sūr**tningsmidderl

And ...

I'd like some more.	**Jeg vil gjerne ha litt mer.**	yæi vil **yæ**ʳner haa lit māyr
Can I have more ...?	**Kan jeg få litt mer ...?**	kahn yæi faw lit māyr
Just a small portion.	**Bare en liten porsjon.**	**baa**rer ehn **lee**tern poo**shōōn**
Nothing more, thanks.	**Takk, ikke mer.**	tahk **ik**ker māyr

Breakfast *Frokost*

Most hotels offer a continental breakfast as well as a buffet, consisting of a variety of breads, butter, cheese, cold cuts, eggs, herring, jam, cereals, fruit juice, milk, coffee and tea.

I'd like breakfast, please.	**Jeg vil gjerne ha frokost.**	yæi vil **yær**ner haa **froo**kost
I'll have a/an/ some ...	**Jeg tar ...**	yæi taar
bacon and eggs	**egg og bacon**	ehg o(g) **bæi**kern
boiled egg	**et kokt egg**	eht kookt ehg
soft/hard	**bløtkokt/hardkokt**	**blurt**kookt/**haar**kookt
cereal	**frokostblanding**	**froo**kostblahning
cheese	**ost**	oost
eggs	**egg**	ehg
fried egg	**et speilegg**	eht **spæil**ehg
scrambled eggs	**eggerøre**	**eh**gerrurrer
fruit juice	**juice**	yewss
grapefruit	**grapefrukt-**	**grayp**frewkt-
orange	**appelsin-**	ahperl**seen**-
ham and eggs	**egg og skinke**	ehg o(g) **shing**ker
jam	**syltetøy**	**sewl**tertoy
marmalade	**appelsinmarmelade**	ahperl**seen**mahrmerlaader
omelet	**omelett**	oomer**leht**
porridge	**grøt**	grurt
roll	**et rundstykke**	eht **rewn**stewker
toast	**litt ristet brød**	lit **ris**tert brur
yoghurt	**en yoghurt**	ehn **yo**gewrt
May I have some ...?	**Kan jeg få ...?**	kahn yæi faw
bread	**litt brød**	lit brur
butter	**litt smør**	lit smurr
(hot) chocolate	**(varm) sjokolade**	(vahrm) shookoo**laa**der
coffee	**kaffe**	**kah**fer
decaffeinated	**koffeinfri**	koffeh**een**free
black	**svart**	svahrt
with cream	**med fløte**	meh(d) **flur**ter
honey	**litt honning**	lit **hon**ning
(cold/hot) milk	**litt (kald/varm) melk**	lit (kahl/vahrm) mehlk
pepper	**litt pepper**	lit **peh**perr
salt	**litt salt**	lit sahlt
tea	**te**	tay
with milk/lemon	**med melk/sitron**	meh(d) mehlk/si**troon**
(hot) water	**litt (varmt) vann**	lit (vahrmt) vahn

What's on the menu? *Hva står på menyen?*

Many restaurants display their menu (*spisekart/meny*) outside. In addition to the à la carte menu, some restaurants offer a dish of the day (*dagens rett*).

Under the headings below you'll find alphabetical lists of dishes that might be offered on a Norwegian menu, with their English equivalent. You can simply show the book to the waiter. If you want some cheese, for instance, let *him* point to what's available on the appropriate list. Use pages 36 and 37 for ordering in general.

Reading the menu *Å lese spisekartet*

Dagens rett/suppe/ grønnsaker	Dish/Soup/Vegetables of the day
Barnemeny	Children's menu
Vegetar ...	Vegetarian ...
Kjøkkensjefen anbefaler ...	The chef proposes ...
Som vår kjøkkensjef liker det	As our chef likes it
(Husets) Spesialiteter	Specialities (of the house)
Serveres/Servert med ...	Served with ...
Velg mellom ...	Choice of ...
Valgfritt tilbehør	Choice of side dishes
På bestilling	Made on request
... med ass. ...	... with assorted ...
... m/ ...	... with ...
... inkl.	... included

dessert	dehss**æ̅r**	dessert
drikker	**drik**kerr	drinks
fisk	fisk	fish
forretter	**for**rehterr	starters (appetizers)
frukt	frewkt	fruit
fugl	fe̅w̅l	poultry
hovedretter	**ho̅o̅**verdrehterr	main courses (entrees)
is(krem)	**ees**(kra̅y̅m)	ice cream
kaker	**kaa**kerr	pastries/cakes
kjøtt	khurt	meat
koldtbord	**kolt**bo̅o̅r	smorgasbord
leskedrikk	**lehs**kerdrik	soft drinks
ost	oost	cheese
pastaretter	**pahs**tahrehterr	pasta dishes
risretter	**rees**rehterr	rice dishes
salatbar	sah**laat**baar	salad bar
smørbrød	**smurr**bru̅r̅	open sandwiches
supper	**sew**perr	soups
varme smørbrød	**vahr**mer **smurr**bru̅r̅	sandwiches with hot meat, fish, etc.
varmretter	**vahrm**rehterr	hot dishes
vilt	vilt	game

Open sandwiches *Smørbrød*

Smørbrød means bread and butter, which is quite an understatement when you consider Scandinavia's reputation for elaborate open sandwiches. Almost anything may turn up on one of these appetizing *smørbrød*, most of which are served cold. Two or three open sandwiches will generally satisfy most appetites. *Landgang* (**lahn**gahng), literally "gangway", is a halved French loaf with several different toppings (fish, egg, meat, cheese, etc.).

I'd like an open sandwich with ...	**Jeg vil gjerne ha et smørbrød med ...**	yæi vil **yæ**ʳner haa eht **smurr**brūr meh(d)

egg og ansjos (ehg o[g] ahng**shōōss**)	sliced egg and marinated sprats
italiensk salat (eetahlee**āy**nsk sah**laat**)	"Italian" salad; sliced ham, apple, potato, onion, carrot, peas in mayonnaise dressing
reker (**rāy**kerr)	prawns (shrimp) with mayonnaise
rekesalat (**rāy**kersahlaat)	prawn (shrimp) salad; prawns, apple, celery, sometimes in a tomato dressing, sometimes in a mayonnaise dressing
roastbiff (**rost**bif)	sliced roast beef, often served with a herb-flavoured mayonnaise sauce
røkelaks (**rūr**kerlahkss)	sliced smoked salmon, often served with scrambled eggs
sildesalat (**sill**ersahlaat)	herring salad; pickled herring, potato, beetroot, apple, egg, onion in cream-and-beetroot dressing

Smorgasbord *Koldtbord*

The Swedish name, *smørgåsbord* ("sandwich table"), is better known than its Norwegian equivalent, *koldtbord* ("cold table"). Some restaurants and mountain hotels specialize in this bountiful self-service buffet. A scaled-down version of the *koldtbord* is often prepared in Norwegian homes for special occasions, particularly during the Christmas season.

Dishes may vary according to season, but there is always a variety of fish (marinated and smoked herring, herring salads, cold salmon, trout or halibut in aspic) and seafood, meat (cold cuts, pâtés, hot sausages, meatballs), vegetables, egg dishes, salads, fruit, cheese and bread.

One of the mainstays of *koldtbord*, particularly in summer and early autumn, is *spekemat* (**spay**kermaat) or cured meat. Norway has a long tradition of curing meat, originating from the time when there was no other way of conserving food. Usually *spekemat* is eaten with scrambled eggs and a crisp, paper-thin barley-and-wheat or barley-and-rye cracker called *flatbrød* (**flaht**brur).

Another speciality that may be found among *koldtbord* dishes is *rømmegrøt* (**rur**mergrurt), a tasty, refreshing and filling porridge made from thick sour cream, flour and milk, which is topped with butter, sugar and cinnamon.

Start with the fish dishes. Use a fresh plate for meat, salad and egg dishes, and another for cheese and fruit. Don't hurry yourself; the whole point of *koldtbord* is to enjoy a large meal with as many trips back to the buffet as desired, and all at a leisurely pace.

Aquavit and beer go particularly well with this spread. It is rare to drink wine with *koldtbord*.

I'd like to try some Norwegian specialities.	**Jeg vil gjerne prøve noen norske spesialiteter.**	yæi vil **yæ**ʳner **prur**ver **noo**ern **nosh**ker spehsseeahli**tay**terr
What do you recommend?	**Hva anbefaler du?**	vaa **ahn**berfaalerr dew

fenalår (**fay**nahlawr) — cured leg of mutton

spekepølse (**spay**kerpurlser) — slices of smoked, cured sausage made from different meats that range in colour from pinkish to black

spekeskinke (**spay**kershingker) — smoked, cured ham, as a main dish often served with thick sour cream (*rømme*) and boiled potatoes

Starters (Appetizers) *Forretter*

Except on special occasions, Norwegians are usually content with soup as a starter. In more elegant restaurants, however, there will be a choice of appetizing hors d'œuvres; maybe one of the dishes from the *koldtbord*, a mixed salad or a selection of scaled-down *smørbrød* called *snitter* (**snit**terr).

I'd like a starter (an appetizer).	**Jeg vil gjerne ha en forrett.**	yæi vil yæ'ner haa ehn **for**reht
blåskjell	**blaw**shehl	mussels
froskelår	**fros**kerlawr	frogs' legs
gåselever	**gaws**serlehverr	goose liver
hummer	**hoom**merr	lobster
kaviar	**kah**veeaar	caviar
krabbe	**krah**ber	crab
laks	**lahkss**	salmon
gravet	**graa**vert	cured
røkt/røkelaks	rurkt/**rūr**kerlahkss	smoked
rekecocktail	**rāy**kerkoktæil	prawn (shrimp) cocktail
(speke)skinke	(**spāy**ker)**shing**ker	(smoked, cured) ham
skinke med melon	**shing**ker meh(d) meh**lōōn**	ham with melon
snegler	**snæi**lerr	snails
sursild	**sēw**shil	marinated herring
tomatjuice	too**maat**yēwss	tomato juice
østers	**ur**stersh	oysters
ål i gelé	awl ee sheh**lāy**	jellied eel

fiskekabaret (**fis**kerkahbah**rāy**) assorted seafood and vegetables in aspic, usually served with bread, butter and a mayonnaise sauce

gravlaks (**graav**lahkss) salt-and-sugar-cured salmon (same as *gravet laks*), often served with a sweet mustard-and-dill sauce

rakørret (**raa**kurreht) specially processed, salt-cured and fermented trout, often served with small potatoes, sour cream and *flatbrød*

(ferske) reker ([**fæsh**ker] **rāy**kerr) (unshelled) prawns (shrimp), usually served with lemon, toast and butter

sildebrikke (**sil**lerbrikker) a variety of herring, served with bread and butter

sjømannsskjell (**shūr**mahnsshehl) mussels simmered in white wine with onion and parsley

Soups *Supper*

I'd like some soup.	**Jeg vil gjerne ha en suppe.**	yæi vil **yæ**ʳner haa ehn **sew**per
What do you recommend?	**Hva foreslår du?**	vaa **faw**rershlawr dew

aspargessuppe	ah**spahr**ggerssewper	asparagus soup
betasuppe	**bāy**tahsewper	thick meat-and-vegetable soup
blomkålsuppe	**blom**kawlsewper	cauliflower soup
buljong	bewl**yong**	consommé
fiskesuppe	**fis**kersewper	fish soup
fransk løksuppe	frahnsk **lūrk**sewper	French onion soup
grønnsaksuppe	**grurn**saaksewper	vegetable soup
gul ertesuppe	gewl **æ**ʳtersewper	yellow pea soup
hummersuppe	**hoom**merrsewper	lobster soup
kjøttsuppe	**khurt**sewper	meat soup
løksuppe	**lūrk**sewper	onion soup
neslesuppe	**nehsh**lersewper	nettle soup
oksehalesuppe	**ook**serhahlersewper	oxtail soup
rekesuppe	**rāy**kersewper	prawn (shrimp) soup
sellerisuppe	sehler**ree**sewper	celery soup
sjampinjongsuppe	shahmpin**yong**sewper	button mushroom soup
soppsuppe	**sop**sewper	field mushroom soup
tomatsuppe	too**maat**sewper	tomato soup

Salads *Salater*

Many restaurants offer an appetizing self-service salad bar (*salatbar*—sah**laat**baar).

What salads do you have?	**Hva slags salater har dere?**	vaa shlahkss sah**laa**ter haar **dāy**rer

agurksalat (ah**gewrk**sahlaat)	cucumber salad, usually with a vinegar-sugar dressing
blandet salat (**blah**nert sah**laat**)	mixed salad (lettuce, tomatoes, cucumber, etc., with oil-and-vinegar dressing); accompanies many main courses
størje-/tunfisksalat (**sturr**yer-/**tēwn**fisk-sahlaat)	tuna fish salad—Norwegian version of salad Niçoise
skalldyrsalat (**skahl**dēwrsahlaat)	seafood salad (mostly mussels and prawns, but also lobster or crab)

Egg dishes *Eggeretter*

eggerøre	**eh**gerrurrer	scrambled eggs
forlorent egg	forloorernt ehg	poached egg
omelett	oomer**leht**	omelet
med kryddergrønt	meh(d) **krew**derr-grurnt	with fine herbs
med ost	meh(d) oost	with cheese
med skinke	meh(d) **shing**ker	with ham
med sjampinjong	meh(d) shahmpin**yong**	with button mush-rooms
med sopp	meh(d) sop	with mushrooms
med -stuing	meh(d) -**stew**ing	with ... sauce
pannekake	**pah**nerkaaker	pancake
speilegg/stekt egg	**spæil**ehg/stehkt ehg	fried egg

Fish and seafood (shellfish) *Fisk og skalldyr*

Fish plays no less an important part in the diet of Norwegians today than it did a thousand years ago. Nowadays, however, visitors will be offered a much wider choice of fish and seafood, prepared in a variety of imaginative and interesting ways.

What kind of ... do you have?	**Hva slags ... har dere?**	vaa shlahkss ... haar **day**rer
fish	**fisk**	fisk
seafood (shellfish)	**skalldyr**	**skahl**dewr

abbor	**ah**bor	perch
ansjos	ahng**shooss**	marinated sprats
blekksprut	**blehk**sprewt	octopus
blåskjell	**blaw**shehl	mussels
brasme	**brah**smer	bream
brisling	**brish**ling	sprat/brisling
flyndre	**flewn**drer	flounder
gjedde	**yeh**der	pike
hellefisk	**heh**lerfisk	halibut
hummer	**hoom**merr	lobster
hvitting	**vit**ting	whiting
hyse	**hew**sser	haddock
kamskjell	**kahm**shehl	scallop
karpe	**kahr**per	carp
klippfisk	**klip**fisk	salted and dried cod
knurr	knewr	gurnard

kolje	**kol**yer	haddock
krabbe	**krah**ber	crab
kreps	krehpss	freshwater crayfish
kveite	**kvæi**ter	halibut
lake	**laa**ker	burbot
laks	lahkss	salmon
lysing	**lew**ssing	hake
makrell	mah**krehl**	mackerel
piggvar	**pig**vaar	turbot
regnbueørret	**ræin**bewerurreht	rainbow trout
reker	**ray**kerr	prawns (shrimp)
rogn	rongn	roe
rødspette	**rur**spehter	plaice
røye	**roy**er	char
sardell	sahʳ**dehl**	anchovy
sardin	sahʳ**deen**	sardine
sei	sæi	coalfish (pollack)
sik	seek	whitefish
sild	sil	herring
sjøtunge	**shur**toonger	sole
sjøørret	**shur**urreht	sea trout
slettvar	**shleht**vaar	brill
steinbit	**stæin**beet	catfish
stør	sturr	sturgeon
størje	**sturr**yer	tuna
torsk	toshk	cod
tunfisk	**tewn**fisk	tuna
uer	**ew**ehr	rosefish
ørret	urreht	trout
østers	**urs**tersh	oysters
åbor	**aw**boor	perch
ål	awl	eel

au gratin	**gratinert**	grahti**nay**ʳ**t**
boiled	**kokt**	kookt
breaded	**griljert/panert**	gril**yay**ʳ**t**/pah**nay**ʳ**t**
deep fried	**fritert/frityrstekt**	fri**tay**ʳ**t**/fri**tew**shtehkt
fried	**stekt**	stehkt
grilled (broiled)	**grillet/grillstekt**	**gril**lert/**gril**stehkt
marinated	**marinert**	mahri**nay**ʳ**t**
poached	**pochert/kokt**	poo**shay**ʳ**t**/kookt
simmered	**lettkokt**	**leht**kookt
smoked	**røkt**	rurkt
steamed	**dampet/dampkokt**	**dahm**pert/**dahmp**kookt

fiskeboller/ fiskepudding (fiskerbollerr/ fiskerpewding)	fish balls/fish pudding; served poached and laid in a béchamel or shrimp sauce, or fried, with boiled potatoes and vegetables
fritert flyndrefilet (frita̅y̅ʳt **flew**ndrerfilla̅y̅)	(deep) fried fillets of flounder; usually served with boiled potatoes or chips (French fries), a cucumber or mixed salad and a herb-flavoured mayonnaise sauce
gravet laks/gravlaks (**graa**vert lahkss/ **graa**vlahkss)	salt-and-sugar-cured salmon flavoured with dill; often served with sliced potatoes in a white sauce
kokt torsk (kookt toshk)	poached cod; normally served with cod liver, boiled potatoes, lemon and melted butter
kokt/dampet ørret (kookt/**dah**mpert urrert)	poached trout; usually served with boiled potatoes, hollandaise sauce or thick sour cream and cucumber salad
lutefisk (**le̅w̅**terfisk)	stockfish soaked in lye; simmered and served with boiled potatoes, peas, mustard, pepper and melted butter or dripping or alternatively a béchamel sauce (a traditional Christmas dish)
seibiff med løk (**sæi**bif meh[d] lu̅r̅k)	fried fillets of coalfish (pollack) with onions, served with boiled potatoes and vegetables or salad
spekesild (**spa̅y̅**kersil)	salted herring; served with boiled potatoes, onion rings, pickled beetroot, butter and often cabbage or mashed swedes (rutabaga)

Meat *Kjøtt*

What kind of meat is this?	**Hva slags kjøtt er dette?**	vaa shlahkss khurt ær **deh**ter
beef	**oksekjøtt**	**ook**serkhurt
lamb	**lammekjøtt**	**lah**merkhurt
mutton	**fårekjøtt**	**faw**rerkhurt
pork	**svinekjøtt**	sveenerkhurt
veal	**kalvekjøtt**	**kahl**verkhurt
I'd like some ...	**Jeg vil gjerne ha ...**	yæi vil **yæʳ**ner haa
biff	bif	beef steak
frikadeller	frikah**deh**lerr	meat balls
fårestek	**faw**rersta̅y̅k	roast leg of mutton or lamb

kalvebrissel	**kahl**verbrisserl	sweetbread
kalverlever	**kahl**verlehverr	calf's liver
kalvemedaljonger	**k**ahlvermehdahlyongerr	small round fillets of veal
kalvenyrestek	**kahl**vernewrerstayk	roast loin of veal
karbonade(kake)	kahrboo**naa**der(kaaker)	hamburger
kjøttboller	**khurt**bollerr	meat balls
kjøttkaker	**khurt**kaakerr	small hamburgers
kjøttpudding	**khurt**pewding	meat loaf
-knoke	-**knoo**ker	... bone
-kotelett	-kotter**leht**	... chop
lammebog	**lah**merboog	shoulder of lamb
lammebryst	**lah**merbrewst	brisket of lamb
lammelår	**lah**merlawr	leg of lamb
lammesadel	**lah**mersaaderl	saddle of lamb
lammestek	**lah**merstayk	roast lamb
-lever	-**leh**verr	... liver
lungemos	**loong**ermoos	minced pork lungs and onions
medisterkaker	meh**dis**terrkaakerr	small pork-and-veal hamburgers
medisterpølse	meh**dis**terrpurlser	pork-and-veal sausage
mørbradstek	**murr**braadstayk	roast sirloin
-nyrer	-**new**rerr	... kidneys
oksebryst	**ook**serbrewst	brisket of beef
oksefilet	**ook**serfillay	fillet of beef
oksekam	**ook**serkahm	loin
okserulader	**ook**serrewlaaderr	braised beef rolls
oksestek	**ook**serstayk	roast beef
pølse	**purl**ser	sausage
-ragu	-rah**gew**	... ragout
roastbiff	**rost**bif	roast beef
skinke	**shing**ker	ham
kokt	kookt	boiled
røkt	rurkt	smoked
spekeskinke	**spay**kershingker	smoked, cured ham
-stek	-stayk	roast ...
svinefilet	**svee**nerfillay	fillet of pork
svinekam	**svee**nerkahm	loin of pork
svineribbe	**svee**nerribber	sparerib
svinestek	**svee**nerstayk	roast pork
svor	svoor	crackling
sylte	**sewl**ter	brawn (headcheese)
tartarbiff	tah^{r}**taar**bif	steak tartare
T-benstek	**tay**-baynstayk	T-bone steak
-tunge	-**toong**er	... tongue
wienerschnitzel	**vee**nershnitserl	breaded veal escalope

boiled	**kokt**	kookt
braised	**braisert**	brahs**sayrt**
breaded	**griljert/panert**	gril**yayrt**/pah**nayrt**
fried	**stekt**	stehkt
grilled (broiled)	**grillet/grillstekt**	grillert/grilstehkt
roast	**ovnsstekt**	ovnsstehkt
sautéed	**sautert/brunet**	so**tayrt**/**brew**nert
smoked	**røkt**	rurkt
stuffed	**fylt**	fewlt
whole roasted	**helstekt**	**hayl**stehkt
underdone (rare)	**råstekt**	**raw**stehkt
medium	**medium stekt**	**may**diewm stehkt
well-done	**godt stekt**	got stehkt

benløse fugler (**bayn**lursser **few**lerr) fried rolled slices of veal or beef stuffed with forcemeat, served with gravy, potatoes and vegetables or salad

biff med løk (bif meh[d] lurk) thick beef steak topped with fried onion, usually served with chips (French fries) and salad

fårikål (**faw**rikawl) mutton or lamb in cabbage stew, cooked in a big pot and served with boiled potatoes (a national dish)

kjøttkaker med løk (**khurt**kaakerr meh[d] lurk) small hamburgers with fried onions, boiled potatoes and vegetables

lapskaus (lahpskouss) a tasty stew that comes either "brown" (*brun* or *bifflapskaus*), with diced fried beef, potatoes and onions, or "white" (*lys* or *saltkjøttlapskaus*), with diced, salted boiled meat (usually pork), potatoes and different root vegetables; traditionally eaten with *flatbrød*

pinnekjøtt (**pin**nerkhurt) salted and dried ribs of mutton steamed on twigs; usually served with boiled potatoes and mashed swedes (rutabaga) or as a *koldtbord* dish (a Christmas speciality)

stekt ribbe/juleribbe (stehkt **rib**ber/ **yew**lerribber) roast spareribs; usually served with sweet-and-sour cabbage stew and boiled potatoes or as a *koldtbord* dish (a Christmas speciality)

Game and poultry *Vilt og fugl*

Game is normally served with a rich and heavy cream sauce, boiled potatoes, vegetables and cranberries.

I'd like some game.	**Jeg vil gjerne ha en viltrett.**	yæi vil **yæ^{r}**ner haa ehn **vilt**reht
What poultry dishes do you serve?	**Hva slags fugleretter har dere?**	vah shlahkss **few**lerrehterr haar **day**rer
and	ahn	duck
bekkasin	berkah**seen**	snipe
broiler	**broy**lerr	chicken
dyrestek	**dew**rerstayk	roast venison
elg	ehlg	elk
elgbiff	**ehlg**bif	elk steak
elgfilet	**ehlg**fillay	fillet of elk
elgstek	**ehlg**stayk	roast elk
fasan	fah**ssaan**	pheasant
gås	gawss	goose
hane	**haa**ner	cock
hare	**haa**rer	hare
harestek	**haa**rerstayk	roast hare
hjort	yo^{r}t	deer
hjortesadel	**yor**tersaaderl	saddle of deer
høne	**hur**ner	hen
jerpe	**yær**per	hazelhen
kalkun	kahl**kewn**	turkey
kanin	kah**neen**	rabbit
kylling	**khew**ling	chicken
orre/orrfugl	**or**rer/**or**fewl	black grouse
rapphøne	**rahp**hurner	partridge
reinsdyr/rensdyr	**ræins**dewr/**rayns**dewr	reindeer
reinsdyrmedaljonger	**ræins**dewrmehdahlyongerr	small, round fillets of reindeer
reinsdyrstek	**ræins**dewshtayk	roast reindeer
rugde	**rewg**der	woodcock
rype	**rew**per	ptarmigan
rådyr	**raw**dewr	venison
rådyrsadel	**raw**dewshaaderl	saddle of venison
rådyrstek	**raw**dewshtayk	roast venison
tiur	**tee**ewr	woodgrouse (capercaillie)
vaktel	**vahk**terl	quail
villand	**vil**ahn	wild duck
årfugl	**awr**fewl	black grouse

Vegetables *Grønnsaker*

Could I have some vegetables?	**Kan jeg få litt grønnsaker?**	kahn yæi faw lit **grurn**saakerr
agurk	ah**gewrk**	cucumber
artisjokker	ah^{r}**tishok**kerr	artichokes
asparges	ah**spahr**ggers	asparagus
aubergine	obæ**sheen**	aubergine (eggplant)
blomkål	**blom**kawl	cauliflower
brekkbønner	**brehk**burnerr	French (cut green) beans
bønner	**bur**nerr	beans
erter	æ^{r}terr	peas
gresskar	**grehs**kaar	marrow
grønnkål	**grurn**kawl	curly kale
gulrøtter	**gewl**rurterr	carrots
hodesalat	**hoo**dersahlaat	lettuce
kantareller	kahntah**reh**lerr	chanterelle mushrooms
kål	kawl	cabbage
kålrabi/kålrot	kawlraabi/**kawl**root	swede (rutabaga)
løk	lurk	onions
linser	**lin**serr	lentils
mais	maayss	sweet corn (corn)
maiskolbe	**maays**kolber	corn on the cob
nepe	**nay**per	turnips
paprika	**paa**prikkah	sweet pepper
purre	**pew**rer	leeks
reddiker	**reh**dikkerr	radishes
rosenkål	**roo**ssernkawl	Brussels sprouts
rødbeter	**rur**behterr	beetroot
rødkål	**rur**kawl	red cabbage
salat	sah**laat**	salad
selleri	sehler**ree**	celery
sjampinjonger	shahmpin**yon**gerr	button mushrooms
sopp	sop	mushrooms
sylteagurk	**sewl**terahgewrk	pickled gherkin
tomater	too**maa**terr	tomatoes
spinat	spin**naat**	spinach

baked	**bakte**	**bahk**ter
boiled	**kokte**	**kook**ter
au gratin	**gratinerte**	grahti**nay**^{r}ter
in a sauce	**stuede**	**stew**erder
stuffed	**fylte**	**fewl**ter

Potatoes, rice and pasta *Poteter, ris og pasta*

bakt potet	bahkt poo**tayt**	baked potato
komper	**koom**perr	potato dumplings
kokte poteter	**kook**ter poo**tay**terr	boiled potatoes
kumler	**koom**lerr	potato dumplings
nudler	**newd**lerr	noodles
nypoteter	**new**pootayterr	new potatoes
pommes frites	pom frit	chips (French fries)
potet	poo**tayt**	potato
potetgull	poo**tayt**gewl	potato crisps (chips)
potetkroketter	poo**tayt**krookehterr	potato croquettes
potetmos/-puré/-stappe	poo**tayt**mooss/-pewray/-stahper	mashed potatoes
potetsalat	poo**tayt**sahlaat	potato salad
raspeball	**rahs**perbahl	potato dumplings
ris	reess	rice
stekte poteter	**stehk**ter poo**tay**terr	sautéed potatoes
stuede poteter	**stew**erder poo**tay**terr	potatoes in a white sauce

sildeball (**si**llerbahl) potato dumplings with a filling of minced salted herring, onion, bacon and flour; served with melted butter and pickled beetroot

Sauces *Sauser*

ansjossmør	ahng**shooss**murr	butter with chopped marinated sprats
brun saus	brurn souss	gravy
dillsaus	**dil**souss	sweet-and-sour béchamel sauce with dill
fløtesaus	**flur**tersouss	cream sauce
hvitløksmør	**veet**lurksmurr	garlic butter
hvit saus	veet souss	béchamel sauce
kryddersmør	**krew**derrsmurr	herb butter
løksaus	**lur**ksouss	onion sauce
majones	mahyoo**nayss**	mayonnaise
pepperrotsaus	**peh**perrootsouss	horseradish sauce
persillesmør	pæ**shil**lersmurr	parsley butter
rekesaus	**ray**kersouss	prawn (shrimp) sauce
rømme	**rur**mer	thick sour cream
smeltet smør	**smehl**tert smurr	melted butter
viltsaus	**vilt**souss	rich cream sauce served with game

Some of the herbs, *urter*, and spices, *krydder*, you may come across:

dill	dil	dill
eine(r)bær	**æi**ner(r)bǣr	juniper berries
gressløk	**greh**slūrk	chives
hvitløk	**veet**lūrk	garlic
ingefær	**inger**fǣr	ginger
kanel	kah**nāyl**	cinnamon
kapers	**kaa**persh	capers
karri	**kah**ri	curry seasoning
karve	**kah**rver	caraway seeds
nellik	**neh**lik	clove
persille	pæ**shil**ler	parsley
pepper	**peh**perr	pepper
salvie	sahl**vee**	sage
salt	sahlt	salt
timian	**tee**meeahn	thyme

Cheese *Ost*

Cheese is mostly eaten on *smørbrød*. Some cheeses are home-grown versions of well-known continental cheeses, while others are indigenous Norwegian.

gammelost (**gah**merloost)	"old-fashioned" pungent "cheese" made with skimmed milk
Jarlsbergost (**yaa**ʳlsbærgoost)	mild, slightly sweet, semi-hard; a taste that falls between Gouda and Emmental
normannaost (noor**mah**nahoost)	blue-veined cow's milk cheese; sharp taste
ridderost (**rid**derroost)	semi-hard with nutty flavour; eaten young or mature

The square brown (goat's) cheeses found on Norwegian breakfast and lunch tables come in different varieties:

ekte geitost (**eh**kter **yæi**toost)	"real" goat's cheese, the most pungent, is made from the whey of goat's milk
Gudbrandsdalsost (**gewd**brahnsdaalsoost)	milder, consists of goat's and cow's milk
fløtemysost (**flūr**termēwssoost)	mild and sweet, made from the whey of cow's milk with cream added

Fruit *Frukt*

Do you have (fresh) fruit?	**Har dere (frisk) frukt?**	haar **dāy**rer (frisk) frewkt
I'd like a fruit salad.	**Jeg vil gjerne ha en fruktsalat.**	yæi vil **yǣ^{r}**ner haa ehn **frewkt**sahlaat
ananas	**ah**nahnahss	pineapple
appelsin	ahperl**seen**	orange
aprikos	ahpri**kkooss**	apricot
banan	bah**naan**	banana
bjørnebær	**byūr^{r}**nerbǣr	blackberries
blåbær	**blaw**bǣr	bilberries (blueberries)
bringebær	**bring**erbǣr	raspberries
dadler	**dahd**lerr	dates
druer	**drēw**err	grapes
blå	blaw	black
grønne	**grur**ner	white
eple	**eh**pler	apple
fersken	**fæsh**kern	peach
fikener	**fee**kernerr	figs
grapefrukt	**grāyp**frewkt	grapefruit
hasselnøtter	**hahs**serlnurterr	hazelnuts
jordbær	**yoor**bǣr	strawberries
kastanjer	kah**stahn**yerr	chestnuts
kirsebær	**khi**sherbǣr	cherries
kokosnøtt	**koo**koosnurt	coconut
korinter	koo**rin**terr	currants
mandler	**mahn**dlerr	almonds
markjordbær	**mahrk**yoorbǣr	wild strawberries
melon	meh**lōōn**	melon
moreller	moo**reh**lerr	morello cherries
multer	**mewl**terr	arctic cloudberries
nøtter	**nur**terr	nuts
plommer	**ploom**merr	plums
pære	**pǣ**rer	pear
rabarbra	rah**bahr**brah	rhubarb
rips	ripss	redcurrants
rognebær	**rong**nerbǣr	rowanberries
rosiner	roo**ssee**nerr	raisins
sitron	si**trōōn**	lemon
solbær	**sōōl**bǣr	blackcurrants
stikkelsbær	**stik**kerlsbǣr	gooseberries
svisker	**svis**kerr	prunes
tyttebær	**tew**terbǣr	cranberries
valnøtter	**vaal**nurterr	walnuts
vannmelon	**vahn**mehlōōn	watermelon

Dessert *Dessert*

I'd like a dessert, please.	**Jeg vil gjerne ha en dessert.**	yæi vil **yær**ner haa ehn dehs**sær**
Something light, please.	**Noe lett, takk.**	**noo**er leht tahk
With/Without ...	**Med/Uten ...**	meh(d)/**ew**tern
cream	**fløte**	**flur**ter
whipped cream	**krem**	kraym
jam	**syltetøy**	**sewl**tertoy
(varm) eplekake med krem	(vahrm) **ehp**lerkaaker meh(d) kraym	(hot) apple pie with whipped cream
frityrstekt camembert med solbærsyltetøy	fri**tew**shtehkt kahmang**bær** meh(d) **sool**bærsewltertoy	deep-fried camembert with blackcurrant jam
fruktkompott	**frewkt**koompot	stewed fruit
is(krem)	**eess**(kraym)	ice cream
jordbær-	**yoor**bær-	strawberry
sjokolade-	shookoo**laa**der-	chocolate
vanilje-	vah**nil**yer-	vanilla
karamellpudding	kahrah**mehl**pewding	creme caramel
mandelkake	**mahn**derlkaaker	almond cake
multer med krem	**mewl**terr meh(d) kraym	arctic cloudberries with whipped cream
pannekaker	**pah**nerkaakerr	pancakes
riskrem	**rees**kraym	creamed rice with red berry sauce
rødgrøt	**rur**grurt	fruit pudding with cream
sjokoladepudding	shookoo**laa**derpewding	chocolate mousse
sorbett	sor**beht**	sorbet (sherbet)
sufflé	sew**flay**	soufflé
terte	**tær**ter	fruit cake
vafler med syltetøy	**vah**flerr meh(d) **sewl**tertoy	waffles with jam

Hoffdessert (**hof**dehssær) layers of meringue and whipped cream, topped with chocolate sauce and toasted almonds

pære Belle Helene (**pæ**rer behl heh**layn**) poached pears with vanilla ice cream and chocolate

tilslørte bondepiker (**til**shlurter **boon**nerpeekerr) layers of stewed apples, biscuit (cookie) crumbs, sugar and whipped cream

Drinks *Drikkevarer*

Alcohol* is expensive because of high taxes. Elegant restaurants are licensed to serve spirits (liquor), but only after 3 p.m., and never on Sundays. Beer and wine are served in a larger number of restaurants — but by no means all of them — even on Sundays, after 12 noon.

Beer *Øl*

Norwegian beer meets international standards. *Pils* (pilss) is the generic term for lager, *bayerøl* (**bah**yerrurl) is medium-strong and dark, *bokkøl* (**book**url) is strong and dark, and *exportøl* (ehks**po^{r}t**url) is strong and light-coloured. If you're driving, stick to low-alcohol beer (*lettøl*—**leht**url or *lagerøl*—**laa**gerrurl) or the nonalcoholic *Zero* (**sa̅y̅**roo). *Vørterøl* (**vur^{r}**terrurl) is a nonalcoholic dark and rather sweet "beer".

I'd like a beer, please.	**Jeg vil gjerne ha en øl.**	yæi vil **yæ^{r}**ner haa ehn url
Do you have ...?	**Har dere ...?**	haar **da̅y̅**rer
bottled beer	**flaskeøl**	**flahs**kerurl
draught (tap) beer	**fatøl**	**faat**url
foreign beer	**utenlandsk øl**	**e̅w̅**ternlahnsk url
light/dark beer	**lyst/mørkt øl**	le̅w̅st/murrkt url
A bottle of ...	**En flaske ...**	ehn **flahs**ker
A glass of ...	**Et glass ...**	eht glahss
Half a litre of lager, please.	**En halv pils, takk.**	ehn hahl pilss tahk

Aquavit *Akevitt*

This traditional Norwegian drink is served ice-cold in tiny glasses and goes well with herring hors d'œuvres, *spekemat* and rich food. *Akevitt* (ahker**vit**), which is usually served with a beer chaser, contains about 40% pure alcohol. It is distilled from potatoes or grain, flavoured with aromatic seeds (mostly

---

* If you want to buy wine or spirits, a branch of *Vinmonopolet* (**veen**moonoopo̅o̅ler), the State Wine Monopoly, is the place to go to.

caraway) and spices and matured in oak casks. *Linjeakevitt* (**lin**yerahkervit—“line” aquavit) is aquavit which has crossed the equator circle stored in the holds of a Norwegian ship; the rolling motion of the ship is said to produce a unique taste.

Wine *Vin*

Wine is imported from many countries. You’ll find excellent Bordeaux and Burgundy vintages in better hotels and restaurants, together with less expensive wines which can be ordered by the carafe or the glass.

Do you have a wine list?	**Har dere et vinkart?**	haar **da̅y̅**rer eht **veen**kah^{r}t
May I have the wine list, please?	**Kan jeg få se vinkartet?**	kahn yæi faw sa̅y̅ **veen**kah^{r}ter
Do you have any open wines?	**Har dere åpne viner?**	haar **da̅y̅**rer **awp**ner **vee**nerr
I’d like to try a glass of ...	**Jeg vil gjerne prøve et glass ...**	yæi vil **yæ^{r}**ner **pru̅r̅**ver eht glahss
Can you recommend a good white wine?	**Kan du anbefale en god hvitvin?**	kahn dew **ahn**berfaaler ehn go̅o̅(d) **veet**veen
I’d like a ... of red wine.	**Jeg vil gjerne ha ... rødvin.**	yæi vil **yæ^{r}**ner haa ... **ru̅r̅**veen
bottle	**en flaske**	ehn **flah**sker
carafe	**en karaffel**	ehn kah**rah**ferl
glass	**et glass**	eht glahss
half bottle	**en halv flaske**	ehn hahl **flah**sker
A bottle of champagne, please.	**En flaske champagne, takk.**	ehn **flah**sker shahm**pah**nyer tahk
Please bring me another ...	**Kan jeg få en ... til?**	kahn yæi faw ehn ... til
Where does this wine come from?	**Hvor kommer denne vinen fra?**	voor **kom**merr **deh**ner **vee**nern fraa
It’s excellent.	**Den er meget god.**	dehn ær **ma̅y̅**gert go̅o̅(d)
Do you have any nonalcoholic wines?	**Har dere alkoholfrie viner?**	haar **da̅y̅**rer ahlkoo**ho̅o̅l**freeyer **vee**nerr

red	**rødvin**	ru̅r̅veen
white	**hvitvin**	**veet**veen
rosé	**rosévin**	roo**ssa̅y̅**veen
dry	**tørr**	turr
full-bodied	**fyldig**	**fewl**di
sparkling	**musserende**	mew**ssa̅y̅**rehner
very dry	**meget tørr**	**ma̅y̅**gert turr
sweet	**søt**	su̅r̅t
chilled	**avkjølt**	**aav**khurlt
at room temperature	**værelses-temperert**	**vær**erlsers-tehmper**ra̅y̅**ʳt

Other alcoholic drinks *Andre alkoholholdige drikker*

You can get almost all the drinks you're used to at home. The customary international names are used, and the drinks are mixed the same way.

I'd like a/an ..., please.	**Jeg vil gjerne ha ...**	yæi vil **yæ**ʳner haa
aperitif	**en aperitiff**	ehn ahperri**tif**
brandy	**brandy**	"brandy"
cognac	**et glass konjakk**	eht glahss **kon**yahk
gin and tonic	**en gin tonic**	ehn "gin tonic"
liqueur	**et glass likør**	eht glahss li**ku̅r̅r**
port	**et glass portvin**	eht glahss **poo**ʳtveen
rum	**rom**	room
sherry	**et glass sherry**	eht glahss **shæ**ri
vermouth	**et glass vermut**	eht glahss **vær**mewt
vodka	**vodka**	**vod**kah
whisky	**whisky**	**vis**ki
neat (straight)	**bar**	baar
on the rocks	**med is**	meh(d) eess
with water	**med vann**	meh(d) vahn
with soda water	**med soda**	me(h)d **so̅o̅**dah

SKÅL!
(skawl)
CHEERS!

Nonalcoholic drinks *Alkoholfrie drikker*

Of course, you don't have to order wine or spirits. If you prefer, ask for a soft drink.

I don't drink alcohol.	**Jeg drikker ikke alkohol.**	yæi **drik**kerr **ik**ker ahlkoo**hool**
A bottle of mineral (spring) water, please.	**En flaske naturlig mineralvann, takk.**	ehn **flah**sker nah**tewr**li minerr**aal**vahn tahk
fizzy (sparkling)	**med kullsyre**	meh(d) **kewl**sewrer
still (natural)	**uten kullsyre**	**ew**tern **kewl**sewrer
I'd like a/an ...	**Jeg vil gjerne ha ...**	yæi vil **yær**ner haa
apple juice	**eplesaft**	**ehp**lersahft
grapefruit juice	**grapefruktjuice**	**grayp**frewktyewss
iced tea	**iste**	**ees**tay
lemonade	**sitronbrus**	si**troon**brewss
(glass of) milk	**(et glass) melk**	(eht glahss) mehlk
low-fat milk	**lettmelk**	**leht**mehlk
milkshake	**en milkshake**	ehn "milkshake"
orange juice	**appelsinjuice**	ahperl**seen**yewss
pineapple juice	**ananasjuice**	**ah**nahnahsyewss
soft drink	**leskedrikk**	**leh**skerdrik

Hot drinks *Varme drikker*

The best place to go for your afternoon tea or coffee is a *konditori*, teashop (coffee shop). Pay for your cake or pastry at the counter and then take it through to the seating area. In more elegant or old-fashioned cafés you'll be served at the table.

I'd like a/an ...	**Jeg vil gjerne ha ...**	yæi vil **yær**ner haa
(hot) chocolate	**(varm) sjokolade**	(vahrm) shookoo**laa**der
coffee	**kaffe**	**kah**fer
a pot of	**en kanne**	ehn **kah**ner
decaffeinated	**koffeinfri**	koffer**een**free
espresso	**en espresso**	ehn ehs**preh**ssoo
with cream	**med fløte**	meh(d) **flur**ter
tea	**te**	tay
a cup of	**en kopp**	ehn kop
with lemon	**med sitron**	meh(d) si**troon**
with milk	**med melk**	meh(d) mehlk

Complaints *Klager*

There's a ... missing.	**Det mangler ...**	deh **mahng**lerr
plate	**en tallerken**	ehn tahl**ær**kern
glass	**et glass**	eht glahss
I don't have a ...	**Jeg har ikke noen ...**	yæi haar **ik**ker **nōō**ern
knife	**kniv**	kneev
fork	**gaffel**	**gah**ferl
spoon	**skje**	shāy
That's not what I ordered.	**Dette er ikke det jeg bestilte.**	**deh**ter ær **ik**ker deh yæi ber**stil**ter
I asked for ...	**Jeg ba om ...**	yæi baa om
There must be a mistake.	**Det må være en misforståelse.**	deh maw **vǣ**rer ehn **mis**foshtawerlser
May I change this?	**Kan jeg få byttet dette?**	kahn yæi faw **bew**tert **deh**ter
I asked for a small portion (for the child).	**Jeg ba om en liten porsjon (til barnet).**	yæi baa om ehn **lee**tern poo**shōōn** (til **baa**^{r}ner)
The meat is ...	**Kjøttet er ...**	**khur**ter ær
overdone	**for mye stekt**	for **mēw**er stehkt
underdone	**for lite stekt**	for **lee**ter stehkt
too rare	**for blodig**	for **blōō**di
too tough	**for seigt**	for sæit
This is too ...	**Dette er for ...**	**deh**ter ær for
bitter	**beskt**	behskt
salty	**salt**	sahlt
sweet	**søtt**	surt
This doesn't taste right.	**Dette smaker ikke godt.**	**deh**ter **smaa**kerr **ik**ker got
The food is cold.	**Maten er kald.**	**maa**tern ær kahl
This isn't fresh.	**Dette er ikke ferskt.**	**deh**ter ær **ik**ker fæshkt
What's taking so long?	**Hvorfor tar det så lang tid?**	**voor**for taar deh saw lahng teed
Have you forgotten our drinks?	**Har du glemt drinkene våre?**	haar du glehmt **dring**kerner **vaw**rer
The wine doesn't taste right.	**Vinen smaker ikke godt.**	**vee**nern **smaa**kerr **ik**ker got

This isn't clean.	**Dette er ikke rent.**	**deh**ter ær **ik**ker raynt
I'd like to speak to the head waiter/ manager.	**Kan jeg få snakke med hovmesteren/ bestyreren?**	kahn yæi faw **snah**ker meh(d) **hawv**mehsterrern/ ber**stew**rerren

The bill (check) *Regningen*

The service charge is automatically included in restaurant bills. You can add a little extra if you are satisfied with the meal and the service.

The bill, please.	**Regningen, takk.**	**ræi**ningern tahk
I'd like to pay.	**Jeg vil gjerne betale.**	yæi vil **yæ^{r}**ner bertaaler
We'd like to pay separately.	**Vi vil gjerne betale hver for oss.**	vee vil **yæ^{r}**ner ber**taa**ler vær for oss
I think there's a mistake in this bill.	**Jeg tror det er en feil på regningen.**	yæi troor deh ær ehn fæil paw **ræi**ningern
What's this amount for?	**Hva står dette beløpet for?**	vah stawr **deh**ter ber**lur**per for
Is everything included?	**Er alt inkludert?**	ær ahlt inklew**day^{r}t**
Do you accept traveller's cheques/ Eurocheques?	**Tar dere reisesjekker/ eurosjekker?**	taar **day**rer **ræi**ssershehkerr/ **yew**rooshehkerr
Can I pay with this credit card?	**Kan jeg betale med dette kreditt-kortet?**	kahn yæi ber**taa**ler meh(d) **deh**ter krehdit-ko^{r}ter
This is for you.	**Vær så god.**	vær saw goo(d)
Keep the change.	**Behold veksle-pengene.**	ber**hol** **vehk**shler-pehngerner
That was a delicious meal.	**Det var et utsøkt måltid.**	deh vaar eht **ew**tsurkt **mawl**teed
We enjoyed it, thank you.	**Det var meget godt.**	deh vaar **may**gert got

SERVICE INKLUDERT
SERVICE INCLUDED

TIPPING, see inside back cover

Snacks *Småretter*

For a quick snack, go to a *gatekjøkken*, "street kitchen", where you can get everything from a hot dog to chicken and spring rolls, ice cream and soft drinks. At cafés and cafeterias, you can have pastries, open sandwiches and maybe a salad.

I'll have one of those.	**Jeg vil gjerne ha en av dem.**	yæi vil **yæ^{r}**ner haa ehn ahv dehm
Can I have two of these, please?	**Kan jeg få to av disse?**	kahn yæi faw tōō ahv **dis**ser
to the right/left	**til høyre/venstre**	til **hoy**rer/**vehns**trer
above/below	**ovenfor/nedenfor**	**aw**vernfor/**nāy**dernfor
It's to take away.	**Jeg tar det med meg.**	yæi taar deh meh(d) mæi
I'll eat it here.	**Jeg spiser det her.**	yæi **spee**sserr deh hǣr
A frankfurter with ..., please.	**En pølse med ...**	ehn **purl**ser meh(d)
mashed potatoes	**potetstappe**	poo**tāyt**stahper
a potato pancake	**lompe**	**loom**per
I'd like a/an/some ...	**Jeg vil gjerne ha ...**	yæi vil **yæ^{r}**ner haa
fried sausage	**en grillpølse**	ehn **gril**purlser
in a roll	**med brød**	meh(d) brūr
with chips (fries)	**med pommes frites**	meh(d) pom frit
with onion	**med løk**	meh(d) lūrk
ice cream	**en is(krem)**	ehn **eess**(krāym)
(slice of) pizza	**en (skive) pizza**	ehn (**shee**ver) **pit**sah
soft ice cream	**en softis**	ehn **soft**eess
with nuts	**med nøtter**	meh(d) **nur**terr
with chocolate	**med sjokolade**	meh(d) shookoo**laa**der
spring (egg) roll	**vårrull**	**vawr**rewl
water ice	**en fruktis**	ehn **frewkt**eess
Can I have an open sandwich with eggs and marinated sprats?	**Kan jeg få et smørbrød med egg og ansjos?**	kahn yæi faw eht **smurr**brūr meh(d) ehg o(g) ahng**shōōs**
cheese	**ost**	oost
cod roe	**torskerogn**	**tosh**kerrongn
fish pudding	**fiskepudding**	**fis**kerpewding
ham	**kokt skinke**	kookt **shing**ker
liver paté	**leverpostei**	**leh**verrpoostæi

Pastries and cakes *Bakverk og kaker*

I'd like a piece of ...	**Jeg vil gjerne ha et stykke ...**	yæi vil **yǣʳ**ner haa eht **stew**ker
gâteau (layer cake)	**bløtkake**	**bl͞urt**kaaker
with marzipan	**med marsipan**	meh(d) mahshi**ppaan**
I'd like a/an/ some ...	**Jeg vil gjerne ha ...**	yæi vil **yǣʳ**ner haa
apple pie	**en eplekake**	ehn **ehp**lerkaaker
biscuits (cookies)	**noen småkaker**	**n͞oo**ern **smaw**kaakerr
bun	**en bolle**	ehn **bol**ler
with raisins	**med rosiner**	meh(d) roo**see**nerr
chocolate cake	**en sjokoladekake**	ehn shookoo**laa**derkaaker
coconut macaroons	**noen kokos-makroner**	**n͞oo**ern **koo**kooss-mahkr͞oonerr
cream horn	**et fløtehorn**	eht **fl͞ur**terh͞ooʳn
custard slice (napo-leon)	**en napoleonskake**	ehn nah**p͞oo**lehonskaaker
Danish pastry	**et wienerbrød**	eht **vee**nerrbr͞ur
doughnut	**en smultring**	ehn **smewlt**ring
fruit tart	**en fruktterte**	ehn **frewkt**tæʳter
meringues	**noen marengs**	**n͞oo**ern mah**rehngss**
shortbread	**en sandkake**	ehn **sahn**kaaker
sponge cake	**et sukkerbrød**	eht **sook**kerrbr͞ur
Swiss roll	**en rullekake**	ehn **rew**lerkaaker
with vanilla butter	**med vaniljefyll**	meh(d) vah**nil**yerfewl
with jam	**med syltetøy**	meh(d) **sewl**tertoy
with chocolate cream	**med sjokoladefyll**	meh(d) shookoo**laa**der-fewl

fastelavnsbolle (fahsterl**aavns**-boller) — lenten bun; bun cut in half, filled with whipped cream and topped with icing (confectioners') sugar

julekake (**y͞ew**lerkaaker) — rich fruit cake (a Christmas speciality)

kransekake (**krahn**serkaaker) — cone-shaped pile of almond-macaroon rings decorated with icing (frosting), marzipan flowers, etc.

kringle (**kring**ler) — twisted sweet yeast-bread ring

krumkake (**kroom**kaaker) — wafer cone filled with whipped cream and jam or berries

vaniljebolle (vah**nil**yerboller) — bun filled with vanilla custard and topped with icing sugar

Picnic *Picnic*

Here's a basic list of food and drink that might come in useful when shopping for a picnic.

I'd like a/an/ some ...	**Jeg vil gjerne ha ...**	yæi vil **yæ**^{r}ner haa
apples	**epler**	**ehp**ler
bananas	**bananer**	bah**naa**nerr
beer	**øl**	url
bread	**brød**	brur
rye	**rug**	rewg
white	**loff**	loof
butter	**smør**	smurr
cake	**en kake**	ehn **kaa**ker
cheese	**ost**	oost
cheese spread	**smøreost**	**smur**reroost
chips (Am.)	**potetgull**	poo**tayt**gewl
chocolate bar	**en sjokoladeplate**	ehn shookoo**laa**derplaater
coffee	**kaffe**	**kah**fer
instant coffee	**pulverkaffe**	**pewl**verrkahfer
cold cuts	**kjøttpålegg**	**khurt**pawlehg
crackers	**salte kjeks**	**sahl**ter khehkss
crisps	**potetgull**	poo**tayt**gewl
eggs	**egg**	ehg
grapes	**druer**	**drew**err
ham	**skinke**	**shing**ker
lemon	**en sitron**	ehn si**troon**
liver paté	**leverpostei**	**leh**verrpoostæi
liver sausage	**leverpølse**	**leh**verrpurlser
milk	**melk**	mehlk
mustard *	**sennep**	**seh**nerp
oranges	**appelsiner**	ahperl**see**nerr
pastries	**kaker**	**kaa**kerr
pepper	**pepper**	**peh**perr
pickled gherkins	**sylteagurker**	**sewl**terahgewrkerr
rolls	**rundstykker**	**rewn**stewkerr
salt	**salt**	sahlt
sausage	**pølse**	**purl**ser
soft drink	**leskedrikk**	**lehs**kerdrik
sugar	**sukker**	**sook**kerr
tea	**te**	tay
wine	**vin**	veen

---

* Norwegian mustard is sweet; if you want a sharp one, ask for French mustard (*fransk sennep* – frahnsk **seh**nerp).

Travelling around

Plane *Fly*

Is there a flight to Tromsø?	**Går det et fly til Tromsø?**	gawr deh eht flew til **troom**sur
Is it a direct flight?	**Er det et direkte fly?**	ær deh eht **dee**rehkter flew
When's the next flight to Alta?	**Når går neste fly til Alta?**	nor gawr **neh**ster flew til **ahl**tah
Is there a connection to Kirkenes?	**Fins det en forbindelse til Kirkenes?**	finss deh ehn for**bin**erlser til **khir**kernayss
I'd like to make a reservation for Stavanger.	**Jeg vil gjerne reservere en plass til Stavanger.**	yæi vil **yæ**^{r}ner rehssær**vay**rer ehn plahss til stah**vahng**err
I'd like a ticket to Bergen.	**Jeg vil gjerne ha en billett til Bergen.**	yæi vil **yæ**^{r}ner haa ehn bil**leht** til **bær**gern
single (one-way)	**enkeltbillett**	**ehng**kerltbilleht
return (round-trip)	**tur-returbillett**	tewr-reh**tewr**billeht
aisle seat	**plass ved midtgangen**	plahss veh(d) **mit**gahngern
window seat	**vindusplass**	**vin**dewsplahss
What time ...?	**Når ...?**	nor
do we take off	**går flyet**	gawr **flew**er
should I check in	**må jeg sjekke inn**	maw yæi **sheh**ker in
do we arrive	**er vi fremme**	ær vee **freh**mer
This is cabin luggage.	**Dette er håndbagasje.**	**deh**ter ær **hon**bahgaasher
Is there a bus to/from the airport?	**Går det buss til/fra flyplassen?**	gawr deh bewss til/fraa **flew**plahssern
I'd like to ... my reservation.	**Jeg vil gjerne ... reservasjonen.**	yæi vil **yæ**^{r}ner ... rehssærvah**shoo**nern
cancel/change	**annullere/endre**	ahnew**lay**rer/**ehn**drer
confirm	**bekrefte**	ber**kreh**fter
How long is the ticket valid?	**Hvor lenge er billetten gyldig?**	voor **lehng**er ær bil**leh**tern **yewl**di

ANKOMST	**AVGANG**
ARRIVAL	DEPARTURE

Train *Tog*

Trains in Norway are operated by Norwegian State Railways—Norges Statsbaner (NSB). From Oslo central station (*Oslo Sentralstasjon*) there are connections to Sweden and the Continent via Copenhagen. The main inland destinations are Stavanger, Bergen and Trondheim, with connections to Bodø, Norway's northernmost station (apart from Narvik, which has connections to Sweden only).

Children under four years old travel free. Travellers under 16 pay half price.

Except on local trains, food is available either from a snack trolley (cart; *serveringsvogn*), a kiosk (*togkiosk*), a buffet car (*kafeteriavogn*) or a dining car (*restaurantvogn*). In sleeping cars, men and women can be accommodated separately; there are also family compartments. Most long-distance trains have carriages specially equipped for parents with babies and for disabled people. It's worth reserving a seat, particularly on long-distance trains.

EuroCity-tog (EC) (yēwroo**s**itti-tawg)	International express train with first and second class
Inter-City-tog ("intercity"-tawg)	Day train connecting major towns in southern Norway with Oslo
Ekspresstog (ehks**preh**stawg)	Long-distance express train stopping at few stations
Hurtigtog (**hew**ʳtitawg)	Long-distance express train stopping at more stations than the *ekspresstog*
Lokaltog (loo**kaal**tawg)	Local train stopping at all stations

Coach (Long-distance bus) *Rutebil/Ekspressbuss*

Areas not served by NSB are covered by regional and local bus companies. Tourist information offices and travel agencies have timetables and other details.

Note: Most of the phrases on the following pages can be used for both train and coach travel.

To the railway station *Til jernbanestasjonen*

Where's the railway station?	**Hvor er jernbane-stasjonen?**	voor ær **yæʳn**baaner-stahshoonern
Where's the coach station?	**Hvor er buss-stasjonen?**	voor ær **bews**-stahshoonern
Taxi!	**Drosje!**	**dro**sher
Take me to the ..., please.	**Kjør meg til ...**	khurr mæi til

INNGANG	ENTRANCE
UTGANG	EXIT
TIL TOGENE	TO THE TRAINS
INFORMASJON	INFORMATION

Where's the ...? *Hvor er ...?*

Where is/are (the) ...?	**Hvor er ...?**	voor ær
booking office	**billettkontoret**	bil**leht**koontoorer
cafeteria	**kafeteriaen**	kahfer**tāy**reeahern
currency exchange office	**vekslingskontoret**	**vehk**shlingskoontoorer
left-luggage office (checkroom)	**bagasje-oppbevaringen**	bah**gaa**sher-opbervaaringern
lost property (lost and found) office	**hittegodskontoret**	**hit**tergoodskoontoorer
luggage (baggage) lockers	**oppbevarings-boksene**	**op**bervaarings-bokserner
newsstand	**aviskiosken**	ah**vees**khyoskern
platform 2	**perrong 2**	peh**rong** 2
reservations office	**billettkontoret**	bil**leht**koontoorer
restaurant	**restauranten**	rehstew**rahng**ern
snack bar	**snackbaren**	**snæk**baarern
ticket office	**billettluken**	bil**leht**lewkern
track 5	**spor 5**	spoor 5
waiting room	**ventesalen**	**vehn**tersaalern
Where are the toilets?	**Hvor er toalettet?**	voor ær tooah**leh**ter

TAXI, see page 21

Inquiries *Forespørsler*

In Norway the sign [i] means information office.

When is the ....train to Halden?	**Når går ... tog til Halden?**	nor gawr ... tawg til **hahl**dern
first/last	**første/siste**	**fursh**ter/**sis**ter
When is the next train to Hamar?	**Når går neste tog til Hamar?**	nor gawr **nehs**ter tawg til **haa**mahr
What time does the train to Oslo leave?	**Når går toget til Oslo?**	nor gawr **taw**ger til **oosh**loo
What's the fare to Trondheim?	**Hvor mye koster det til Trondheim?**	voor **mew**er **kos**terr deh til **tron**hæim
Is it a through train?	**Er det et gjennomgående tog?**	ær deh eht **yeh**nom-gawehner tawg
Is there a connection to Elverum?	**Fins det en forbindelse til Elverum?**	finss deh ehn for**bin**-erlser til **ehl**verrewm
Do I have to change trains?	**Må jeg bytte tog?**	maw yæi **bew**ter tawg
Is there enough time to change?	**Rekker jeg å bytte tog?**	**reh**kerr yæi aw **bew**ter tawg
Is the train running on time?	**Er toget i rute?**	ær **taw**ger ee **rew**ter
What time does the train arrive in Åndalsnes?	**Når er toget fremme i Åndalsnes?**	nor ær **taw**ger **freh**mer ee **on**dahlsnayss
Is there a dining car/sleeping car on the train?	**Er det en restaurantvogn/sovevogn i toget?**	ær deh ehn rehstew-**rahng**vongn/**saw**ver-vongn ee **taw**ger
Does the train stop in Asker?	**Stanser toget i Asker?**	**stahn**serr **taw**ger ee **ahs**kerr
Which platform does the train to Skien leave from?	**Fra hvilken perrong går toget til Skien?**	fraa **vil**kern peh**rong** gawr **taw**ger til **shay**ern
Which track does the train from Gjøvik arrive at?	**På hvilket spor kommer toget fra Gjøvik inn?**	paw **vil**kert spoor **kom**merr **taw**ger fraa **yur**veek in
I'd like a timetable, please.	**Jeg vil gjerne ha en rutetabell.**	yæi vil **yær**ner haa ehn **rew**tertahbehl

Det er et gjennomgående tog.	It's a through train.
Du må bytte i ...	You have to change at ...
Bytt i ... og ta lokaltoget.	Change at ... and get a local train.
Perrong 2 er ...	Platform 2 is ...
der borte/opp trappen til høyre/til venstre	over there/upstairs on the right/on the left
Det går et tog til Tønsberg kl. 16.00.	There's a train to Tønsberg at 16.00 (4 p.m.).
Toget går fra spor 8.	Your train will leave from track 8.
Det er ... minutter forsinket.	It's running ... minutes late.
Første klasse er foran/i midten/bakerst.	First class at the front/in the middle/at the rear.

Tickets—Reservation *Billetter – Bestilling*

I'd like a ticket to ...	**Jeg vil gjerne ha en billett til ...**	yæi vil **yæ[r]ner** haa ehn bil**leht** til
single (one-way)	**enkeltbillett**	**ehng**kerltbilleht
return (round-trip)	**tur-returbillett**	tewr-reh**tewr**billeht
first class	**første klasse**	**fursh**ter **klah**sser
second class	**andre/annen klasse**	**ahn**drer/**aa**ern **klah**sser
half price	**halv pris**	hahl preess
Must the child pay full fare?	**Må barnet betale full takst?**	maw **baa[r]**ner ber**taa**ler fewl tahkst
I'd like a window seat.	**Jeg vil gjerne ha vindusplass.**	yæi vil **yæ[r]**ner hah **vin**dewsplahss
I'd like to reserve a ...	**Jeg vil gjerne reservere en ...**	yæi vil **yæ[r]**ner rehssær**vay**rer ehn
couchette	**køye i liggevognen**	**koy**er ee **lig**gervongnern
berth in the sleeping car	**køye i sovevognen**	**koy**er ee **saw**vervongnern
upper berth	**overkøye**	**aw**verrkoyer
middle berth	**midtkøye**	**mit**koyer
lower berth	**underkøye**	**ewn**errkoyer

TIME, see page 153

On the platform *På perrongen*

Is this the platform for the train to Kongsberg?	**Er dette perrongen for toget til Kongsberg?**	ær **deh**ter peh**rong**ern for **taw**ger til **kongs**bærg
Is this the train to Geilo?	**Er dette toget til Geilo?**	ær **deh**ter **taw**ger til **yæi**loo
Is the train from Levanger late?	**Er toget fra Levanger forsinket?**	ær **taw**ger fraa ler**vahng**err fo**shing**kert
What track does the train to Gol arrive on?	**På hvilket spor kommer toget til Gol inn?**	paw **vil**kert spōōr **kom**merr **taw**ger til gōōl in

All aboard *Ta plass*

Excuse me. Could I get by?	**Unnskyld. Kan jeg få komme forbi?**	**ewn**shewl. kahn yæi faw **kom**mer for**bee**
Is this seat taken?	**Er denne plassen opptatt?**	ær **deh**ner **plahs**sern **op**taht

RØYKING TILLATT
SMOKER

RØYKING FORBUDT/ RØYKING IKKE TILLATT
NONSMOKER

I think that's my seat.	**Jeg tror at det er min plass.**	yæi trōōr aht deh ær meen plahss
Would you let me know before we get to Røros?	**Kan du si fra før vi kommer til Røros?**	kahn dew see fraa fūrr vee **kom**merr til **rūr**rawss
What station is this?	**Hvilken stasjon er dette?**	**vil**kern stah**shōōn** ær **deh**ter
How long does the train stop here?	**Hvor lenge står toget her?**	voor **lehng**er stawr **taw**ger hǣr
When do we get to Voss?	**Når kommer vi til Voss?**	nor **kom**merr vee til voss
Where are we now?	**Hvor er vi nå?**	voor ær vee naw
Where's the ...?	**Hvor er ...**	voor ær
dining car	**restaurantvognen**	rehstew**rahng**vongnern
buffet car	**kafeteriavognen**	kahfer**tāy**reeahvongnern
kiosk	**togkiosken**	**tawg**khyoskern

Sleeping *I sovevognen*

Are there any free compartments in the sleeping car?	**Fins det noen ledige kupéer i sovevognen?**	finss deh **nōōern lāy**deeyer kew**pāy**err ee **saw**vervongnern
Where's the sleeping car?	**Hvor er sovevognen?**	voor ær **saw**vervongnern
Where's my berth?	**Hvor er min køye?**	voor ær meen **koy**er
I'd like a lower berth.	**Jeg vil gjerne ha en underkøye.**	yæi vil **yæʳ**ner haa ehn **ewn**errkoyer
Would you make up our berths?	**Kan du gjøre i stand køyene våre?**	kahn dew **yūr**rer ee stahn **koy**erner **vaw**rer
Would you wake me at 7 o'clock?	**Kan du vekke meg kl. 7?**	kahn dew **veh**ker mæi **klok**kern 7

Baggage and porters *Bagasje og bærere*

Can you help me with my luggage?	**Kan du hjelpe meg med bagasjen?**	kahn dew **yehl**per mæi meh(d) bah**gaa**shern
Are there any ...?	**Fins det ... her?**	finss deh ... hær
luggage trolleys (carts)	**bagasjetraller**	bah**gaa**shertrahlerr
luggage (baggage) lockers	**oppbevarings-bokser**	**op**bervaaringsbokserr
Where are they?	**Hvor er de?**	voor ær dee
Where's the left-luggage office (checkroom)?	**Hvor er bagasje-oppbevaringen?**	voor ær bah**gaa**sher-opbervaaringern
I'd like to leave my luggage, please.	**Jeg vil gjerne levere inn bagasjen til oppbevaring.**	yæi vil **yæʳ**ner leh**vāy**rer in bah**gaa**shern til **op**bervaaring
I'd like to register (check) my luggage.	**Jeg vil gjerne ekspedere bagasjen.**	yæi vil **yæʳ**ner ehksper**dāy**rer bah**gaa**shern
I'd like to take out luggage insurance.	**Jeg vil gjerne tegne en reisegodsforsikring.**	yæi vil **yæʳ**ner **tæi**ner ehn **ræis**sergoodsfoshikring

REISEGODSEKSPEDISJON

REGISTERING LUGGAGE (BAGGAGE CHECKING)

PORTERS, see also page 18

Bus—Tram (Streetcar) *Buss – Trikk*

Single tickets are available from the driver. In Oslo, it's worth buying a booklet of tickets (valid for transfers within one hour) if you plan to travel around.

I'd like a booklet of tickets.	**Jeg vil gjerne ha et billetthefte.**	yæi vil **yæ**ʳner haa eht bil**leht**hehfter
Which tram (streetcar) goes to the town centre?	**Hvilken trikk går til sentrum?**	**vil**kern trik gawr til **sehn**trewm
Does this bus stop at ...?	**Stanser denne bussen ved ...?**	**stahn**serr **deh**ner **bews**sern veh(d)
Where can I get a bus to the Folk Museum?	**Hvorfra går bussen til Folkemuseet?**	**voor**fra gawr **bews**sern til **fol**kermewssāyer
Which tram do I take to Vigeland Park?	**Hvilken trikk går til Vigelandsparken?**	**vil**kern trik gawr til **vee**gerlahnspahrkern
Where's the ...?	**Hvor er ...?**	voor ær
bus stop tram stop	**bussholdeplassen** **trikkeholdeplassen**	**bews**hollerplahssern **trik**kerhollerplahssern
When is the ... bus to the town centre?	**Når går ... buss til sentrum?**	nor gawr ... bewss til **sehn**trewm
first/next/last	**første/neste/siste**	**fursh**ter/**neh**ster/**sis**ter
How much is the fare to ...?	**Hvor mye koster det til ...?**	voor **mēw**er **kos**terr deh til
Do I have to change buses?	**Må jeg bytte buss?**	maw yæi **bew**ter bewss
How many stops are there to ...?	**Hvor mange holdeplasser er det til ...?**	voor **mahng**er **hol**ler-plahsserr ær deh til
Will you tell me when to get off?	**Kan du si fra når jeg skal gå av?**	kahn dew see fraa nor yæi skahl gaw ahv
I want to get off at ...	**Jeg skal av ved ...**	yæi skahl ahv veh(d)

BUSSHOLDEPLASS
BUS STOP

Underground (Subway) *T-bane*

Oslo's underground railway extends from the centre of the city to the suburbs. Maps of the system are displayed at stations and aboard trains. You can transfer from bus or tram to underground (subway) on the same ticket.

Where's the nearest underground station?	**Hvor er nærmeste T-banestasjon?**	voor ær **nær**mehster **tāy**-baanerstahshōōn
Does this train go to Holmenkollen?	**Går denne banen til Holmenkollen?**	gawr **deh**ner **baa**nern til **hol**mernkollern
Where do I change for ...?	**Hvor må jeg bytte for å komme til ...?**	voor maw yæi **bew**ter for aw **kom**mer til
Is the next station ...?	**Er neste stasjon ...?**	ær **neh**ster stah**shōōn**
Which line should I take to ...?	**Hvilken linje skal jeg ta til ...?**	**vil**kern **lin**yer skahl yæi taa til

Boat—Ship *Båt – Skip*

Travelling by car in western Norway involves numerous fjord crossings by ferry. The frequency of services depends on the season. In rural areas, local hotels will always be able to tell you exact ferry times. At the height of the summer tourist season, try to reserve a place for your car or you may find yourself spending hours in queues. Fares vary according to size and weight of vehicle.

In Oslo, there are guided cruises of the harbour and around the islands, as well as regular boat services to the museums on the Bygdøy peninsula.

When does the boat/ferry for ... leave?	**Når går båten/ fergen til ...?**	nor gawr **baw**tern/ **fær**ggern til
Where's the embarkation point?	**Ved hvilken kai legger båten til?**	veh(d) **vil**kern kahy **leh**gerr **baw**tern til
How long does the crossing take?	**Hvor lang tid tar overfarten?**	voor lahng teed taar **aw**verrfah[r]tern

When do we call at Molde?	**Når legger vi til i Molde?**	nor **leh**gerr vee til ee **mol**der
I'd like to take a boat trip/harbour tour.	**Jeg vil gjerne ta en båttur/havne-rundtur.**	yæi vil **yæ**^{r}ner taa ehn **bawt**tewr/**hahv**ner-rewntewr
boat	**en båt**	ehn bawt
cabin	**en lugar**	ehn lew**gaar**
single/double	**enkel/dobbel**	**ehng**kerl/**dob**berl
canoe	**en kano**	ehn **kaa**noo
cruise	**et cruise**	eht "cruise"
deck	**et dekk**	eht dehk
ferry	**en ferge/ferje**	ehn **fær**gger/**fær**yer
car ferry	**bilferge**	**beel**færgger
gangway	**en landgang**	ehn **lahn**gahng
hydrofoil	**en hydrofoil**	ehn hewdroo**foil**
jetty	**en brygge**	ehn **brew**ger
kayak	**en kajakk**	ehn **kah**yahk
life belt	**et livbelte**	eht **leev**behlter
life boat	**en livbåt**	ehn **leev**bawt
life jacket	**en flytevest**	ehn **flew**tervehst
motorboat	**en motorbåt**	ehn **moo**toorbawt
pier	**en pir**	ehn peer
port	**en havn**	ehn hahvn
rowing boat	**en robåt**	ehn **roo**bawt
sailing boat	**en seilbåt**	ehn **sæil**bawt
ship	**et skip**	eht sheep
steamer	**en dampbåt**	ehn **dahmp**bawt

Other means of transport *Andre transportmidler*

bicycle	**en sykkel**	ehn **sew**kerl
cable car	**en taubane**	ehn **tou**baaner
helicopter	**et helikopter**	eht hehli**kop**terr
moped	**en moped**	ehn moo**payd**
motorbike	**en motorsykkel**	ehn **moo**tooshewkerl
scooter	**en scooter**	ehn **skew**terr
I'd like to hire (rent) a bicycle.	**Jeg vil gjerne leie en sykkel.**	yæi vil **yæ**^{r}ner **læi**er ehn **sew**kerl

Or perhaps you prefer:

to hike	**å vandre**	aw **vahn**drer
to hitchhike	**å haike**	aw **hah**yker
to walk	**å spasere**	aw spah**ssay**rer

Car *Bil*

All the basic rules for right-hand traffic apply. The use of seat belts (*bilbelte*) is obligatory, and that includes back-seat passengers if the car is so equipped. A red reflector warning triangle must be carried. Crash helmets are compulsory for both drivers and passengers on motorcycles and scooters. Fines for drinking and driving are prohibitive and may involve loss of licence and imprisonment.

Where's the nearest filling station?	**Hvor er nærmeste bensinstasjon?**	voor ær **nær**mehster behn**seen**stahshōōn
Fill it up, please.	**Full tank, takk.**	fewl tahngk tahk
Give me ... litres of petrol (gasoline).	**... liter bensin, takk.**	... **lee**terr behn**seen** tahk
super (premium)	**super**	**sēw**perr
regular	**normal**	noor**maal**
unleaded	**blyfri**	**blēw**free
diesel	**diesel**	**dee**sserl
Please check the ...	**Vær snill å kontrollere ...**	vær snil aw koontroo**lāy**rer
battery	**batteriet**	bahterr**ee**yer
brake fluid	**bremsevæsken**	**brehm**servehskern
oil/water	**oljen/vannet**	**ol**yern/**vah**ner
Would you check the tyre pressure?	**Kan du kontrollere trykket i dekkene?**	kahn dew koontroo**lāy**rer **trew**ker ee **deh**kerner
1.6 front, 1.8 rear.	**1,6 foran, 1,8 bak.**	1 **kom**mah 6 **for**ahn 1 **kom**mah 8 baak
Could you check the spare tyre, too?	**Kan du kontrollere reservedekket også?**	kahn dew koontroo**lāy**rer reh**sær**verdehker **os**so
Can you mend this puncture (fix this flat)?	**Kan du reparere denne punkteringen?**	kahn dew rehpah**rāy**rer **deh**ner poong**tāy**ringern
Would you change the ..., please?	**Kan du skifte ...**	kahn dew **shif**ter
bulb	**pæren**	**pǣ**rern
fan belt	**vifteremmen**	**vif**terrehmern
spark(ing) plugs	**tennstiftene**	**tehn**stifterner
tyre	**dekket**	**deh**ker
wipers	**vindusviskerne**	**vin**dewsviskæʳner

Would you clean the windscreen (windshield)?	**Kan du vaske frontruten?**	kahn dew **vahs**ker **front**re̅w̅tern
Where can I get my car cleaned?	**Hvor kan jeg få vasket bilen?**	voor kahn yæi faw **vahs**kert **bee**lern
Is there a car wash here/nearby?	**Er det en bilvask her/i nærheten?**	ær deh ehn **beel**vahsk hǣr/ee **nǣr**hehtern

Asking the way *Spørre om veien*

In which direction is ...?	**I hvilken retning ligger ...?**	ee **vil**kern **reht**ning **lig**gerr
Can you tell me the way to ...?	**Kan du vise meg veien til ...?**	kahn dew **vee**sser mæi **væi**ern til
Can you tell me where ... is?	**Kan du si meg hvor ... ligger?**	kahn dew see mæi voor ... **lig**gerr
How do I get to ...?	**Hvordan kommer jeg til ...?**	**voo^{r}**dahn **kom**merr yæi til
this place	**dette stedet**	**deh**ter **stāy**der
this address	**denne adressen**	**deh**ner ah**drehs**sern
Am I on the right road for ...?	**Er dette veien til ...?**	ær **deh**ter **væi**ern til
How far is the next village?	**Hvor langt er det til neste tettsted?**	voor lahngt ær deh til **nehs**ter **teht**stāy(d)
How far is it to ... from here?	**Hvor langt er det til ... herfra?**	voor lahngt ær deh til ... **hær**frah
Is there a motorway (expressway) to ...?	**Fins det en motorvei til ...?**	finss deh ehn **mōō**toorvæi til
Is there a road with little traffic?	**Fins det en vei med lite trafikk?**	finss deh ehn væi meh(d) **lee**ter trah**fik**
Can I drive to the centre of town?	**Kan jeg kjøre inn i sentrum?**	kahn yæi **khūr**rer in ee **sehn**trewm
How long does it take by car/on foot?	**Hvor lang tid tar det med bil/til fots?**	voor lahng teed taar deh meh(d) beel/til footss
Where does this road lead to?	**Hvor fører denne veien?**	voor **fūr**rerr **deh**ner **væi**ern
Can you show me on the map where I am?	**Kan du vise meg på kartet hvor jeg er?**	kahn dew **vee**sser mæi paw **kah^{r}**ter voor yæi ær

Du har kjørt feil.	You're on the wrong road.
Kjør rett frem.	Go straight ahead.
Det er der borte til høyre/venstre.	It's down there on the right/left.
midt imot/bak ...	opposite/behind ...
ved siden av/etter ...	next to/after ...
nord/sør/øst/vest	north/south/east/west
Kjør til første/annet kryss.	Go to the first/second crossroads (intersection).
Sving til venstre ved trafikklyset.	Turn left at the traffic lights.
Ta til høyre ved neste kryss.	Turn right at the next corner.
Ta E 6.	Take the E 6.
Det er en enveisgate.	It's a one-way street.
Du må kjøre tilbake til ...	You have to go back to ...
Følg skiltene til Moss.	Follow signs for Moss.

Parking *Parkering*

Where can I park?	**Hvor kan jeg parkere?**	voor kahn yæi pahr**kāy**rer
Is there a ... nearby?	**Fins det en ... i nærheten?**	finns deh ehn ... ee **nǣr**hehtern
car park (parking lot)	**parkeringsplass**	pahr**kāy**ringsplahss
multistorey car park (parking garage)	**parkeringshus**	pahr**kāy**ringshew̄ss
May I park here?	**Kan jeg parkere her?**	kahn yæi pahr**kāy**rer hǣr
How long can I park here?	**Hvor lenge kan jeg stå her?**	voor **lehng**er kahn yæi staw hǣr
What's the charge per hour?	**Hvor mye koster det pr. time?**	voor **mew̄**er **kos**terr deh pær **tee**mer
Do you have some change for the parking meter?	**Har du vekslepenger til parkometeret?**	haar dew **vehk**shlerpehngerr til pahrkoo**māy**terrer

Breakdown—Road assistance *Motorstopp – Hjelp på veien*

Where's the nearest garage (auto repair shop)?	**Hvor er nærmeste bilverksted?**	voor ær **nær**mehster **beel**værksteh(d)
My car has broken down.	**Jeg har fått motorstopp.**	yæi haar fot **mo͞o**tooshtop
I've had a breakdown at ...	**Jeg har fått motorstopp ved ...**	yæi haar fot **mo͞o**tooshtop veh(d)
Can you send a mechanic?	**Kan du sende en mekaniker?**	kahn dew **seh**ner ehn meh**kaa**nikkerr
My car won't start.	**Bilen starter ikke.**	**bee**lern **staa**^{r}terr **ik**ker
The battery is dead.	**Batteriet er flatt.**	bahter**ree**yer ær flaht
I've run out of petrol (gas).	**Jeg har kjørt tom.**	yæi haar khūr^{r}t tom
I have a flat tyre.	**Jeg har punktert.**	yæi haar poong**tāy**^{r}**t**
The engine is overheating.	**Motoren har gått varm.**	**mo͞o**toorern haar got vahrm
There is something wrong with the ...	**Det er noe i veien med ...**	deh ær **no͞o**er ee **væi**ern meh(d)
brakes	**bremsene**	**brehm**serner
carburettor	**forgasseren**	for**gahs**serrern
exhaust (tail) pipe	**eksosrøret**	ehk**so͞os**rūrer
ignition	**tenningen**	**teh**ningern
indicator	**blinklyset**	**blingk**lēwsser
radiator	**kjøleren**	**khūr**lerrern
steering	**styringen**	**stēw**ringern
wheel	**hjulet**	y**ūr**ler
Can you send a breakdown van (tow truck)?	**Kan du sende en kranbil?**	kahn dew **seh**ner ehn **kraan**beel
How long will you be?	**Når kommer du?**	nor **kom**merr dew
Can you lend me a/some ...?	**Kan du låne meg ...?**	kahn dew **law**ner mæi
jack	**en jekk**	ehn yehk
jerry can	**en bensinkanne**	ehn behn**seen**kahner
pliers	**en tang**	ehn tahng
spanner	**en skrunøkkel**	ehn **skrēw**nurkerl
tools	**noe verktøy**	**no͞o**er **værk**toy
towrope	**et slepetau**	eht **shlāy**pertou

Accident—Police *Ulykke – Politi*

Please call the police.	**Vær så snill å ringe politiet.**	vær saw snil aw **ringer** polit**tee**yer
There's been an accident.	**Det har skjedd en ulykke.**	deh haar shehd ehn **ew**lewker
It's about 2 km. from ...	**Det er ca. 2 km fra ...**	deh ær **sir**rkah 2 **khil**loomayterr fraa
Where's there a telephone?	**Hvor fins det en telefon?**	voor finss deh ehn tehler**foon**
Call a doctor/an ambulance quickly.	**Ring etter lege/sykebil!**	ring **eh**terr **lay**ger/**sew**kerbeel
There are people injured.	**Det er noen som er skadet.**	deh ær **noo**ern som ær **skaa**dert
Here's my driving licence.	**Her er førerkortet mitt.**	hær ær **fur**rerkoʳter mit
What's your name and address?	**Kan jeg få navn og adresse?**	kahn yæi faw nahvn o(g) ah**dreh**sser
What's your insurance company?	**Hvilket forsikrings-selskap har du?**	vilkert fos**hik**rings-sehlskaap haar dew

Road signs *Trafikkskilt*

ALL STANS FORBUDT	No stopping
DATOPARKERING	Parking according to date*
FERIST	Cattle grid
GRUSVEI	Gravelled road
INNKJØRSEL FORBUDT	No entry
KJØR SAKTE	Drive slowly
LØS GRUS	Gravelled road
MØTEPLASS	Road passing place
FORBIKJØRING FORBUDT	No overtaking (passing)
OMKJØRING	Diversion (Detour)
PARKERING (FORBUDT)	(No) Parking
RASFARE	Falling rocks
SVAKE KANTER	Soft shoulders
TELELØSNING/TELELØYSE	Potholes due to frost
TOLL	Customs
UTKJØRSEL	Exit
VEIARBEID/VEGARBEID	Roadworks (Men working)

* Night parking on one side of the street only (even numbers on even days, odd numbers on odd days).

Sightseeing

Where's the tourist office?	**Hvor er turist-kontoret?**	voor ær tew**rist**-koont**o͞o**rer
What are the main points of interest?	**Hva er hoved-severdighetene?**	vah ær **ho͞o**verd-sehværdihehterner
We're here for ...	**Vi skal være her ...**	vee skahl vǣrer hǣr
a few hours	**et par timer**	eht pahr **tee**merr
a day/a week	**en dag/en uke**	ehn daag/ehn **e͞w**ker
Can you recommend a/an ...?	**Kan du anbefale en ...?**	kan dew **ahn**berfaaler ehn
sightseeing tour	**sightseeingtur**	"**sight**seeing"te͞wr
excursion	**utflukt**	**e͞wt**flewkt
Where do we leave from?	**Hvor starter vi fra?**	voor **staa**^{r}terr vee fraa
Will the bus pick us up at the hotel?	**Kommer bussen og henter oss ved hotellet?**	**k**ommerr **bews**sern o(g) **hehn**terr oss veh(d) hoo**teh**ler
How much does the tour cost?	**Hvor mye koster turen?**	voor **me͞w**er **kos**terr **te͞w**rern
What time does the tour start?	**Når starter turen?**	nor **staa**^{r}terr **te͞w**rern
Is lunch included?	**Er lunsj inkludert?**	ær lurnsh inklew**da͞y**^{r}**t**
What time do we get back?	**Når er vi tilbake?**	nor ær vee til**baa**ker
Do we have free time in ...?	**Har vi fri tid til disposisjon i ...?**	haar vee free teed til dispoosi**sho͞o**n ee
Is there an English-speaking guide?	**Fins det en engelsk-talende guide der?**	finss deh ehn **ehng**erlsk-taalerner "guide" dǣr
I'd like to hire a private guide for ...	**Jeg vil gjerne ha en privat guide for ...**	yæi vil **yǣ**^{r}ner haa ehn pree**vaat** "guide" for
half a day	**en halv dag**	ehn hahl daag
a day	**en dag**	ehn daag
I'd like to see the ...	**Jeg vil gjerne se ...**	yæi vil **yǣ**^{r}ner sa͞y
Are there any special events going on?	**Foregår det noen spesielle begiven-heter her for tiden?**	**faw**rergawr deh **no͞o**ern spehsseey**eh**ler ber**yee**-vernhehterr hǣr for **tee**dern

Where is/are the ...?	**Hvor er ...?**	voor ær
amusement park	**fornøyelsesparken**	fo^{r}**noyer**lserspahrkern
aquarium	**akvariet**	ah**kvaa**reeyer
art gallery	**kunstgalleriet**	**kewnst**gahlerreeyer
botanical gardens	**den botaniske hagen**	dehn boo**taa**nisker **haa**gern
bridge	**broen**	**broo**ern
building	**bygningen**	**bewg**ningern
business district	**forretningskvarteret**	for**reht**ningskvah^{r}tayrer
castle	**slottet**	**shlot**ter
cathedral	**domkirken**	**dom**khirkern
cave	**hulen**	**hew**lern
cemetery	**gravlunden**	**graav**lewnern
chapel	**kapellet**	kah**peh**ler
church	**kirken**	**khir**kern
citadel	**festningen**	**fehst**ningern
city centre	**sentrum**	sehntrewm
concert hall	**konserthuset**	koon**sæ^{r}t**hewsser
conference centre/ congress hall	**kongresshallen**	kong**grehs**hahlern
court house	**tinghuset**	**ting**hewsser
downtown area	**sentrum**	**sehn**trewm
exhibition	**utstillingen**	**ewt**stillingern
factory	**fabrikken**	fah**brik**kern
fair	**messen**	**meh**ssern
flea market	**loppemarkedet**	**lop**permahrkerder
fortress	**borgen**	**bor**ggern
fountain	**fontenen**	fon**tay**nern
gardens	**hagene**	**haa**gerner
grotto	**grotten**	**grot**tern
harbour	**havnen**	**hahv**nern
lake	**(inn)sjøen**	**(in)shur**ern
library	**biblioteket**	biblyoo**tay**ker
market	**torghandelen**	**torg**hahnderlern
memorial	**minnesmerket**	**min**nersmærker
monastery	**klostret**	**klos**trer
monument	**monumentet**	moonew**mehn**ter
museum	**museet**	mew**ssay**er
observatory	**observatoriet**	obsærvah**too**ryer
old town	**gamlebyen**	**gahm**lerbewern
opera house	**operahuset**	**oo**perrahhewsser
palace	**slottet**	**shlot**ter
park	**parken**	**pahr**kern
parliament building	**Stortinget**	**stoo^{r}**tinger
planetarium	**planetariet**	plahner**taa**ryer
royal palace	**det kongelige slott**	deh **kong**erleeyer shlot

ruins	**ruinene**	rew**ee**nerner
shopping area	**handlestrøket**	**hahn**dlerstrurker
square	**plassen/torget**	**plahs**sern/**tor**gger
stadium	**stadion**	**staad**yoon
statue	**statuen**	**staa**tewern
stave church	**stavkirken**	**staav**khirkern
stock exchange	**børsen**	**bur**shern
theatre	**teatret**	tay**aa**trer
tomb	**graven**	**graa**vern
tower	**tårnet**	**taw**[r]ner
town (city) hall	**rådhuset**	**rawd**hewsser
university	**universitetet**	ewnivæshi**tay**ter
zoo	**dyrehagen**	**dew**rerhaagern

Admission *Adgang*

Is ... open on Sundays?	**Er ... åpent på søndager?**	ær ... **aw**pernt paw **surn**daagerr
When is it open?	**Når er det åpent?**	nor ær deh **aw**pernt
When does it open/close?	**Når åpner/stenger det?**	nor **awp**nerr/**stehng**err deh
What's the entrance fee?	**Hva koster inngangs-billetten?**	vah **kos**terr **in**gahngs-billehtern
2 adults and 1 child	**2 voksne og 1 barn**	2 **voks**ner o(g) 1 baa[r]n
Is there any reduction for (the) ...?	**Er det noen rabatt for ...?**	ær deh **noo**ern rah**baht** for
children	**barn**	baa[r]n
disabled	**bevegelseshemmede**	ber**vay**gerlsershehmerder
groups	**grupper**	**grew**perr
pensioners (senior citizens)	**pensjonister**	pahngshoo**nis**terr
students	**studenter**	stew**dehn**terr
Do you have a guide-book (in English)?	**Har du en guidebok (på engelsk)?**	haar dew ehn "**guide**"-book (paw **ehng**erlsk)
Can I buy a catalogue?	**Kan jeg få kjøpt en katalog?**	kahn yæi faw khurpt ehn kahtah**lawg**
Is it all right to take pictures?	**Er det tillatt å fotografere?**	ær deh **til**laht aw footoograh**fay**rer

GRATIS ADGANG	ADMISSION FREE
FOTOGRAFERING FORBUDT	NO CAMERAS ALLOWED

Who—What—When? *Hvem – Hva – Når?*

What's that building?	**Hvilken bygning er det?**	vilkern **bew**gning ær day
Who was the ...?	**Hvem var ...?**	vehm vaar
architect	**arkitekten**	ahrki**tehk**tern
artist	**kunstneren**	**kewnst**nerrern
painter	**maleren**	**maa**lerrern
sculptor	**billedhuggeren**	**bil**lerdhewgerrern
Who built it?	**Hvem har bygd den?**	vehm haar bewgd dehn
Who painted that picture?	**Hvem har malt det bildet?**	vehm haar maalt day **bil**der
When did he live?	**Når levde han?**	nor **lehv**der hahn
When was it built?	**Når ble det bygd?**	nor bleh deh bewgd
Where's the house where ... lived?	**Hvor er huset hvor ... bodde?**	vohr ær **hew**sser voor ... **boo**dder
We're interested in ...	**Vi interesserer oss for ...**	vee interreh**ssay**rerr oss for
antiques	**antikviteter**	ahntikvi**tay**terr
archaeology	**arkeologi**	ahrkehoolo**oggee**
art	**kunst**	kewnst
botany	**botanikk**	boota**hnik**
ceramics	**keramikk**	khæra**hmik**
coins	**mynter**	**mewn**terr
folk art	**folkekunst**	**fol**kerkewnst
furniture	**møbler**	**murb**lerr
geology	**geologi**	gayoolo**oggee**
handicrafts	**kunsthåndverk**	**kewnst**honværk
history	**historie**	his**too**ryer
maritime history	**sjøfartshistorie**	**shur**fahʳtshistooryer
medicine	**medisin**	mehdi**sseen**
modern art	**moderne kunst**	moo**dæʳ**ner kewnst
music	**musikk**	mew**ssik**
natural history	**naturhistorie**	nah**tewr**histooryer
ornithology	**ornitologi**	oornitoolo**oggee**
painting	**maleri**	mahler**ree**
pottery	**pottemakerkunst**	**pot**termaakerrkewnst
religion	**religion**	rehliggee**oon**
sculpture	**skulptur**	skewlp**tewr**
zoology	**zoologi**	soolo**oggee**
Where's the ... department?	**Hvor er avdelingen for ...?**	voor ær ahv**day**lingern for

It's ...	**Det er ...**	deh ær
amazing	**praktfullt**	**prahkt**fewlt
awful	**forferdelig**	for**fær**derli
beautiful	**vakkert**	**vah**ker^{r}t
fantastic	**fantastisk**	fahn**tahs**tisk
gloomy	**dystert**	**dews**ter^{r}t
impressive	**imponerende**	impoo**na̅y̅**rerner
interesting	**interessant**	interehs**sahngt**
magnificent	**storslagent**	**sto̅o̅**shlaagernt
pretty	**søtt**	surt
romantic	**romantisk**	roo**mahn**tisk
strange	**underlig**	**ewn**derli
superb	**ypperlig**	**ew**perli
terrible	**forferdelig**	for**fær**derli
tremendous	**forskrekkelig**	fo**shkreh**kerli
ugly	**stygt**	stewkt

Churches—Religious services *Kirker – Gudstjenester*

Norway has a Lutheran state church, but freedom of religion is assured, and other denominations have their own places of worship.

Most churches are open to visitors except, of course, when a service is being conducted.

Is there a ... nearby?	**Fins det en ... i nærheten?**	finss deh ehn ... ee **nær**hehtern
Catholic church	**katolsk kirke**	kah**to̅o̅**lsk khirker
Protestant church	**protestantisk kirke**	prooter**stahn**tisk **khir**ker
mosque	**moské**	moos**ka̅y̅**
synagogue	**synagoge**	sewnah**go̅o̅**gger
At what time is ...?	**Når begynner ...?**	nor ber**yew**nerr
mass	**messen**	**mehs**sern
the service	**gudstjenesten**	**gewds**tyehnerstern
Where can I find a ... who speaks English?	**Hvor kan jeg få tak i en ... som snakker engelsk?**	voor kahn yæi faw taak ee ehn ... som **snah**kerr **ehng**erlsk
priest	**katolsk prest**	kah**to̅o̅lsk** prehst
minister	**protestantisk prest**	prooter**stahn**tisk prehst
rabbi	**rabbiner**	rah**bee**nerr
I'd like to visit the church.	**Jeg vil gjerne se kirken.**	yæi vil **yæ**^{r}ner sa̅y̅ **khir**kern

In the countryside *På landet*

Is there a scenic route to ...?	**Fins det en naturskjønn vei til ...?**	finss deh ehn nah**tewr**shurn væi til
How far is it to ...?	**Hvor langt er det til ...?**	voor lahngt ær deh til
Can we walk there?	**Kan man spasere dit?**	kahn mahn spah**ssay**rer deet
How high is that mountain?	**Hvor høyt er det fjellet?**	voor hoyt ær day **fyeh**ler
What kind of ... is that?	**Hva slags ... er det?**	vaa shlahkss ... ær day
animal/bird	**dyr/fugl**	dewr/fewl
flower/tree	**blomst/tre**	blomst/tray

Landmarks *Landemerker*

cliff	**en klippe**	ehn **klip**per
coast	**en kyst**	ehn khewst
farm	**en bondegård**	ehn **boon**ergawr
field	**et jorde**	eht **yoo**rer
fjord	**en fjord**	ehn fyoor
footpath	**en sti**	ehn stee
forest	**en skog**	ehn skoog
garden	**en hage**	ehn **haa**ger
hill	**en høyde**	ehn **hoy**der
house	**et hus**	eht hewss
inlet	**en vik**	ehn veek
island	**en øy**	ehn oy
meadow	**en eng**	ehn ehng
mountain	**et fjell**	eht fyehl
ocean	**et hav**	eht haav
path	**en sti**	ehn stee
peak	**en topp**	ehn top
pond	**en dam**	ehn dahm
ridge	**en ås**	ehn awss
river	**en elv**	ehn ehlv
sea	**en sjø**	ehn shur
spring	**en kilde**	ehn **khil**der
stream	**en bekk**	ehn behk
valley	**en dal**	ehn daal
wall	**en mur**	ehn mewr
waterfall	**en foss**	ehn foss
well	**en brønn**	ehn brurn

ASKING THE WAY, see page 76

Relaxing

Cinema (Movies)—Theatre *Kino – Teater*

To find out what's on, check the newspapers and advertizing posters, or the weekly/monthly tourist publication in Oslo and other towns.

All films are shown in the original language with Norwegian subtitles. Advance booking is essential for theatres and the opera.

I'd like to ... tonight.	**Jeg har lyst til å ... i kveld.**	yæi haar lewst til aw ... ee kvehl
go to the cinema	**gå på kino**	gaw paw **khee**noo
go to the teatre	**gå i teatret**	gaw ee tāȳ**aa**trer
What's on at the cinema tonight?	**Hvilke filmer vises på kino i kveld?**	**vil**ker **fil**merr **vee**ssers paw **khee**noo ee kvehl
What's playing at the National Theatre?	**Hva spilles på Nationaltheatret?**	vah **spil**lerss paw nahshoo**naal**tāȳaatrer
What sort of play is it?	**Hva slags stykke er det?**	vah shlahkss **stew**ker ær deh
Who's it by?	**Hvem har skrevet det?**	vehm haar **skrāȳ**vert deh
Can you recommend a ...?	**Kan du anbefale en ...?**	kahn dew **ahn**berfaaler ehn
good film	**god film**	goo(d) film
comedy	**komedie**	koo**māȳd**yer
musical	**musikal**	mewssi**kaal**
revue	**revy**	reh**vēw̄**
Where's that new film directed by ... being shown?	**Hvor går den nye filmen av ...?**	voor gawr dehn **nēw̄**er **fil**mern ahv
Who's in it?	**Hvem spiller i den?**	vehm **spil**lerr ee dehn
Who's playing the lead?	**Hvem spiller hoved-rollen?**	vehm **spil**lerr **hōō**verd-rollern
Who's the director?	**Hvem har regissert den?**	vehm haar rehshis**sāȳ**ʳt dehn

At which theatre is that new play by ... being performed?	**På hvilket teater går det nye stykket av ...?**	paw **vil**kert tayaaterr gawr deh **new**er **stew**ker ahv
What time does it begin/finish?	**Når begynner/ slutter det?**	nor ber**yew**nerr/ **shlew**terr deh
How long does it last?	**Hvor lenge varer det?**	voor **leh**nger **vaa**rerr deh
Are there any tickets for tonight?	**Fins det fremdeles billetter til i kveld?**	finss deh frehm**day**lerss bil**leh**terr til ee kvehl
How much are the tickets?	**Hvor mye koster billettene?**	voor **mew**er **kos**terr bil**leh**terner
I'd like to reserve 2 tickets for the show on Friday evening.	**Jeg vil gjerne bestille 2 billetter til forestillingen på fredag kveld.**	yæi vil **yær**ner ber**stil**ler 2 bil**leh**terr til **faw**rerstillingern paw **fray**dah(g) kvehl
Can I have a ticket for the matinée on Tuesday?	**Kan jeg få en billett til matinéen på tirsdag?**	kahn yæi faw ehn bil**leht** til mahti**nay**ern paw **teesh**dah(g)
I'd like a seat in the stalls (orchestra).	**Jeg vil gjerne ha en plass i parkett.**	yæi vil **yær**ner haa ehn plahss ee pahr**keht**
Not too far back.	**Ikke for langt bak.**	**ik**ker for lahngt baak
Somewhere in the middle.	**Et sted i midten.**	eht stay(d) ee **mit**tern
How much are the tickets for the circle (mezzanine)?	**Hvor mye koster billettene på balkongen?**	voor **mew**er **kos**terr bil**leh**terner paw bahl**kong**ern
May I have a programme, please?	**Kan jeg få et program?**	kahn yæi faw eht proo**grahm**
Where's the cloakroom?	**Hvor er garderoben?**	voor ær gahrder**roo**bern

Dessverre, det er utsolgt.	I'm sorry, we're sold out.
Det er bare noen få plasser igjen på balkongen.	There are only a few seats left in the circle (mezzanine).
Kan jeg få se billetten?	May I see your ticket?
Dette er din plass.	This is your seat.

DAYS OF THE WEEK, see page 150

Opera—Ballet—Concert *Opera – Ballett – Konsert*

Can you recommend a/an ...?	**Kan du anbefale en ...?**	kahn dew **ahn**berfaaler ehn
ballet/concert opera/operetta	**ballett/konsert opera/operette**	bah**leht**/koon**sæ^{r}t** **oo**perrah/ooper**reh**ter
Where's the opera house/the concert hall?	**Hvor er operahuset/ konserthuset?**	voor ær **oo**perrahhewsser/ koon**sæ^{r}t**hewsser
What's on at the opera tonight?	**Hva spilles på operaen i kveld?**	vah **spil**lerss paw **oo**perrahern ee kvehl
Who's singing/ dancing?	**Hvem synger/ danser?**	vehm **sewng**err/ **dahn**serr
Which orchestra is playing?	**Hvilket orkester spiller?**	**vil**kert or**kehs**terr **spil**lerr
What are they playing?	**Hva spilles?**	vah **spil**lerss
Who's the conductor/soloist?	**Hvem er dirigent/ solist?**	vehm ær dirri**ggehnt**/ soo**list**

Nightclubs *Nattklubber*

Can you recommend a good nightclub?	**Kan du anbefale en bra nattklubb?**	kahn dew **ahn**berfaaler ehn braa **naht**klewb
Is there a floor show?	**Vises det noe show?**	**vee**sserss deh **noo**er "show"
What time does the show start?	**Når begynner showet?**	nor ber**yew**nerr **"schow"**er
Do I have to wear a tie?	**Er det slipstvang?**	ær deh **shlips**tvahng

Discos *Diskoteker*

Where can we go dancing?	**Hvor kan man gå og danse?**	voor kahn mahn gaw o(g) **dahn**ser
Is there a discotheque in town/ nearby?	**Fins det et diskotek i byen/i nærheten?**	finss deh eht diskoo**tayk** ee **bew**ern/ee **nær**heh-tern
Would you like to dance?	**Skal vi danse?**	skahl vee **dahn**ser

Sports *Sport*

Are there any sporting events going on?	**Holdes det noe sportsstevne her for tiden?**	hollerss deh **nōōer** **spoʳts**stehvner hǣr for **tee**dern

athletics (track-and-field) meeting	**friidrettsstevne**	**free**eedrehtsstehvner
bicycle racing	**sykkelløp**	**sew**kerllūrp
car racing	**billøp**	**beel**lūrp
football (soccer) match	**fotballkamp**	**foot**bahlkahmp
horse racing	**hesteveddeløp**	**heh**stervehderlūrp
ice hockey match	**ishockeykamp**	**ees**hokkikahmp
regatta	**regatta**	reh**gah**tah
speed skating	**skøyteløp**	**shoy**terlūrp
ski race	**skirenn**	**shee**rehn
ski jumping	**skihopping**	**shee**hopping
tennis match	**tenniskamp**	**teh**niskahmp

Is there a football (soccer) match anywhere this Saturday?	**Er det en fotball-kamp noe sted på lørdag?**	ær deh ehn **foot**bahl-kahmp **nōōer** stāy(d) paw **lūrʳ**dah(g)
Which teams are playing?	**Hvilke lag spiller?**	vilker laag **spill**err
Can you get me a ticket?	**Kan du skaffe meg en billett?**	kahn dew **skah**fer mæi ehn bill**eht**
I'd like to see an ice-hockey match.	**Jeg vil gjerne se en ishockeykamp**	yæi vil **yǣʳ**ner sāy ehn **ees**hokkikahmp
What's the admission charge?	**Hva koster inngangs-billetten?**	vah **kost**err **in**gahngs-billehtern
Where's the race course (track)?	**Hvor er heste-veddeløpsbanen?**	voor ær **hehs**ter-vehderlūrpsbaanern

And if you want to take a more active part:

Is there a golf course/tennis court nearby?	**Fins det en golf-bane/tennisbane i nærheten?**	finss deh ehn **golf**baaner/**teh**nisbaaner ee **nær**-hehtern
I'd like to play golf/tennis.	**Jeg vil gjerne spille golf/tennis.**	yæi vil **yǣʳ**ner **spill**er golf/**teh**niss

What's the charge per ...?	**Hva koster det pr. ...?**	vah **kos**terr deh pær
day/round/hour	**dag/runde/time**	daag/**rewn**der/**tee**mer
Can I hire (rent) rackets?	**Kan man leie racketer?**	kahn mahn **læi**er **reh**keh^{r}terr
Is there any good fishing around here?	**Fins det en bra fiske-plass i nærheten?**	finss deh ehn braa **fis**ker-plahss ee **nǣr**hehtern
Do I need a permit?	**Må man ha fiske-kort?**	maw mahn haa **fis**kerko^{r}t
Can one swim in the lake/river?	**Kan man bade i (inn)sjøen/elven?**	kahn mahn **baa**der ee **(in)shū**rern/**ehl**vern
Is there a swimming pool here?	**Er det et svømme-basseng her?**	ær deh eht **svur**mer-bahssehng hǣr
Is it an open-air or indoor pool?	**Er det utendørs eller innendørs?**	ær deh **ēw**terndūrsh **eh**lerr **in**nerndūrsh
Is it heated?	**Er det oppvarmet?**	ær deh **op**vahrmert
Is there a sandy beach?	**Fins det en sand-strand her?**	finss deh ehn **sahn**-strahn hǣr

bicycling	**sykling**	**sewk**ling
(horse-back) riding	**ridning**	**reed**ning
fishing	**fiske**	**fis**ker
mountain climbing	**fjellklatring**	**fyehl**klahtring
rowing	**roing**	**rōō**ing
sailing	**seiling**	**sæi**ling
swimming	**svømming**	**svur**ming

On the beach *På stranden*

Is it safe to swim/dive here?	**Er det trygt å bade/dykke her?**	ær deh trewkt aw **baa**der/**dew**ker hǣr
Is there a lifeguard?	**Fins det badevakt?**	finss deh **baa**dervahkt
Is it safe for children?	**Er det trygt for barn?**	ær deh trewkt for baa^{r}n
Could I have swimming lessons?	**Kan man ta svømme-timer?**	kahn mahn taa **svur**mer-teemerr
Are there any dangerous currents?	**Fins det noen farlige strømmer?**	finss deh **nōō**ern **faa**^{r}-leeyer **strur**merr
How deep is it?	**Hvor dypt er det?**	voor dewpt ær deh

Is it shallow?	**Er det langgrunt?**	ær deh **lahng**grewnt
What's the temperature of the water?	**Hvor mange grader er det i vannet?**	voor **mahng**er **graa**derr ær deh ee **vah**ner
I want to hire (rent) a/some ...	**Jeg vil gjerne leie ...**	yæi vil **yæ**ʳner **læi**er
bathing hut (cabana)	**et badehus**	eht **baa**derhe͞wss
skin-diving equipment	**et dykkerutstyr**	eht **dew**kerre͞wtste͞wr
sunshade	**en parasoll**	ehn pahrah**sol**
water-skis	**vannski**	**vahn**shee
windsurfer	**et seilbrett**	eht **sæil**breht

BADING FORBUDT	NO SWIMMING
FISKING FORBUDT	NO FISHING

Winter sports *Vintersport*

Is there a skating rink near here?	**Fins det en skøytebane i nærheten?**	finss deh ehn **shoy**terbaaner ee **nǣr**hehtern
I'd like to ski.	**Jeg vil gjerne gå på ski.**	yæi vil **yǣ**ʳner gaw paw shee
downhill	**utforkjøring**	**ewt**forkhūrring
cross-country skiing	**langrenn**	**lahng**rehn
Are there any ski runs for ...?	**Fins det noen skibakker for ...?**	finss deh **no͞o**ern **shee**bahkerr for
beginners	**begynnere**	ber**yew**nerrer
average skiers	**middelsgode skiløpere**	**mid**derlsgo͞o(d)er **shee**lūrperrer
good skiers	**gode skiløpere**	**go͞o**(d)er **shee**lūrperrer
Which way are the ski lifts?	**I hvilken retning ligger skiheisene?**	ee **vil**kern **reht**ning **lig**gerr **shee**hæisserner
Are there any good ski tracks (trails) nearby?	**Fins det noen gode skiløyper i nærheten?**	finss deh **no͞o**ern **go͞o**(d)er **shee**loyperr ee **nǣr**hehtern
Are there floodlit ski tracks?	**Fins det lysløyper?**	finss deh **le͞ws**loyperr
I'd like to hire ...	**Jeg vil gjerne leie ...**	yæi vil **yǣ**ʳner **læi**er
skates/skis	**skøyter/ski**	**shoy**terr/shee
ski boots/poles	**skistøvler/staver**	**shee**sturvlerr/**staa**verr

Making friends

Introduction *Presentasjon*

May I introduce ...?	**Får jeg presentere ...?**	fawr yæi prehssern**tay**rer
John, this is ...	**John, dette er ...***	John **deh**ter ær
My name is ...	**Mitt navn er ...**	mit nahvn ær
Pleased to meet you!	**Hyggelig å treffes!**	**hew**gerli aw **treh**ferss
What's your name?	**Hva heter du?**	vah **hay**terr dew
How are you?	**Hvordan står det til?**	**voo**^{r}dahn stawr deh til
Fine, thanks. And you?	**Bare bra, takk. Og med deg?**	**baa**rer braa tahk. o(g) meh(d) dæi

Follow up *Nærmere bekjentskap*

How long have you been here?	**Hvor lenge har du vært her?**	voor **lehng**er haar dew væ^{r}t hær
I've been here a week.	**Jeg har vært her en uke.**	yæi haar væ^{r}t hær ehn **ew**ker
We're on a 3-day visit.	**Vi er her på et 3-dagers besøk.**	vee ær hær paw eht **3**-daagersh ber**surk**
Is this your first visit to Oslo?	**Er det første gang du er i Oslo?**	ær deh **fursh**ter gahng dew ær ee **oosh**loo
How do you like Norway?	**Hva synes du om Norge?**	vah **sew**nerss dew om **nor**gger
We like it here.	**Vi liker oss her.**	vee **lee**kerr oss hær
What do you think of the country/the people?	**Hva synes du om landet/folket?**	vah **sew**nerss dew om **lah**ner/**fol**ker
The scenery is beautiful.	**Naturen er vakker.**	nah**tew**rern ær **vah**kerr
Where do you come from?	**Hvor kommer du fra?**	voor **kom**mer dew fraa
I'm from ...	**Jeg er fra ...**	yæi ær fraa

* The terms Mr., Mrs. and Miss (*herr* – hærr, *fru* – frew, *frøken* – **frur**kern) are very rarely used. People are introduced by their full name.

COUNTRIES, see page 146

What nationality are you?	**Hvilken nasjonalitet har du?**	vilkern nahshoo-nahlit**āy**t haar dew
I'm ...	**Jeg er ...**	yæi ær
American	**amerikaner**	ahm(er)rik**aa**nerr
British	**brite**	**bree**ter
Canadian	**kanadier**	kah**naad**yer
English	**englender**	**ehng**lehnder
Irish	**irlender**	**eer**lehnderr
Where are you staying?	**Hvor bor du her?**	voor bōor dew hǣr
Are you on your own?	**Er du her alene?**	ær dew hǣr ahl**āy**ner
I'm with my ...	**Jeg er her med ...**	yæi ær hǣr meh(d)
wife/husband	**min kone/min mann**	meen **kōo**ner/meen mahn
family	**min familie**	meen fah**meel**yer
children	**mine barn**	**mee**ner baa[r]n
parents	**mine foreldre**	**mee**ner for**ehl**drer
boyfriend/girlfriend	**min venn/venninne**	meen vehn/veh**nin**ner

father/mother	**far/mor**	faar/mōor
son/daughter	**sønn/datter**	surn/**dah**terr
brother/sister	**bror/søster**	brōor/**surs**terr
uncle/aunt	**onkel/tante**	**oong**kerl/**tahn**ter
nephew/niece	**nevø/niese**	neh**vūr**/nee**āy**sser
cousin	**fetter */kusine ****	**feh**terr/kews**see**ner

* masc., ** fem.

Are you married/single?	**Er du gift/ugift?**	ær dew yift/**ēw**yift
Do you have children?	**Har du barn?**	haar dew baa[r]n
What do you do?	**Hvilket yrke har du?**	vilkert **ewr**ker haar dew
I'm a student.	**Jeg er student.**	yæi ær stew**dehnt**
What are you studying?	**Hva studerer du?**	vah stew**dāy**rerr dew
I'm here on a business trip.	**Jeg er her på forretningsreise.**	yæi ær hǣr paw forr**eht**ningsræisser
Do you travel a lot?	**Reiser du mye?**	ræisserr dew **mēw**er
Do you play cards/chess?	**Spiller du kort/sjakk?**	**spil**lerr dew ko[r]t/shahk

The weather *Været*

What a lovely day!	**Hvilken herlig dag!**	vilkern **hǣ^{r}**li daag
What awful weather!	**For et forferdelig vær!**	for eht for**fær**derli vǣr
Isn't it cold/hot today?	**Er det ikke kaldt/ varmt i dag?**	ær deh **ik**ker kahlt/ vahrmt ee daag
Is it usually as rainy/warm as this?	**Pleier det å være så regnfullt/varmt?**	**plæi**err deh aw **vǣ**rer saw **ræin**fewlt/vahrmt
Do you think it's going to ... tomorrow?	**Tror du det kommer til å ... i morgen?**	tro͞or dew deh **kom**merr til aw ... ee **maw**er^{r}n
be a nice day	**bli pent vær**	blee pa͞ynt vǣr
rain	**regne**	**ræi**ner
snow	**snø**	snu͞r
What's the weather forecast?	**Hva er vær-utsiktene?**	vah ær **vǣ**rewtsikterner

cloud	**sky**	she͞w
fog	**tåke**	**taw**ker
frost	**frost**	frost
hail	**hagl**	hahgl
ice	**is**	eess
lightning	**lyn**	le͞wn
midnight sun	**midnattssol**	**mid**nahtsso͞ol
moon	**måne**	**maw**ner
rain	**regn**	ræin
sky	**himmel**	**him**merl
snow	**snø**	snu͞r
star	**stjerne**	**styǣ^{r}**ner
sun	**sol**	so͞ol
thunder	**torden**	**toor**dern
thunderstorm	**tordenvær**	**toor**dernvǣr
wind	**vind**	vin

Invitations *Innbydelser*

Would you like to have dinner with us on ...?	**Vil du spise middag med oss på ...?**	vil dew **spee**sser **mid**-dah(g) meh(d) oss paw
May I invite you to lunch?	**Får jeg by på lunsj?**	fawr yæi be͞w paw lurnsh

DAYS OF THE WEEK, see page 150

Can you come round for a drink this evening?	**Kan du komme til en drink i kveld?**	kahn dew **kom**mer til ehn dringk ee kvehl
We're having a party. Can you come?	**Vi skal ha fest. Kan du komme?**	vee skahl haa fehst. kahn dew **kom**mer
Great. I'd love to come.	**Mange takk. Jeg kommer gjerne.**	**mahng**er tahk. yæi kommerr **yæ^{r}**ner
What time shall I come?	**Når skal jeg komme?**	nor skahl yæi **kom**mer
May I bring a friend?	**Kan jeg ta med en venn?**	kahn yæi taa meh(d) ehn vehn
I'm afraid we've got to leave now.	**Vi må dessverre gå nå.**	vee maw **dehs**værer gaw naw
Next time you (pl.) must come to visit us.	**Neste gang må dere besøke oss.**	**neh**ster gahng maw **da̅y**rer bers**u̅r**ker oss
Thanks for the evening.	**Takk for i kveld.**	tahk for ee kvehl
It was great.	**Det var veldig hyggelig.**	det vaar **vehl**di **hew**gerli

Dating *Stevnemøte*

Do you mind if I smoke?	**Har du noe imot at jeg røyker?**	haar dew **no͞o**er eem**o͞o**t aht yæi **roy**kerr
Would you like a cigarette?	**Vil du ha en sigarett?**	vil dew haa ehn siggah**reht**
Do you have a light, please?	**Har du fyr?**	haar dew f**e̅w̅**r
Why are you laughing?	**Hvorfor ler du?**	**voor**for l**a̅y̅**r dew
Is my Norwegian that bad?	**Snakker jeg så dårlig norsk?**	**snah**kerr yæi saw **daw^{r}**li noshk
Do you mind if I sit down here?	**Har du noe imot at jeg setter meg her?**	haar dew **no͞o**er eem**o͞o**t aht yæi **seh**terr mæi h**æ̅**r
Would you like a drink?	**Har du lyst på en drink?**	haar dew lewst paw ehn dringk
Are you waiting for someone?	**Venter du på noen?**	**vehn**terr dew paw **no͞o**ern

Are you free this evening?	**Er du ledig i kveld?**	ær dew **la̅y̅**di ee kvehl
Would you like to go out with me tonight?	**Skal vi gå ut i kveld?**	skahl vee gaw e̅w̅t ee kvehl
Would you like to go dancing?	**Har du lyst til å gå ut og danse?**	haar dew lewst til aw gaw e̅w̅t o(g) **dahn**ser
I know a good discotheque.	**Jeg vet om et bra diskotek.**	yæi va̅y̅t om eht braa diskoo**ta̅y̅k**
Shall we go to the cinema (movies)?	**Skal vi gå på kino?**	skahl vee gaw paw **khee**noo
Would you like to go for a drive?	**Har du lyst til å kjøre en tur?**	haar dew lewst til aw **khu̅r̅**rer ehn te̅w̅r
Where shall we meet?	**Hvor skal vi møtes?**	voor skahl vee **mu̅r̅**terss
I'll pick you up at your hotel.	**Jeg henter deg på hotellet.**	yæi **hehn**terr dæi paw hoo**teh**ler
I'll call for you at 8.	**Jeg henter deg kl. 8.**	yæi **hehn**terr dæi **klok**kern 8
May I take you home?	**Kan jeg få følge deg hjem?**	kahn yæi faw **fur**ler dæi yehm
Can I see you again tomorrow?	**Skal vi ses igjen i morgen?**	skahl vee sa̅y̅ss ee**yehn** ee **mawer**^{r}n
I hope we'll meet again.	**Jeg håper vi ses igjen.**	yæi **haw**perr vee sa̅y̅ss ee**yehn**

… and you might answer:

I'd love to, thank you.	**Takk, det vil jeg gjerne.**	tahk deh vil yæi **yæ**^{r}ner
That's very kind of you.	**Det er veldig snilt av deg.**	deh ær **vehl**di snilt ahv dæi
Thank you, but I'm busy.	**Takk, men jeg er dessverre opptatt.**	tahk mehn yæi ær dehs**vær**er **op**taht
Leave me alone, please.	**Vær så snill å la meg være i fred.**	væ̅r̅ saw snill aw laa mæi **væ̅**rer ee fra̅y̅(d)
Thank you, it's been a wonderful evening.	**Takk, det har vært en veldig hyggelig kveld.**	tahk deh haar væ^{r}t ehn **vehl**di **hew**gerli kvehl

Shopping guide

This shopping guide is designed to help you find what you want with ease, accuracy and speed. It features:

1. A list of all major shops, stores and services (p. 98).
2. Some general expressions required when shopping to allow you to be specific and selective (p. 100).
3. Full details of the shops and services most likely to concern you. Here you'll find advice, alphabetical lists of items and conversion charts listed under the headings below.

LAUNDRY, see page 29/HAIRDRESSER, see page 30

Shops, stores and services *Butikker og servicenæringer*

Hours vary, but most shops are open from 9 a.m. to 5 p.m., Monday to Friday, and from 9 a.m. to 2 p.m. on Saturdays. Centrally located kiosks selling newspapers, tobacco and sweets may stay open till 11 p.m. Fruit, vegetable and flower markets normally open from 7 or 8 a.m. to 2 or 3 p.m., Monday to Saturday.

Where can I find a/an ...?	**Hvor er det ...?**	voor ær deh
antique shop	**en antikvitets-forretning**	ehn ahntikvi**ttayts**-forrehtning
art gallery	**et kunstgalleri**	eht **kewnst**gahlerree
baker's	**et bakeri**	eht baaker**ree**
bank	**en bank**	ehn bahngk
barber's	**en herrefrisør**	ehn **hærerfrissurr**
beauty salon	**en skjønnhetssalong**	ehn **shurn**hehtssahlong
bookshop	**en bokhandel**	ehn **book**hahnderl
butcher's	**en slakter**	ehn **shlahk**terr
cake shop	**et konditori**	eht koondittoo**ree**
camera shop	**en fotoforretning**	ehn **foo**tooforrehtning
candy store	**en godtebutikk**	ehn **go**terbewtik
cheese shop	**en osteforretning**	ehn **oo**sterforrehtning
chemist's	**et apotek**	eht ahpoo**tayk**
china shop	**et glassmagasin**	eht **glahs**mahgahsseen
dairy	**en melkebutikk**	ehn **mehl**kerbewtik
delicatessen	**en delikatesse-forretning**	ehn dehlikka**tehs**ser-forrehtning
dentist	**en tannlege**	ehn **tahn**layger
department store	**et stormagasin**	eht **stoor**mahgahsseen
doctor	**en lege**	ehn **lay**ger
drugstore	**et apotek**	eht ahpoo**tayk**
dry cleaner's	**et renseri**	eht rehnser**ree**
electrical goods shop	**en elektrisitets-forretning**	ehn ehlehktrissi**tayts**-forrehtning
fishmonger's	**en fiskebutikk**	ehn **fis**kerbewtik
flea market	**et loppemarked**	eht **lop**permahrkerd
florist's	**en blomsterbutikk**	ehn **blom**sterrbewtik
furrier's	**en pelsforetning**	ehn **pehls**forrehtning
greengrocer's	**en grønnsakhandel**	ehn **grurn**saakhahnderl
grocer's	**en matvarehandel**	ehn **maat**vaarerhahnderl
hairdresser (ladies/men)	**en frisør (dame-/herre-)**	ehn fri**ssurr** (**daa**mer-/**hæ**rer-)
hardware store	**en jernvarehandel**	ehn **yæ^{r}n**vaarerhahnderl

health food shop	**en helsekost-forretning**	ehn **hehl**serkost-forrehtning
hospital	**et sykehus**	eht **sew**kerhewss
ironmonger's	**en jernvarehandel**	ehn **yærn**vaarerhahnderl
jeweller's	**en gullsmed**	ehn **gewl**smay(d)
launderette	**et selvbetjenings-vaskeri**	eht **sehl**bertyaynings-vahskerree
laundry	**et vaskeri**	eht vahsker**ree**
library	**et bibliotek**	eht biblyoo**tayk**
liquor store	**et vinmonopol**	eht **veen**moonoopool
market	**en torghandel**	ehn **torg**hahnderl
newsstand	**en aviskiosk**	ehn ah**vees**khyosk
optician	**en optiker**	ehn **op**tikkerr
pastry shop	**et konditori**	eht koondittoo**ree**
perfumery	**et parfymeri**	eht pahrfewmer**ree**
pharmacy	**et apotek**	eht ahpoo**tayk**
photographer	**en fotograf**	ehn footoo**graaf**
police station	**en politistasjon**	ehn poolit**tee**stahshoon
post office	**et postkontor**	eht **post**koontoor
second-hand shop	**en marsjandise-forretning**	ehn mahshahn**dee**sser-forrehtning
shoemaker's (repairs)	**en skomaker**	ehn **skoo**maakerr
shoe shop	**en skoforretning**	ehn **skoo**forrehtning
shopping centre	**et butikksenter**	eht bew**tik**sehnterr
souvenir shop	**en suvenirbutikk**	ehn sewver**neer**bewtik
sporting goods shop	**en sportsforretning**	ehn **sports**forrehtning
stationer's	**en papirhandel**	ehn pah**peer**hahnderl
supermarket	**et supermarked**	eht **sew**perrmahrkerd
sweet shop	**en godtebutikk**	ehn **go**terbewtik
tailor's	**en skredder**	ehn **skreh**derr
telegraph office	**et telesenter**	eht **tay**lerssehnterr
tobacconist's	**en tobakkshandel**	ehn too**bahks**hahnderl
toy shop	**en leketøysbutikk**	ehn **lay**kertoysbewtik
travel agency	**et reisebyrå**	eht **ræi**sserbewraw
vegetable store	**en grønnsakhandel**	ehn **grurn**saakhahnderl
veterinarian	**en dyrlege**	ehn **dewr**layger
watchmaker's	**en urmaker**	ehn **ewr**maakerr
wine merchant	**et vinmonopol**	eht **veen**moonoopool

INNGANG	ENTRANCE
UTGANG	EXIT
NØDUTGANG	EMERGENCY EXIT

General expressions *Vanlige uttrykk*

Where? *Hvor?*

Where's there a good ...?	**Hvor fins det en god ...?**	voor finss deh ehn goo(d)
Where can I find a ...?	**Hvor finner jeg en ...?**	voor **fin**nerr yæi ehn
Where's the (main) shopping area?	**Hvor er (det største) handlestrøket?**	voor ær (deh **sturshter**) **hahn**dlerstrūrker
Is it far from here?	**Er det langt herfra?**	ær deh lahngt **hær**frah
How do I get there?	**Hvordan kommer jeg dit?**	**voo**^{r}dahn **kom**merr yæi deet

(UT)SALG	SALE
TILBUDSVARE	BARGAIN

Service *Betjening*

Can you help me?	**Kan du hjelpe meg?**	kahn dew **yehl**per mæi
I'm just looking.	**Jeg bare ser meg omkring.**	yæi **baa**rer sāyr mæi om**kring**
Do you sell ...?	**Selger dere ...?**	**sehl**err **dāy**rer
I'd like to buy ...	**Jeg vil gjerne kjøpe ...**	yæi vil **yæ**^{r}ner **khūr**per
Can you show me ...?	**Kan du vise meg ...?**	kahn dew **vee**sser mæi
this/that	**dette/det**	**deh**ter/deh
the one in the window	**den i vinduet**	dehn ee **vin**dewer
the one in the display case	**den i monteren**	dehn ee **mon**terrern
Do you have any ...?	**Har du noen ...?**	har dew **nōo**ern
Where's the ...?	**Hvor er ...?**	voor ær
... department	**-avdelingen**	-ahv**dāy**lingern
lift (elevator)	**heisen**	**hæi**ssern
escalator	**rulletrappen**	**rew**lertrahpern
Where do I pay?	**Hvor betaler man?**	voor ber**taa**lerr mahn

Defining the article *Varebeskrivelse*

I'd like a ... one.	**Jeg vil gjerne ha en ...**	yæi vil **yæ[r]ner** haa ehn
big	**stor**	stoor
cheap	**rimelig**	**ree**merli
dark	**mørk**	murrk
good	**god**	goo(d)
heavy	**tung**	toong
large	**stor**	stoor
light (weight)	**lett**	leht
light (colour)	**lys**	lewss
oval	**oval**	oo**vaal**
rectangular	**rektangulær**	rehktahngew**lær**
round	**rund**	rewn
small	**liten**	**lee**tern
square	**firkantet**	**fir**kahntert
sturdy	**robust/solid**	roo**bewst**/soo**leed**
I don't want anything too expensive.	**Jeg vil ikke ha noe for dyrt.**	yæi vil **ik**ker haa **noo**er for dew[r]t

Preference *Jeg foretrekker ...*

Can you show me some others?	**Kan du vise meg noen andre?**	kahn dew **vee**sser mæi **noo**ern **ahn**drer
Don't you have anything ...?	**Har du ikke noe ...?**	haar dew **ik**ker **noo**er
cheaper/better	**rimeligere/bedre**	**ree**merleeyerrer/**bay**drer
larger/smaller	**større/mindre**	**stur**rer/**min**drer
It's too ...	**Den er for ...**	den ær for
big/small	**stor/liten**	stoor/**lee**tern
dark/light	**mørk/lys**	murrk/lewss

How much? *Hvor mye?*

How much is this?	**Hvor mye koster dette?**	voor **mew**er **kos**terr **deh**ter
How much are they?	**Hvor mye koster de?**	voor **mew**er **kos**terr dee
I don't understand.	**Jeg forstår ikke.**	yæi fosh**tawr** **ik**ker
Please write it down.	**Kan du skrive det?**	kahn dew **skree**ver deh
I don't want to spend more than ... kroner.	**Jeg vil ikke gi mer enn ... kroner.**	yæi vil **ik**ker yee mayr ehn ... **kroo**nerr

COLOURS, see page 113

Decision *Avgjørelse*

I'll take it.	**Jeg tar det.**	yæi taar deh
No, I don't like it.	**Nei, jeg liker det ikke.**	næi yæi **lee**kerr deh **ik**ker
It's not quite what I want.	**Det er ikke akkurat det jeg hadde tenkt meg.**	deh ær **ik**ker ahkew**raat** deh yæi **hah**der tehngkt mæi

Ordering—Delivery *Bestilling – Levering*

Can you order it for me?	**Kan du bestille det til meg?**	kahn dew ber**stil**ler deh til mæi
How long will it take?	**Hvor lang tid tar det?**	voor lahng teed taar deh
I'll take it with me.	**Jeg tar det med meg.**	yæi taar deh meh(d) mæi
Deliver it to the ... Hotel.	**Kan du levere det til ... hotell?**	kahn dew leh**vāy**rer deh til ... hoo**tehl**
Please send it to this address.	**Kan du sende det til denne adressen?**	kahn dew **seh**ner deh til **deh**ner ah**drehs**sern
Will I have any difficulties with the customs?	**Kan jeg få problemer i tollen?**	kahn yæi faw proo**blāy**merr ee **tol**lern

Paying *Betaling*

How much is it?	**Hvor mye blir det?**	voor **mēw**er bleer deh
Can I pay by traveller's cheque?	**Kan jeg betale med reisesjekk?**	kahn yæi ber**taa**ler meh(d) **ræi**ssershehk
Do you accept dollars/pounds?	**Tar dere dollar/pund?**	taar **dāy**rer **dol**lahr/pewn
Do you accept credit cards?	**Tar dere kreditt-kort?**	taar **dāy**rer kreh**dit**ko^r^t
Can I get the VAT (sales tax) back?	**Får jeg tilbakebetalt momsen?**	fawr yæi til**baa**kerbertaalt **moom**sern
Could I have a receipt?	**Kan jeg få kvittering?**	kahn yæi faw kvit**tāy**ring
I think there's a mistake in the bill.	**Jeg tror det er en feil på regningen.**	yæi trōōr deh ær ehn fæil paw **ræi**ningern

Anything else? *Noe annet?*

No, thanks, that's all.	**Nei takk. Det var alt.**	næi tahk. deh vaar **ahlt**
Yes, I'd like ...	**Ja, jeg vil gjerne ha ...**	yaa yæi vil **yǣrner** haa
May I have a bag, please?	**Kan jeg få en bærepose?**	kahn yæi faw ehn **bæ**rerpōōsser
Could you wrap it up for me, please?	**Kan du pakke det inn for meg?**	kahn dew **pah**ker deh in for mæi

Dissatisfied? *Misfornøyd?*

Can you exchange this, please?	**Kan jeg få byttet dette?**	kahn yæi faw **bew**tert **deh**ter
I want to return this.	**Jeg vil gjerne levere tilbake dette.**	yæi vil **yǣrner** lehvāyrer til**baa**ker **deh**ter
Could I have a refund?	**Kan jeg få pengene tilbake?**	kahn yæi faw **pehng**erner til**baa**ker.
Here's the receipt.	**Her er kvitteringen.**	hǣr ær kvit**tāy**ringern

Kan jeg hjelpe deg?	Can I help you?
Hva skal det være?	What would you like?
Hvilken ... vil du ha?	What ... would you like?
farge/form	colour/shape
Jeg beklager. Det har vi ikke.	I'm sorry, we don't have any.
Det er vi utsolgt for.	We're out of stock.
Skal vi bestille det?	Shall we order it for you?
Tar du det med eller skal vi sende det?	Will you take it with you or shall we send it?
Skal det være noe annet?	Anything else?
Det blir ... kroner, takk.	That comes to ... kroner.
Kassen er der borte.	The cash desk is over there.

Bookshop—Stationer's *Bokhandel – Papirhandel*

In Norway, books and stationery are usually sold in the same shop. You'll find newspapers, magazines and paperbacks at newsstands and tobacconists.

Where's the nearest ...?	**Hvor er nærmeste ...?**	voor ær **nær**mehster
bookshop	**bokhandel**	**bōōk**hahnderl
stationer's	**papirhandel**	pah**peer**hahnderl
newsstand	**aviskiosk**	ah**vees**khyosk
Where can I buy an English-language newspaper?	**Hvor kan jeg få kjøpt en engelsk-språklig avis?**	voor kahn yæi faw khurpt ehn **ehng**erlsk-sprawkli ah**veess**
Where's the guide-book section?	**Hvor står reise-håndbøkene?**	voor stawr **ræi**sser-honbūrkerner
Where are the English books?	**Hvor står de engelske bøkene?**	voor stawr dee **ehng**erlsker **būr**kerner
Do you have any of ...'s books in English?	**Har dere noen av ...s bøker på engelsk?**	haar **day**rer **nōō**ern ahv ...s **būr**kerr paw **ehng**erlsk
I'd like a/an/some ...	**Jeg vil gjerne ha ...**	yæi vil **yæ**^{r}ner haa
address book	**en adressebok**	ehn ah**drehs**serbōōk
adhesive tape	**limbånd**	**leem**bon
ball-point pen	**en kulepenn**	ehn **kēw**lerpehn
blotting paper	**trekkpapir**	**trehk**pahpeer
book	**en bok**	ehn bōōk
calendar	**en kalender**	ehn kah**lehn**derr
carbon paper	**blåpapir**	**blaw**pahpeer
chalk	**kritt**	krit
crayons	**fargeblyanter**	**fahr**ggerblēwahnterr
dictionary	**en ordbok**	ehn **ōōr**bōōk
pocket	**lomme-**	**loom**mer-
Norwegian-English	**norsk-engelsk**	noshk-**ehng**erlsk
drawing pad	**en tegneblokk**	ehn **tæi**nerblok
drawing pins	**tegnestifter**	**tæi**nerstifterr
envelopes	**noen konvolutter**	**nōō**ern koonvoo**lew**terr
eraser	**et viskelær**	eht **vis**kerlær
exercise book	**en skrivebok**	ehn **skree**verbōōk
felt-tip pen	**en tusjpenn**	ehn **tewsh**pehn
fountain pen	**en fyllepenn**	ehn **few**lerpehn
gift wrapping paper	**gavepapir**	**gaa**verpahpeer

glue	**lim**	leem
grammar book	**en grammatikk**	ehn grahmah**tik**
guidebook	**en reisehåndbok**	ehn **ræi**sserhonbook
ink	**blekk**	blehk
(self-adhesive) labels	**noen (selvklebende) etiketter**	**noo**ern (**sehl**klayberner) ehti**keh**terr
magazine	**et ukeblad**	eht **ew**kerblaa(d)
map	**et kart**	eht kah^{r}t
street map of ...	**et kart over ...**	eht kah^{r}t **aw**verr
road map of ...	**et veikart over ...**	eht **væi**ka^{r}t **aw**verr
mechanical pencil	**en skrublyant**	ehn **skrew**blewahnt
newspaper	**en avis**	ehn ah**veess**
American	**amerikansk**	ahm(eh)ri**kaansk**
English	**engelsk**	**ehng**erlsk
notebook	**en notiskbok**	ehn noo**tees**book
note paper	**brevpapir**	**bray**vpahpeer
phrase book	**en parlør**	ehn pah^{r}**lurr**
paintbox	**et malerskrin**	eht **maa**lerrskreen
paper	**papir**	pah**peer**
paperback	**en pocketbok**	ehn **pok**kertbook
paperclips	**binders**	**bin**dersh
paper napkins	**papirservietter**	pah**peer**særvyehterr
pen	**penn**	pehn
pencil	**en blyant**	ehn **blew**ahnt
pencil sharpener	**en blyantspisser**	ehn **blew**ahntspisserr
picturebook	**en billedbok**	ehn **bil**lerdbook
playing cards	**spillkort**	**spil**ko^{r}t
pocket calculator	**en lommekalkulator**	ehn **lom**merkahlkewlaatoor
postcard	**et postkort**	eht **post**ko^{r}t
propelling pencil	**en skrublyant**	ehn **skrew**blewahnt
refill (for a pen)	**en refill**	ehn "refill"
rubber	**et viskelær**	eht **vis**kerlær
rubber bands	**gummistrikker**	**gew**mistrikkerr
ruler	**en linjal**	ehn lin**yaal**
stapler	**en heftemaskin**	ehn **hehf**termahsheen
staples	**heftestifter**	**hehf**terstifterr
string	**hyssing**	**hew**ssing
thumbtacks	**tegnestifter**	**tæi**nerstifterr
tissue paper	**silkepapir**	**sil**kerpahpeer
travel guide	**en reisehåndbok**	ehn **ræi**sserhonbook
typewriter ribbon	**et fargebånd (til skrivemaskin)**	eht **fahr**ggerbon (til **skree**vermahsheen)
typing paper	**skrivemaskinpapir**	**skree**vermahsheenpahpeer
(box of) watercolors	**et malerskrin**	eht **maa**lerrskreen
wrapping paper	**innpakningspapir**	**in**pahkningspahpeer
writing pad	**en skriveblokk**	ehn **skree**verblok
writing paper	**skrivepapir**	**skree**verpahpeer

Camping equipment *Campingutstyr*

I'd like a/an/ some ...	**Jeg vil gjerne ha ...**	yæi vil **yæ**^{r}ner haa
air bed (mattress)	**en luftmadrass**	ehn **lewft**mahdrahss
aluminum foil (Am.)	**aluminiumsfolie**	ahlew**meen**yewmsfoolyer
backpack	**en ryggsekk**	ehn **rewg**sehk
bottle-opener	**en flaskeåpner**	ehn **flahs**kerawpnerr
bucket	**en bøtte**	eht **bur**ter
butane gas	**butangass**	bew**taan**gahss
camp bed	**en campingseng**	ehn **kæm**pingsehng
candles	**stearinlys**	stehah**reen**lewss
can opener	**en boksåpner**	ehn **boks**awpnerr
charcoal briquets	**trekullbriketter**	**tray**kewlbrikkehterr
clothes pegs (pins)	**klesklyper**	**klay**sklewperr
compass	**et kompass**	eht koom**pahss**
cool bag	**en kjøleboks**	ehn **khur**lerbokss
corkscrew	**en korketrekker**	ehn **kor**kertrehkerr
crockery	**et servise**	eht sær**vee**sser
deck chair	**en fluktstol**	ehn **flewkt**stool
dish detergent	**et oppvaskmiddel**	eht **op**vahskmidderl
fire lighter	**tennvæske**	**tehn**vehsker
fishing tackle	**fiskeutstyr**	**fis**kerewtstewr
flashlight	**en lommelykt**	ehn **loom**merlewkt
folding chair	**en klappstol**	ehn **klahp**stool
folding table	**et klappbord**	eht **klahp**boor
food box	**en matboks**	ehn **maat**bokss
frying pan	**en stekepanne**	ehn **stay**kerpahner
groundsheet	**et teltunderlag**	eht **tehl**tewnerrlaag
hammer	**en hammer**	ehn **hah**merr
hammock	**en hengekøye**	ehn **hehng**erkoyer
ice chest	**en kjøleboks**	ehn **khur**lerbokss
(cooler) ice packs	**kjøleelementer**	**khur**lerehlermehnterr
insect spray (killer)	**en insektgift**	ehn **in**sehktyift
kerosene	**parafin**	pahrah**feen**
(oil) lamp	**en (olje)lampe**	ehn (**ol**yer)**lahm**per
lantern	**en lykt**	ehn lewkt
matches	**fyrstikker**	**fewsh**tikkerr
(foam rubber) mattress	**en (skumgummi-) madrass**	ehn (**skoom**gewmi-) mah**drahss**
mosquito net	**et myggnett**	eht **mewg**neht
paper napkins	**papirservietter**	pah**peer**særvyehterr
paper towel	**husholdningspapir**	hew**shol**ningspahpeer
paraffin	**parafin**	pahrah**feen**
penknife	**en lommekniv**	ehn **lom**merkneev
picnic basket	**en picnickurv**	ehn **pik**nikkewrv

CAMPING, see page 32

plastic bags	**plastposer**	**plahst**poosserr
pliers	**en tang**	ehn tahng
pocketknife	**en lommekniv**	ehn **lom**merkneev
pot holders	**grytekluter**	**grew**terklewterr
primus stove	**en primus**	ehn **pree**mewss
pump	**en pumpe**	ehn **poom**per
rope	**et tau**	eht tou
rucksack	**en ryggsekk**	ehn **rewg**sehk
saucepan	**en kasserolle**	ehn kahsser**rol**ler
scissors	**en saks**	ehn sahkss
screwdriver	**en skrutrekker**	ehn **skrew**trehkerr
sleeping bag	**en sovepose**	ehn **saw**verpoosser
stew pot	**en gryte**	ehn **grew**ter
tent	**et telt**	eht tehlt
tent pegs	**teltplugger**	**tehlt**plewgerr
tent pole	**en teltstang**	ehn **tehlt**stahng
tinfoil	**aluminiumsfolie**	ahlew**meen**yewmsfoolyer
tin opener	**en boksåpner**	ehn **boks**awpnerr
torch	**en lommelykt**	ehn **loom**merlewkt
vacuum flask	**en termosflaske**	ehn **tær**moosflahsker
washing powder	**vaskepulver**	**vahs**kerpewlverr
water flask	**en feltflaske**	ehn **fehlt**flahsker

Crockery *Servise*

cups	**kopper**	**kop**perr
mugs	**krus**	krewss
dishes	**fat**	faat
bowls	**skåler**	**skaw**lerr
plates	**tallerkener**	tah**lær**kernerr
saucers	**skåler (til kopper)**	**skaw**lerr (til **kop**perr)
tumblers	**drikkeglass**	**drik**kerglahss
(made of) cardboard	**(av) papp**	(ahv) pahp

Cutlery (Flatware) *Bestikk*

forks	**gafler**	**gah**flerr
knives	**kniver**	**knee**verr
spoons	**skjeer**	**shay**err
teaspoons	**teskjeer**	**tay**shayerr
(made of) plastic	**(av) plast**	(ahv) plahst
(made of) stainless steel	**(av) rustfritt stål**	(ahv) **rewst**frit stawl

Chemist's (Drugstore) *Apotek*

Norwegian pharmacies don't stock the wide range of goods that you'll find in Britain or the U.S. For example, they don't sell photographic equipment or toys. And for perfume, cosmetics, etc., you have to go to a *parfymeri* (pahrfewmer**ree**). You need a prescription for most medicine.

In the window you'll see a notice telling you where the nearest all-night pharmacy is.

This section is divided into two parts:

1. Pharmaceutical—medicine, first-aid, etc.
2. Toiletry—toilet articles, cosmetics

General *Allment*

Where's the nearest (all-night) chemist's?	**Hvor er nærmeste (vakthavende) apotek?**	voor ær **nær**mehster (**vahkt**haaverner) ahpoo**tayk**
What time does the chemist's open/close?	**Når åpner/stenger apoteket?**	nor **awp**nerr/**stehng**err ahpoo**tay**ker

1. Pharmaceutical *Medisiner*

I'd like something for ...	**Jeg vil gjerne ha noe mot ...**	yæi vil **yær**ner haa **noo**er moot
a cold	**forkjølelse**	for**khur**lerlser
a cough	**hoste**	**hoo**ster
a headache	**hodepine**	**hoo**derpeener
hay fever	**høysnue**	**hoy**snewer
insect bites	**insektstikk**	**in**sehktstik
sunburn	**solforbrenning**	**sool**forbrehning
travel sickness	**reisesyke**	**ræi**ssersewker
an upset stomach	**urolig mage**	ewrooli **maa**ger
Can you make up this prescription for me?	**Kan du gjøre i stand denne resepten for meg?**	kahn dew **yur**rer ee stahn **deh**ner reh**ssehp**tern for mæi
Can I get it without a prescription?	**Kan jeg få det uten resept?**	kahn yæi faw deh **ew**tern reh**ssehpt**
Shall I wait?	**Skal jeg vente?**	skahl yæi **vehn**ter

DOCTOR, see page 137

Can I have a/an/ some ...?	**Kan jeg få ...?**	kahn yæi faw
absorbent cotton	**bomull**	**boo**mewl
analgesic	**et analgetikum**	eht ahnahl**gay**tikewm
antiseptic cream	**en antiseptisk salve**	ehn ahntis**sehp**tisk **sahl**ver
aspirin	**aspirin**	ahspir**reen**
bandage	**en bandasje**	ehn bahn**daa**sher
elastic bandage	**et elastisk bind**	eht ehl**ah**stisk bin
Band-Aids	**plaster**	**plah**sterr
... capsules	**-kapsler**	**-kahp**shlerr
charcoal tablets	**kulltabletter**	**kewl**tahblehterr
condoms	**kondomer**	koon**doo**merr
contraceptives	**et preventivmiddel**	eht **pray**vahngteevmidderl
corn plasters	**liktornplaster**	**leek**too^{r}nplahsterr
cotton wool	**bomull**	**boo**mewl
cough drops	**halspastiller**	**hahls**pahstillerr
cough syrup	**hostesaft**	**hoo**stersahft
disinfectant	**et desinfeksjons-middel**	eht dehssinfehk**shoons**-midderl
ear drops	**øredråper**	**ur**rerdrawperr
Elastoplast	**plaster**	**plah**sterr
eye drops	**øyendråper**	**oy**erndrawperr
first-aid kit	**et førstehjelpsskrin**	eht **fursh**teryehlpsskreen
(roll of) gauze	**(en rull) gasbind**	(ehn rewl) **gahs**bin
insect repellent	**et insektmiddel**	eht in**sehkt**midderl
iodine	**jod**	yod
laxative	**et laksermiddel**	eht lahk**sayr**midderl
mouthwash	**et munnvann**	eht **mewn**vahn
nose drops	**nesedråper**	**nay**sserdrawperr
... ointment	**-salve**	**-sahl**ver
painkiller	**et smertestillende middel**	eht **smæ**^{r}terstillerner **mid**derl
sanitary towels (napkins)	**sanitetsbind**	sahni**tayts**bin
suppositories	**stikkpiller**	**stik**pillerr
... tablets	**-tabletter**	-tah**bleh**terr
tampons	**tamponger**	tahm**pong**err
thermometer	**termometer**	tærmoo**may**terr
throat lozenges	**halstabletter**	**hahls**tahblehterr
vitamin pills	**vitaminpiller**	vittah**meen**pillerr

GIFT	POISON
KUN TIL UTVENDIG BRUK	FOR EXTERNAL USE ONLY

2. Toiletry *Toalettartikler*

I'd like a/an/ some ...	**Jeg vil gjerne ha ...**	yæi vil **yæʳ**ner haa
after-shave lotion	**et etterbarberings-vann**	eht **eh**terrbahrbayrings-vahn
bath salts	**et badesalt**	eht **baa**dersahlt
blusher	**en rouge**	ehn roosh
bubble bath	**et skumbad**	eht **skoom**baad
cosmetics	**noe kosmetikk**	nooer koosmer**tik**
cream	**en krem**	ehn kraym
cleansing cream	**en rensekrem**	ehn **rehn**serkraym
foot cream	**en fotkrem**	ehn **foot**kraym
foundation cream	**en underlagskrem**	ehn **ew**nerrlaagskraym
hand cream	**en håndkrem**	ehn **hon**kraym
moisturizing cream	**en fuktighetskrem**	ehn **fook**tihehtskraym
night cream	**en nattkrem**	ehn **naht**kraym
sun-tan cream	**en solkrem**	ehn **sool**kraym
cuticle remover	**en neglebåndsfjerner**	ehn **næi**lerbonsfyæʳnerr
deodorant	**en deodorant**	ehn dehoodoo**rahnt**
emery boards	**sandpapirfiler**	**sahn**pahpeerfeelerr
eyebrow pencil	**en øyenbrynsstift**	ehn **oy**ernbrewnsstift
eye liner	**en eyeliner**	ehn "eyeliner"
eye shadow	**en øyenskygge**	ehn **oy**ernshewger
face flannel	**en ansiktsklut**	ehn **ahn**siktsklewt
face powder	**pudder**	**pew**derr
lipbrush	**en leppestiftpensel**	ehn **leh**perstiftpehnserl
lipsalve (balm)	**en leppepomade**	ehn **leh**perpoomaader
lipstick	**en leppestift**	ehn **leh**perstift
make-up bag	**en sminkepung**	ehn **sming**kerpoong
make-up remover pads	**bomullspads**	**boom**ewls"pads"
mascara	**en øyensverte**	ehn **oy**ernsvæʳter
nail brush	**en neglebørste**	ehn **næi**lerburshter
nail clippers	**en negleklipper**	ehn **næi**lerklipperr
nail file	**en neglefil**	ehn **næi**lerfeel
nail polish	**en neglelakk**	ehn **næi**lerlahk
nail polish remover	**en neglelakkfjerner**	ehn **næi**lerlahkfyæʳnerr
nail scissors	**en neglesaks**	ehn **næi**lersahkss
perfume	**en parfyme**	ehn pahr**few**mer
powder	**pudder**	**pew**derr
powder puff	**en pudderkvast**	ehn **pew**derrkvahst
razor	**en barberhøvel**	ehn bahr**bayr**hurverl
razor blades	**barberblader**	bahr**bayr**blaaderr
safety pins	**sikkerhetsnåler**	**sik**kerrhehtsnawlerr
shaving brush	**en barberkost**	ehn bahr**bayr**koost

shaving cream	**en barberkrem**	ehn bahr**bayr**kraym
soap	**en såpe**	ehn **saw**per
sponge	**en svamp**	ehn svahmp
sponge bag	**en toalettmappe**	ehn tooah**leht**mahper
sun-tan oil	**en sololje**	ehn **soo**lolyer
talcum powder	**en talkum**	ehn **tahl**kewm
(facial) tissues	**papirlommetørklær**	pah**peer**loommerturrklær
toilet paper	**toalettpapir**	tooah**leht**pahpeer
toiletries bag	**en toalettmappe**	ehn tooah**leht**mahper
toilet water	**en eau de toilette**	en aw deh tooah**leht**
toothbrush	**en tannbørste**	ehn **tahn**burshter
toothpaste	**en tannpasta**	ehn **tahn**pahstah
towel	**et håndkle**	eht **hong**kleh
tweezers	**en pinsett**	ehn pin**seht**
washcloth	**en ansiktsklut**	ehn **ahn**siktsklewt

For your hair *For håret*

barrette	**en hårspenne**	ehn **haw**shpehner
bobby pins	**hårklemmer**	**hawr**klehmerr
colour shampoo	**en fargesjampo**	ehn **fahr**ggershahmpoo
comb	**en kam**	ehn kahm
curlers (rollers)	**hårruller**	**hawr**rewlerr
dry shampoo	**tørrsjampo**	**turr**shahmpoo
hairbrush	**en hårbørste**	ehn **hawr**burshter
hair dye	**et hårfargingsmiddel**	eht **hawr**fahrgingsmidderl
hair (styling) gel	**en hårgelé**	ehn **hawr**shehlay
hairgrips	**hårklemmer**	**hawr**klehmerr
hair lotion	**hårvann**	**hawr**vahn
hair mousse	**et hårskum**	eht **haw**shkoom
hairpins	**hårnåler**	**haw^r**nawlerr
hair slide	**en hårspenne**	ehn **haw**shpehner
hair spray	**hårlakk**	**haw^r**lahk
setting lotion	**et leggevann**	eht **leh**gervahn
shampoo	**en sjampo**	ehn **shahm**poo
for dry/greasy (oily) hair	**for tørt/fett hår**	for tur^{r}t/feht hawr
tint	**et hårtoningsmiddel**	eht **haw^r**tooningsmidderl
wig	**en parykk**	ehn pah**rewk**

For the baby *For babyen*

baby food	**barnemat**	**baa^r**nermaat
dummy (pacifier)	**en narresmokk**	ehn **nah**rersmook
feeding bottle	**en tåteflaske**	ehn **taw**terflahsker
nappies (diapers)	**bleier**	**blæi**err

Clothing *Klær*

If you want to buy something specific, prepare yourself in advance. Look at the list of clothing on page 116. Get some idea of the colour, material and size you want. They're all listed on the next few pages.

General *Allment*

I'd like ...	**Jeg vil gjerne ha ...**	yæi vil **yǣʳ**ner haa
I'm just looking.	**Jeg bare ser meg omkring.**	yæi **baa**rer sāyr mæi om**kring**
I'd like ... for a 10-year-old boy/girl.	**Jeg vil gjerne ha ... til en gutt/pike på 10 år.**	yæi vil **yǣʳ**ner haa ... til ehn gewt/**pee**ker paw 10 awr
I'd like something like this.	**Jeg vil gjerne ha noe i denne stilen.**	yæi vil **yǣʳ**ner haa **nōō**er ee **deh**ner **stee**lern
I like the one in the window.	**Jeg liker den i vinduet.**	yæi **lee**ker dehn ee **vin**dewer
How much is that per metre?	**Hvor mye koster det pr. meter?**	voor **mēw**er **kos**terr deh pær **māy**terr

1 centimetre (cm.)	= 0.39 in.	1 inch	= 2.54 cm.
1 metre (m.)	= 39.37 in.	1 foot	= 30.5 cm.
10 metres	= 32.81 ft.	1 yard	= 0.91 m.

Colour *Farge*

I'd like something in ...	**Jeg vil gjerne ha noe i ...**	yæi vil **yǣʳ**ner haa **nōō**er ee
I'd like a darker/lighter shade.	**Jeg vil gjerne ha en mørkere/lysere nyanse.**	yæi vil **yǣʳ**ner haa en **murr**kerrer/**lēw**sserrer new**ahng**ser
I'd like something to match this.	**Jeg vil gjerne ha noe som står til dette.**	yæi vil **yǣʳ**ner haa **nōō**er som stawr til **deh**ter
I don't like the colour/pattern.	**Jeg liker ikke fargen/mønstret.**	yæi **lee**kerr **ik**ker **fahr**ggern/**murn**strer

beige	**beige**	baysh
black	**svart**	svah^{r}t
blue	**blå**	blaw
brown	**brun**	brewn
golden	**gullfarget**	**gewl**fahrggert
green	**grønn**	grurn
grey	**grå**	graw
mauve	**lilla**	lillah
orange	**oransje**	oo**rahngsh**
pink	**rosa**	roossah
purple	**fiolett**	feeoo**leht**
red	**rød**	rur
scarlet	**skarlagenrød**	skah^r**laa**gernrur
silver	**sølvfarget**	**surl**fahrggert
turquoise	**turkis**	tewr**keess**
white	**hvit**	veet
yellow	**gul**	gewl
light ...	**lyse-**	**lew**sser-
dark ...	**mørke-**	**murr**ker-

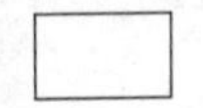

ensfarget
(**ayns**fahrggert)

stripet
(**stree**pert)

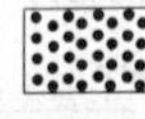

prikket
(**prik**kert)

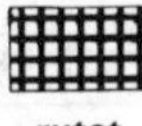

rutet
(**rew**tert)

mønstret
(**murn**strert)

Fabric *Tøystoff*

Do you have anything in ...?	**Har du noe i ...?**	haar dew **noo**er ee
Is that ...?	**Er det ...?**	ær deh
handmade	**håndlaget**	**hon**laagert
imported	**importert**	impo^r**tay**^{r}**t**
made in Norway	**laget i Norge**	**laa**gert ee **nor**gger
What fabric/material is it?	**Hva slags stoff/ materiale er det?**	vah shlahkss stof/ maht(er)ree**aa**ler ær deh
I'd like something thinner.	**Jeg vil gjerne ha noe tynnere.**	yæi vil **yæ**^{r}ner haa **noo**er **tew**nerrer
Do you have anything of better quality?	**Har du en bedre kvalitet?**	haar dew ehn **bay**drer kvahli**tayt**

What's it made of?	**Hva er det laget av?**	vaa ær deh **laa**gert ahv

cambric	**batist**	bah**tist**
camelhair	**kamelhår**	kah**ma̅y̅**lhawr
chiffon	**chiffon**	shif**fong**
corduroy	**kordfløyel**	**kaw**^{r}**d**floyerl
cotton	**bomull**	**boo**mewl
crepe	**krepp**	krehp
denim	**denim**	deh**neem**
felt	**filt**	filt
flannel	**flanell**	flah**nehl**
gabardine	**gabardin**	gahbah^{r}**deen**
lace	**knipling**	**knip**ling
leather	**lær**	læ̅r
linen	**lin**	leen
poplin	**poplin**	**pop**lin
satin	**sateng**	sah**tehng**
silk	**silke**	**sil**ker
suede	**semsket skinn**	**sehm**skert shin
towelling	**frotté**	froo**ta̅y̅**
velvet	**fløyel**	**floy**erl
velveteen	**bomullsfløyel**	**boo**mewlsfloyerl
wool	**ull**	ewl
worsted	**kamgarn**	kahmgaa^{r}n

Is it ...?	**Er det ...?**	ær deh
pure cotton/wool	**ren bomull/ull**	ra̅y̅n **boo**mewl/ewl
synthetic	**syntetisk**	sewn**ta̅y̅**tisk
colourfast	**fargeekte**	**fahr**ggerehkter
crease resistant (wrinkle-free)	**krøllfritt**	**krurl**frit
Is it hand washable/ machine washable?	**Skal det vaskes for hånd/i maskin?**	skahl deh **vahs**kerss for hon/ee mah**sheen**
Will it shrink?	**Krymper det?**	**krewm**perr deh

Size *Størrelse*

I take size 38.	**Jeg bruker størrelse 38.**	yæi **bre̅w̅**kerr **stur**rerlser 38
Could you measure me?	**Kan du ta mål av meg?**	kahn dew taa mawl ahv mæi
I don't know the Norwegian sizes.	**Jeg kjenner ikke de norske størrelsene.**	yæi **kheh**nerr **ik**ker dee **nosh**ker **stur**rerlserner

Sizes vary from country to country and from one manufacturer to another, so be sure to try on the clothes before you buy.

Women *Kvinner*

Dresses/Suits						
American	8	10	12	14	16	18
British	10	12	14	16	18	20
Continental	36	38	40	42	44	46

Stockings						
American / British	8	$8\frac{1}{2}$	9	$9\frac{1}{2}$	10	$10\frac{1}{2}$
Continental	1		2		3	

Shoes				
American	$5\frac{1}{2}$	$6\frac{1}{2}$	$7\frac{1}{2}$	$8\frac{1}{2}$
British	4	5	6	7
Continental	37	38	39	40

Men *Menn*

Suits/Overcoats						
American / British	36	38	40	42	44	46
Continental	46	48	50	52	54	56

Shirts				
American / British	15	16	17	18
Continental	38	40	42	44

Shoes								
American	$6\frac{1}{2}$	7	$7\frac{1}{2}$	8	$8\frac{1}{2}$	9	10	11
British	5	6	7	8	9	10	11	12
Continental	38	39	40	41	42	43	44	45

A good fit? *Passer det?*

Can I try it on?	**Kan jeg få prøve den?**	kahn yæi faw **prūrver** dehn
Where's the changing room?	**Hvor er prøverommet?**	voor ær **prūrver**-roommer
Is there a mirror?	**Fins det et speil her?**	finss deh eht spæil hær
It fits very well.	**Den passer meget bra.**	dehn **pah**sserr **māy**gert braa
It doesn't fit.	**Den passer ikke.**	dehn **pah**sser **ik**ker

NUMBERS, see page 147

It's too ...	**Den er for ...**	dehn ær for
short/long	**kort/lang**	ko^{r}t/lahng
tight/loose	**trang/vid**	trahng/vee(d)
How long will it take to alter it?	**Hvor lang tid tar det å endre den?**	voor lahng teed taar deh aw **ehn**drer dehn

Clothes and accessories *Klær og tilbehør*

I would like a/an/some ...	**Jeg vil gjerne ha ...**	yæi vil **yæ**^{r}ner haa
anorak	**en anorakk**	ehn ahnoo**rahk**
bathing cap	**en badehette**	ehn **baa**derhehter
bathrobe	**en badekåpe**	ehn **baa**derkawper
blouse	**en bluse**	ehn **blew**sser
bow tie	**en flue**	ehn **flew**er
bra	**en behå**	ehn **bay**haw
braces	**et par seler**	eht pahr **say**lerr
cap	**en lue**	ehn **lew**er
cardigan	**en golfjakke**	ehn **golf**yahker
children's ...	**barne-**	**baa**^{r}ner-
coat (man's)	**en frakk**	ehn frahk
coat (woman's)	**en kåpe**	ehn **kaw**per
dress	**en kjole**	ehn **khoo**ler
with long sleeves	**med lange ermer**	meh(d) **laang**er **ær**merr
with short sleeves	**med korte ermer**	meh(d) **ko**^{r}ter **ær**merr
sleeveless	**uten ermer**	**ew**tern **ær**merr
dressing gown	**en morgenkåpe**	ehn **maw**er^{r}nkawper
evening dress (woman's)	**en aftenkjole**	ehn **ahf**ternkhooler
fur coat	**en pels**	ehn pehlss
girdle	**en hofteholder**	ehn **hof**terhollerr
gloves	**et par hansker**	eht pahr **hahn**skerr
handbag	**en håndveske**	ehn **hon**vehsker
handkerchief	**et lommetørkle**	eht **loom**merturrkler
hat	**en hatt**	ehn haht
jacket	**en jakke**	ehn **yah**ker
jeans	**et par jeans**	eht pahr "jeans"
kneesocks	**et par knestrømper**	eht pahr **knay**strurmperr
man's ...	**herre-**	**hær**er-
nightdress (nightgown)	**en nattkjole**	ehn **naht**khooler
overalls	**en overall**	ehn **aw**verrol
pair of ...	**et par ...**	eht pahr
panties	**et par truser**	eht pahr **trew**sserr

pants (Am.)	**et par langbukser**	eht pahr **lahng**bookserr
panty hose	**en strømpebukse**	ehn **strurm**perbookser
parka	**en anorakk**	ehn ahnoo**rahk**
pullover	**en genser**	ehn **gehn**serr
crew-neck	**med rund hals**	meh(d) rewn hahlss
polo (turtle)-neck	**høyhalset**	**hoy**hahlsert
V-neck	**V-genser**	**va̅y̅**-gehnserr
pyjamas	**en pyjamas**	ehn pew**shaa**mahss
raincoat	**en regnfrakk**	ehn **ræin**frahk
scarf	**et skjerf**	eht shærf
shirt	**en skjorte**	ehn **shoo^{r}**ter
shorts	**et par shorts**	eht pahr "shorts"
skirt	**et skjørt**	eht shur^{r}t
slip	**en underkjole**	ehn **ew**nerrkho̅o̅ler
socks	**et par sokker**	eht pahr **sok**kerr
sportswear	**sportsklær**	**spo^{r}ts**klæ̅r
stockings	**et par strømper**	eht pahr **strurm**perr
suit (man's)	**en dress**	ehn drehss
suit (woman's)	**en drakt**	ehn drahkt
suspenders (Am.)	**et par seler**	eht pahr **sa̅y̅**lerr
sweater	**en genser**	ehn **gehn**serr
sweat suit	**en treningsdrakt**	ehn **tra̅y̅**ningsdrahkt
swimming trunks	**en badebukse**	ehn **baa**derbookser
swimsuit	**en badedrakt**	ehn **baa**derdrahkt
tie	**et slips**	eht shlipss
tights	**en strømpebukse**	ehn **strurm**perbookser
tracksuit	**en treningsdrakt**	ehn **tra̅y̅**ningsdrahkt
trousers	**et par langbukser**	eht pahr **lahng**bookserr
T-shirt	**en T-skjorte**	ehn **ta̅y̅**-shoo^{r}ter
umbrella	**en paraply**	ehn pahrah**ple̅w̅**
underpants	**en underbukse**	ehn **ew**nerrbookser
undershirt	**en trøye**	ehn **troy**er
vest (Am.)	**en vest**	ehn vehst
vest (Br.)	**en trøye**	ehn **troy**er
waistcoat	**en vest**	ehn vehst
woman's ...	**dame-**	**daa**mer-

belt	**et belte**	eht **behl**ter
buckle	**en spenne**	ehn **speh**ner
button	**en knapp**	ehn knahp
collar	**en krage**	ehn **kraa**ger
pocket	**en lomme**	ehn **loo**mmer
press stud (snap fastener)	**en trykknapp**	ehn **trewk**knahp
zip (zipper)	**en glidelås**	ehn **glee**derlawss

Shoes *Sko*

I'd like a pair of ...	**Jeg vil gjerne ha et par ...**	yæi vil **yæ**rner haa eht pahr
athletic shoes	**turnsko**	**tew**rnskoo
boots	**støvler**	**sturv**lerr
lined/unlined	**forede/uforede**	**foo**rerder/**ew**foorerder
moccasins	**mokkasiner**	mookah**ssee**nerr
plimsolls	**turnsko**	**tew**rnskoo
sandals	**sandaler**	sahn**daa**lerr
shoes	**sko**	skoo
flat	**lavhælte**	**laav**hayIter
with a heel	**med hæl**	meh(d) hayl
with leather soles	**med lærsåler**	meh(d) **læ**rsawlerr
with rubber soles	**med gummisåler**	meh(d) **gew**missawlerr
slippers	**tøfler**	**turf**lerr
These are too ...	**Disse er for ...**	**dis**ser ær for
narrow/wide	**smale/vide**	**smaa**ler/**vee**(d)er
big/small	**store/små**	**stoo**rer/smaw
Do you have a smaller/larger size?	**Har du et nummer mindre/større?**	haar dew eht **noom**merr **min**drer/**stur**rer
Do you have the same in black?	**Har du de samme i svart?**	haar dew dee **sah**mer ee svahrt
cloth/leather/rubber/suede	**tøy/lær/gummi/semsket skinn**	toy/lær/**gew**mi/**sehm**skert shin
Is it real leather?	**Er det ekte lær?**	ær deh **ehk**ter lær
I need some ...	**Jeg trenger ...**	yæi **trehng**err
insoles	**innleggssåler**	**in**lehgssawlerr
shoe polish	**skokrem**	**skoo**kraym
shoelaces	**skolisser**	**skoo**lisserr

Shoe repairs *Skoreparasjon*

Can you repair these shoes?	**Kan du reparere disse skoene?**	kahn dew rehpah**ray**rer **dis**ser **skoo**erner
Can you stitch this?	**Kan du sy sammen dette?**	kahn dew sew **sah**mern **deh**ter
I want new soles and heels.	**Jeg vil ha nye såler og hæler.**	yæi vil haa **new**er **saw**ler o(g) **hay**lerr
When will they be ready?	**Når blir de ferdig?**	nor bleer dee **fæ**rdi

COLOURS, see page 113

Electrical appliances *Elektrisk utstyr*

Standard voltage (*strømstyrke*) is 220 volts, 50 cycles A.C.

Do you have a battery for this?	**Har du et batteri til denne?**	haar dew eht bahter**ree** til **deh**ner
This is broken. Can you repair it?	**Denne er gått i stykker. Kan du reparere den?**	**deh**ner ær got ee **stew**kerr. kahn dew rehpah**ray**rer dehn
Can you show me how it works?	**Kan du vise meg hvordan den fungerer?**	kahn dew **vee**sser mæi **voo**^{r}dahn dehn fewn**gay**rerr
How do I switch it on?	**Hvordan setter man den i gang?**	**voo**^{r}dahn **seh**terr mahn dehn ee gahng
I'd like to hire (rent) a video cassette.	**Jeg vil gjerne leie en videokassett.**	yæi vil **yæ**^{r}ner **læi**er ehn **veed**yookahsseht
I'd like a/an/some ...	**Jeg vil gjerne ha ...**	yæi vil **yæ**^{r}ner haa
adaptor	**en adapter**	ehn ah**dahp**terr
amplifier	**en forsterker**	ehn **fosh**tærkerr
bulb	**en lyspære**	ehn **lew**spærer
cassette player	**en kassettspiller**	ehn kahs**seht**spillerr
(radio) cassette recorder	**en (radio)kassett-opptaker**	ehn (**raa**dyoo)kahs**seht**-optaakerr
clock-radio	**en klokkeradio**	ehn **klok**kerraadyoo
electric toothbrush	**en elektrisk tannbørste**	ehn eh**lehk**trisk **tahn**burshter
extension lead (cord)	**en skjøteledning**	ehn **shur**terlaydning
hair dryer	**en hårføner**	ehn **hawr**furnerr
headphones	**et par høre-telefoner**	eht pahr **hur**rer-tehlerfoonerr
(travelling) iron	**et (reise)strykejern**	eht (**ræi**sser)**strew**keryæ^{r}n
lamp	**en lampe**	ehn **lahm**per
personal stereo (pocket radio)	**en lommeradio**	ehn **loom**merraadyoo
portable ...	**bærbar ...**	**bær**baar
radio	**en radio**	ehn **raa**dyoo
record player	**en platespiller**	ehn **plaa**terspillerr
shaver	**en barbermaskin**	ehn bahr**bay**rmahsheen
speakers	**høyttalere**	**hoyt**taalerrer
(colour) television	**en (farge)TV**	ehn (**fahr**gger)**tay**veh
transformer	**en transformator**	ehn trahnsfor**maa**toor
video recorder	**en videokassett-opptaker**	ehn **veed**yookahsseht-optaakerr

Grocer's *Matvarehandel*

I'd like some bread, please.	**Jeg vil gjerne ha litt brød.**	yæi vil **yæ**^{r}ner haa lit brūr
crispbread	**knekkebrød**	**kneh**kerbrūr
sliced bread	**oppskåret brød**	**op**skawrert brūr
white bread	**loff**	loof
What sort of cheese do you have?	**Hva slags ostesorter har du?**	vaa shlakss **oo**sterso^{r}terr haar dew
A piece of that one, please.	**Et stykke av den, takk.**	eht **stew**ker ahv dehn tahk
I'll have one of those, please.	**Kan jeg få en av dem?**	kahn yæi faw ehn ahv dehm
May I help myself?	**Kan jeg ta selv?**	kahn yæi taa sehl
I'd like ...	**Jeg vil gjerne ha ...**	yæi vil **yæ**^{r}ner haa
a kilo of apples	**1 kg epler**	ehn **khee**loo **ehp**lerr
half a kilo of tomatoes	**½ kg tomater**	ehn hahl **khee**loo too**maa**terr
250 grams of coffee	**¼ kg kaffe**	ehn kvah^{r}t **khee**loo **kah**fer
3 hg. (300 g.) of salami	**3 h salami**	trāy **hehk**too sah**laa**mi
a litre of milk	**1 l melk**	ehn **lee**terr mehlk
4 slices of ham	**4 skiver skinke**	**fee**rer **shee**verr **shing**ker
a packet of tea	**en pakke te**	ehn **pah**ker tāy
a jar of jam	**et glass syltetøy**	eht glahss **sewl**tertoy
a tin (can) of peaches	**en boks fersken**	ehn bokss **fæsh**kern
a tube of mustard	**en tube sennep**	ehn **tēw**ber **seh**nerp
a box of chocolates	**en eske sjokolade**	ehn **eh**sker shookoo**laa**der

Weights and measures

1 kilogram or kilo (kg.) = 1,000 grams (g.)

100 g. = 3.5 oz.	½ kg. = 1.1 lb.
200 g. = 7.0 oz.	1 kg. = 2.2 lb.

1 oz. = 28.35 g.
1 lb. = 453.60 g.

1 litre (l.) = 0.88 imp. qt. or 1.6 U.S. qt.

1 imp. qt. = 1.14 l.	1 U.S. qt. = 0.95 l.
1 imp. gal. = 4.55 l.	1 U.S. gal. = 3.80 l.

FOOD, see also page 64

Jeweller's—Watchmaker's *Gullsmed – Urmaker*

Can you show me some jewellery, please?	**Kan jeg få se på noen smykker?**	kahn yæi faw say paw **noo**ern **smew**kerr
I want a present for ...	**Jeg vil gjerne ha en presang til ...**	yæi vil **yæ**^{r}ner haa ehn prehs**sahng** til
Could I see that, please?	**Kan jeg få se på det?**	kahn yæi faw say paw day
Do you have anything in gold?	**Har du noe i gull?**	haar dew **noo**er ee gewl
How many carats is this?	**Hvor mange karat har dette?**	voor **mahng**er kah**raat** haar **deh**ter
Is this real silver?	**Er dette ekte sølv?**	ær **deh**ter **ehk**ter surl
Can you engrave these initials on it?	**Kan du gravere disse initialene?**	kahn dew grah**vay**rer **dis**ser ini(t)see**aa**lerner
Can you repair this watch?	**Kan du reparere denne klokken?**	kahn dew rehpah**ray**rer **deh**ner **klok**kern
I'd like a/an/some ...	**Jeg vil gjerne ha ...**	yæi vil **yæ**^{r}ner haa
alarm clock	**en vekkeklokke**	ehn **veh**kerklokker
bangle	**en armring**	ehn **ahrm**ring
battery	**et batteri**	eht bahter**ree**
bracelet	**et armbånd**	eht **ahrm**bon
chain bracelet	**en armlenke**	ehn **ahrm**lehngker
charm bracelet	**et berlokkarmbånd**	eht bær**lok**ahrmbon
brooch	**en brosje**	ehn **broo**sher
chain	**et kjede**	eht **khay**der
charm	**en berlokk**	ehn bær**lok**
clock	**en klokke**	ehn **klok**ker
cross	**et kors**	eht kosh
cuff links	**et par mansjettknapper**	eht pahr mahn**sheht**knahperr
earrings	**et par øreringer**	eht pahr **ur**rerringerr
gem	**en edelsten**	ehn **ay**derlstayn
jewel box	**et smykkeskrin**	eht **smew**kerskreen
mechanical pencil	**en skrublyant**	ehn **skrew**blewahnt
music box	**en spilledåse**	ehn **spil**lerdawsser
necklace	**et halskjede**	eht **hahls**khayder
pendant	**et hengesmykke**	eht **hehng**ersmewker
pocket watch	**et lommeur**	eht **loom**merewr
powder compact	**en pudderdåse**	ehn **pew**derrdawsser
propelling pencil	**en skrublyant**	ehn **skrew**blewahnt

ring	**en ring**	ehn ring
engagement ring	**en forlovelsesring**	ehn for**law**verlsersring
signet ring	**en signetring**	ehn sing**nāȳ**tring
wedding ring	**en giftering**	ehn **yif**terring
silverware	**noe sølvtøy**	**nōō**er **surl**toy
string (strand) of pearls	**et perlekjede**	eht **pæʳ**lerkhāȳder
tie clip	**en slipsklype**	ehn **shlips**klēw̄per
tie pin	**en slipsnål**	ehn **shlips**nawl
watch	**en klokke**	ehn **klok**ker
automatic	**automatisk**	outoo**maa**tisk
digital/analogue	**digital/analog**	diggi**taal**/ahnah**lawg**
quartz	**kvarts**	kvahʳtss
with a second hand	**med sekundviser**	meh(d) seh**kewn**veesserr
waterproof	**vanntett**	**vahn**teht
watchstrap	**en klokkerem**	ehn **klok**kerrehm
wristwatch	**et armbåndsur**	eht **ahrm**bonsēw̄r

amber	**rav**	raav
amethyst	**ametyst**	ahmer**tewst**
brass	**messing**	**meh**ssing
bronze	**bronse**	**brong**ser
chromium	**krom**	kroom
copper	**kopper**	**kop**perr
coral	**korall**	koo**rahl**
crystal	**krystall**	krew**stahl**
cut glass	**slepet glass**	**shlāȳ**pert glahss
diamond	**diamant**	deeah**mahnt**
emerald	**smaragd**	smah**rahgd**
enamel	**emalje**	eh**mahl**yer
gold	**gull**	gewl
gold plate	**gullbelagt**	**gewl**berlahkt
jade	**jade**	**yaa**der
mother-of-pearl	**perlemor**	**pæʳ**lermōōr
onyx	**onyks**	oo**newkss**
pearl	**perle**	**pæʳ**ler
pewter	**tinn**	tin
platinum	**platina**	**plaa**teenah
ruby	**rubin**	rew**been**
sapphire	**safir**	sah**feer**
silver	**sølv**	surl
silver plate	**sølvplett**	**surl**pleht
topaz	**topas**	too**paass**
turquoise	**turkis**	tewr**keess**

Optician *Optiker*

I've broken my glasses.	**Brillene mine er gått i stykker.**	brillerner **mee**ner ær got ee **staw**kerr
Can you repair them for me?	**Kan du reparere dem for meg?**	kahn dew rehpah**ray**rer dehm for mæi
When will they be ready?	**Når blir de ferdig?**	nor bleer dee **fæ^{r}**di
Can you change the lenses?	**Kan du skifte ut glassene?**	kahn dew **shif**ter ewt **glahs**serner
I'd like tinted lenses.	**Jeg vil gjerne ha fargede glass.**	yæi vil **yæ^{r}**ner haa **fahr**ggerder glahss
The frame is broken.	**Innfatningen er brukket.**	**in**fahtningern ær **brook**kert
I'd like a glasses case.	**Jeg vil gjerne ha et brillefutteral.**	yæi vil **yæ^{r}**ner haa eht **bril**lerfewterraal
I'd like to have my eyesight checked.	**Jeg vil gjerne få kontrollert synet.**	yæi vil **yæ^{r}**ner faw koontroo**lay^{r}t** **sew**ner
I'm ...	**Jeg er ...**	yæi ær
short-sighted	**nærsynt**	**næ^{r}**sewnt
long-sighted	**langsynt**	**lahng**sewnt
I'd like some contact lenses.	**Jeg vil gjerne ha kontaktlinser.**	yæi vil **yæ^{r}**ner haa koon**tahkt**linserr
I've lost one of my contact lenses.	**Jeg har mistet en kontaktlinse.**	yæi haar **mis**tert ehn koon**tahkt**linser
Could you give me another one?	**Kan jeg få en ny?**	kahn yæi faw ehn new
I have hard/soft lenses.	**Jeg har harde/ myke linser.**	yæi haar **haa**rer/ **mew**ker **lin**serr
Do you have any contact-lens fluid?	**Har du en kontakt-linsevæske?**	haar dew ehn koon**tahkt**-linservehsker
I'd like to buy a pair of sunglasses.	**Jeg vil gjerne kjøpe et par solbriller.**	yæi vil **yæ^{r}**ner **khur**per eht pahr **sool**brillerr
May I look in the mirror?	**Kan jeg få se meg i speilet?**	kahn yæi faw say mæi ee **spæi**ler
I'd like to buy a pair of binoculars.	**Jeg vil gjerne kjøpe en kikkert.**	yæi vil **yæ^{r}**ner **khur**per ehn **khikke^{r}t**

Photography *Fotografering*

I'd like a(n) ... camera.	**Jeg vil gjerne ha et ... fotoapparat.**	yæi vil **yæ**^{r}ner haa eht ... **foo**tooahpahraat
automatic	**helautomatisk**	**hay**loutoomaatisk
compact	**kompakt**	koom**pahkt**
simple	**enkelt**	**ehng**kehrlt
Can you show me some video cameras, please?	**Kan jeg få se på noen video-kameraer?**	kahn yæi faw say paw **noo**ern **veed**yoo-kaamerraherr
I'd like to have some passport photos.	**Jeg vil gjerne få tatt noen passfoto.**	yæi vil **yæ**^{r}ner faw taht **noo**ern **pahs**footoo

Film *Film*

I'd like a film (for this camera).	**Jeg vil gjerne ha en film (til dette apparatet).**	yæi vil **yæ**^{r}ner haa ehn film (til **deh**ter ahpah**raa**ter)
black and white	**svart-hvitt**	**svah**^{r}**t**-vit
colour	**farge**	**fahr**gger
colour negative	**fargenegativ**	**fahr**ggernaygahteev
cartridge	**en kassett**	ehn kah**sseht**
disc film	**en disc**	ehn disk
roll film	**en rullefilm**	ehn **rew**lerfilm
slide film	**film for lysbilder**	film for **lews**bilderr
video cassette	**en videokassett**	ehn **veed**yookahsseht
24/36 exposures	**24/36 bilder**	khewer**feer**er/trehti**sehkss** **bil**derr
this size	**dette formatet**	**deh**ter for**maa**ter
this ASA/DIN number	**dette ASA-/DIN-nummeret**	**deh**ter **aa**ssah-/**din**-noommerrer
artificial light type	**for kunstig belysning**	for **kewn**sti ber**lews**ning
daylight type	**for dagslys**	for **dahks**lewss
fast (high-speed)	**hurtig**	**hew**^{r}ti
fine grain	**finkornet**	**feen**koo^{r}nert

Processing *Fremkalling*

Does the price include processing?	**Er fremkalling inkludert i prisen?**	ær **frehm**kahling in-klew**day**^{r}**t** ee **pree**ssern
How much do you charge for processing?	**Hvor mye koster fremkallingen?**	voor **mew**er **kos**terr **frehm**kahlingern

I'd like ... prints of each negative.	**Jeg vil gjerne ha ... kopier av hvert negativ.**	yæi vil **yæ^{r}**ner haa ... koo**pee**yerr ahv væ^{r}t **nay**gahteev
with a mat finish	**med matt overflate**	meh(d) maht **aw**verflaater
with a glossy finish	**med blank overflate**	meh(d) blahngk **aw**verflaater
Will you enlarge this, please?	**Kan du forstørre dette?**	kahn dew fo**shtur**rer **deh**ter
When will the photos be ready?	**Når blir bildene ferdig?**	nor bleer **bil**derner **fæ^{r}**di

Accessories and repairs *Tilbehør og reparasjon*

I'd like a/an/some ...	**Jeg vil gjerne ha ...**	yæi vil **yæ^{r}**ner haa
battery	**et batteri**	eht bahter**ree**
cable release	**en snorutløser**	ehn **snoo**rewtlursserr
camera case	**en kameraveske**	ehn **kaa**merrahvehsker
(electronic) flash	**en (elektronisk) blitz**	ehn (ehlehk**troo**nisk) blitss
filter	**et filter**	eht **fil**terr
for black and white	**for svart-hvitt**	for **svah^{r}t**-vit
for colour	**for farge**	for **fahr**gger
lens	**et objektiv**	eht obyehk**teev**
telephoto lens	**et teleobjektiv**	eht **tay**lerobyehkteev
wide-angle lens	**et vidvinkel-objektiv**	eht **vee(d)**vinkerl-obyehkteev
lens cap	**en linsebeskytter**	ehn **lin**serbershewterr
slide projector	**et lysbildeapparat**	eht **lews**bilderahpahraat
Can you repair this camera?	**Kan du reparere dette apparatet?**	kahn dew rehpah**ray**rer **deh**ter ahpah**raa**ter
The film is jammed.	**Filmen sitter fast.**	**fil**mern **sit**ter fahst
There's something wrong with the ...	**Det er noe i veien med ...**	deh ær **noo**er ee **væi**ern meh(d)
exposure counter	**telleverket**	**teh**lerværker
film winder	**fremtrekkeren**	**frehm**trehkerrern
flash attachment	**blitzaggregatet**	**blits**ahgrergaater
lens	**objektivet**	obyehk**tee**ver
light meter	**lysmåleren**	**lews**mawlerrern
rangefinder	**avstandsmåleren**	**aav**stahnsmawlerrern
self-timing release	**selvutløseren**	**sehl**ewtlursserrern
shutter	**lukkeren**	**look**kerrern

NUMBERS, see page 147

Tobacconist's *Tobakkshandel*

Virtually all international brands of cigarettes, cigars and tobacco are available at tobacconists, in kiosks and supermarkets. Local cigarettes are quite good, and Norwegian pipe tobacco is noted for its quality.

A packet of cigarettes, please.	**En pakke sigaretter, takk.**	ehn **pah**ker siggah**reh**terr tahk
How much are they per ...?	**Hvor mye koster de pr. ...?**	voor **mew**er **kos**terr dee pær
packet/carton	**pakke/kartong**	**pah**ker/kah^{r}**tong**
Could I have a carton, please?	**Kan jeg få en kartong?**	kahn yæi faw ehn kah^{r}**tong**
I'd like a/some ...	**Jeg vil gjerne ha ...**	yæi vil **yæ**^{r}ner haa
candy	**noen godter**	**noo**ern **go**terr
chewing gum	**en pakke tyggegummi**	ehn **pah**ker **tew**ger-gewmi
chewing tobacco	**litt skråtobakk**	lit **skraw**toobahk
chocolate bar	**en sjokoladeplate**	ehn shookoo**laa**derplaater
cigarette case	**et sigarettetui**	eht siggah**reh**tehtewee
cigarette holder	**et sigarett-munnstykke**	eht siggah**reht**-mewnstewker
cigarettes	**sigaretter**	siggah**reh**ter
filter-tipped	**med filter**	meh(d) **fil**terr
without filter	**uten filter**	**ew**tern **fil**terr
light/dark tobacco	**lys/mørk tobakk**	lewss/murrk too**bahk**
mild/strong	**milde/sterke**	**mil**ler/**stær**ker
menthol	**mentol-**	mehn**tool**-
king-size	**king-size**	"king-size"
cigars	**noen sigarer**	**noo**ern si**ggaa**rerr
lighter	**en lighter**	ehn "lighter"
lighter fluid	**lighterbensin**	"lighter"behn**seen**
lighter gas	**lightergass**	"lighter"gahss
matches	**fyrstikker**	**fewsh**tikkerr
pipe	**en pipe**	ehn **pee**per
pipe cleaners	**piperensere**	**pee**perrehnserrer
pipe tobacco	**pipetobakk**	**pee**pertoobahk
postcards	**noen postkort**	**noo**ern **post**ko^{r}t
snuff	**en eske snus**	ehn **eh**sker snewss
stamps	**noen frimerker**	**noo**ern **free**mærkerr
sweets	**noen godter**	**noo**ern **go**terr
tobacco	**tobakk**	too**bahk**
wick	**en veke**	ehn **vay**ker

Miscellaneous *Forskjellig*

Souvenirs *Suvenirer*

The most attractive Norwegian souvenirs to look for are products of home craftsmen, like handmade knitwear—pullovers (sweaters), cardigans, mittens, scarves and ski caps—painted wooden figurines, trolls, sealskin slippers and "rose-painted" wooden articles, such as small boxes, egg cups, plates and miniature bellows; the rococo floral designs are typically Norwegian. Other popular souvenirs include miniature Viking ships of wood, pewter, enamel or silver, dolls in native costume, reindeer-skin rugs, woven runners, table cloths and wall hangings.

I'd like a souvenir from ...	**Jeg vil gjerne ha en suvenir fra ...**	yæi vil **yæ**^{r}ner haa ehn sewver**neer** fraa
Something typically Norwegian, please.	**Noe typisk norsk.**	nooer **tew**pisk noshk
cardigan (with Norwegian design)	**en lusekofte**	ehn **lew**sserkofter
doll in native costume	**en dukke med bunad**	ehn **dew**ker meh(d) **bew**nahd
drinking horn	**et drikkehorn**	eht **drik**kerhoo^{r}n
hunting knife	**en jaktkniv**	ehn **yahkt**kneev
reindeer skin	**et reinsdyrskinn**	eht **ræins**dewrshin
sealskin slippers	**et par selskinnstøfler**	eht pahr **sayl**shinsturflerr
troll	**et troll**	eht trol
Viking ship	**et vikingskip**	eht **vee**kingsheep
wooden figurine	**en trefigur**	ehn **tray**figgewr
woven runner	**en rye**	ehn **rew**er
A "rose-painted" ...	**En rosemalt ...**	ehn **roo**ssermaalt
bowl	**bolle**	**bol**ler
candlestick	**lysestake**	**lew**sserstaaker
plate	**asjett**	ah**sheht**

Records—Cassettes *Plater – Kassetter*

I'd like a ...	**Jeg vil gjerne ha ...**	yæi vil **yæ**^{r}ner haa
cassette	**en kassett**	ehn kahs**seht**
video cassette	**en videokassett**	ehn **veed**yookahsseht
compact disc	**en CD-plate**	ehn **say**-day-plaater

L.P. (33 rpm)	**LP (33 omdreininger)**	**ehl**-pa̅y̅ (trehti**tra̅y̅** **om**dræiningerr)
E.P. (45 rpm)	**EP (45 omdreininger)**	a̅y̅-pa̅y̅ (fur^{r}ti**fehm** **om**dræiningerr)
single	**singel**	**sing**erl

Do you have any records by ...?	**Har du noen plater av ...?**	haar dew **no̅o̅**ern **plaa**terr ahv
Can I listen to this record?	**Kan jeg få høre på denne platen?**	kahn yæi faw **hu̅r̅**rer paw **deh**ner **plaa**tern
chamber music	**kammermusikk**	**kah**merrmewssik
classical music	**klassisk musikk**	**klah**ssisk mew**ssik**
folk music	**folkemusikk**	**fol**kermewssik
folk songs	**folkesanger**	**fol**kersahngerr
instrumental music	**instrumentalmusikk**	instrewmehn**taal**mewssik
jazz	**jazz**	yahss
light music	**underholdnings-musikk**	ewnerr**hold**nings-mewssik
orchestral music	**orkestermusikk**	or**kehs**terrmewssik
pop music	**pop**	pop

Toys and games *Leker og spill*

I'd like a toy/game.	**Jeg vil gjerne ha en leke/et spill.**	yæi vil **yæ**^{r}ner haa ehn **la̅y̅**ker/eht spil
(beach) ball	**en (bade)ball**	ehn (**baa**der)bahl
board/card game	**et brettspill/kortspill**	eht **breht**spil/**ko**^{r}**t**spil
bucket and spade (pail and shovel)	**spann og spade**	spahn o(g) **spaa**der
building blocks (bricks)	**noen byggeklosser**	**no̅o̅**ern **bew**gerklosserr
building set	**et byggesett**	eht **bew**gersseht
chess set	**et sjakkspill**	eht **shahk**spil
doll	**en dukke**	ehn **dew**ker
electronic game	**et elektronisk spill**	eht ehlehk**tro̅o̅**nisk spil
flippers	**et par svømme-føtter**	eht pahr **svur**mer-furterr
roller skates	**et par rulleskøyter**	eht pahr **rew**lershoyter
snorkel	**en snorkel**	ehn **snor**kerl
stuffed animal	**et stoffdyr**	eht **stof**de̅w̅r
toy car	**en lekebil**	ehn **la̅y̅**kerbeel
battery-powered	**batteridrevet**	bahterr**ee**dra̅y̅vert
remote-controlled	**ledningstyrt**	**la̅y̅d**ningstew^{r}t

Your money: banks—currency

At most banks there's sure to be someone who speaks English. You'll find small currency exchange offices in most tourist centres, especially during the summer season. Remember to take your passport along with you, as you may need it for identification.

Traveller's cheques and credit cards are widely accepted in tourist-oriented shops, hotels, restaurants, etc. However, if you're exploring way off the beaten track, you'll probably come across stores where they are not taken. The same goes for garages and filling stations—generally, only major agency garages will accept payment in traveller's cheques or by credit card.

Opening hours. Banks are generally open from 8.15 a.m. to 3.30 p.m., Monday to Wednesday and Fridays, until 5 or 6 p.m. on Thursdays. Between June 1 and August 31, however, they close at 3 p.m. (5 or 5.30 p.m. on Thursdays). At Oslo airport and central railway station, the currency exchange offices have longer hours.

Monetary unit. The Norwegian krone (meaning "crown", pronounced **kroo̅**ner, plural kroner—**kroo̅**nerr, abbreviated kr/kr.) is divided into 100 øre (u̅rrer).

Coins: 10 and 50 øre, kr 1,5 and 10.
Banknotes: kr 50, 100, 500 and 1,000.

Where's the nearest bank?	**Hvor er nærmeste bank?**	voor ær **nær**mehster bahngk
Where's the nearest currency exchange office?	**Hvor er nærmeste vekslingskontor?**	voor ær **nær**mehster **vehk**shlingskoontoo̅r
When is the bank open?	**Når er banken åpen?**	nor ær **bahng**kern **aw**pern
When is the currency exchange office open?	**Når er vekslingskontoret åpent?**	nor ær **vehk**shlingskoontoo̅rer **aw**pernt

At the bank *I banken*

I'd like to change some dollars/ pounds.	**Jeg vil gjerne veksle noen dollar/ pund.**	yæi vil **yæ**^{r}ner **vehk**shler **nōō**ern **dol**lahr/ pewn
I'd like to cash a traveller's cheque.	**Jeg vil gjerne løse inn en reisesjekk.**	yæi vil **yæ**^{r}ner **lūr**sser in ehn **ræi**ssershehk
What's the exchange rate?	**Hva er vekslings-kursen?**	vaa ær **vehk**shlings-kēwshern
How much commission do you charge?	**Hvor mye tar dere i kommisjon?**	voor **mēw**er taar **dāy**rer ee koomi**shōōn**
Can you cash this cheque?	**Kan du løse inn denne sjekken?**	kahn dew **lūr**sser in **deh**ner **sheh**kern
Can you telex my bank in London?	**Kan du sende en telex til min bank i London?**	kahn dew **seh**ner ehn **tāy**lekss til meen bahngk ee **lon**don
I have a/an/ some ...	**Jeg har ...**	yæi haar
credit card	**kredittkort**	kreh**dit**ko^{r}t
Eurocheques	**eurosjekker**	**yēw**rooshehkerr
letter of credit	**et kredittbrev**	eht kreh**dit**brāyv
I'm expecting some money from New York. Has it arrived?	**Jeg venter penger fra New York. Har de kommet?**	yæi **vehn**terr **pehng**err fraa new york. haar dee **kom**mert
Please give me ... in notes (bills) and some small change.	**Gi meg ... i sedler og litt småpenger.**	yee mæi ... ee **sehd**lerr o(g) litt **smaw**pehngerr
Give me ... in large notes and the rest in small notes.	**Gi meg ... i store sedler og resten i små sedler.**	yee mæi ... ee **stōō**rer **sehd**lerr o(g) **rehs**tern ee smaw **sehd**lerr

Deposit—Withdrawal *Innskudd – Uttak*

I'd like to ...	**Jeg vil gjerne ...**	yæi vil **yæ**^{r}ner
open an account	**åpne en konto**	**awp**ner ehn **kon**too
withdraw ... kroner	**ta ut ... kroner**	taa ēwt ... **krōō**nerr
Where should I sign?	**Hvor skal jeg undertegne?**	voor skahl yæi **ewn**errtæiner
I'd like to pay this into my account.	**Jeg vil gjerne sette dette inn på kontoen min.**	yæi vil **yæ**^{r}ner **seh**ter **deh**ter in paw **kon**tooern meen

NUMBERS, see page 147

Business terms *Forretningsuttrykk*

My name is ...	**Mitt navn er ...**	mit nahvn ær
Here's my card.	**Her er mitt kort.**	hær ær mit ko[r]t
I have an appointment with ...	**Jeg har avtalt et møte med ...**	yæi haar **aav**tahlt eht **mur**ter meh(d)
Can you give me an estimate of the cost?	**Kan du gi meg et overslag over kostnadene?**	kahn dew yee mæi eht **aw**vershlaag **aw**verr **kost**nahderner
What's the rate of inflation?	**Hvor høy er inflasjonsraten?**	voor hoy ær inflah**shoons**raatern
Can you provide me with a/an ...	**Kan du skaffe meg en ...**	kahn dew **skah**fer mæi ehn
interpreter	**tolk**	tolk
secretary	**sekretær**	sehkrer**tær**
translation	**oversettelse**	**aw**vershehterlser
translator	**oversetter**	**aw**vershehterr
Where can I make photocopies?	**Hvor kan jeg ta fotokopier?**	voor kahn yæi taa **foo**tookoopeeyerr

amount	**et beløp**	eht ber**lurp**
balance	**en balanse**	ehn bah**lahng**ser
capital	**en kapital**	ehn kahpi**taal**
contract	**en kontrakt**	ehn koon**trahkt**
credit	**en kreditt**	ehn kreh**dit**
discount	**en rabatt**	ehn rah**baht**
expenses	**utgifter**	**ew**tyifterr
interest	**en rente**	ehn **rehn**ter
investment	**en investering**	ehn inver**stay**ring
invoice	**en faktura**	ehn fahk**tew**rah
loan	**et lån**	eht lawn
loss	**et tap**	eht taap
mortgage	**et hypotek**	eht hewpoo**tayk**
payment	**en betaling**	ehn ber**taa**ling
percentage	**en prosentsats**	ehn proo**sehnt**sahtss
profit	**et utbytte**	eht **ew**tbewter
purchase	**et kjøp**	eht khurp
sale	**et salg**	eht sahlg
share	**en aksje**	ehn **ahk**sher
tax	**en skatt**	ehn skaht
transfer	**en overføring**	ehn **aw**verfurring
value	**en verdi**	ehn væ[r]**dee**

At the post office

The post office only handles mail; for fax, telephone and telegram or telex services you have to go to a *telesenter* office.

Business hours are generally from 8 a.m. to 5 or 5.30 p.m., Monday to Friday (4 or 4.30 p.m. in summer), and from 9 a.m. to 1 p.m. on Saturdays.

Letter (mail) boxes are painted red.

Where's the nearest post office?	**Hvor er nærmeste postkontor?**	voor ær **nær**mehster **post**koontōōr
What time does the post office open/close?	**Når åpner/stenger postkontoret**	nor **awp**nerr/**stehng**err **post**koontōōrer
A stamp for this letter/postcard, please.	**Et frimerke til dette brevet/kortet, takk.**	eht **free**mærker til **deh**ter **brāy**ver/**ko**^{r}ter tahk
A ... -kroner stamp, please.	**Et ... -kroners frimerke, takk.**	eht ... -**krōō**nersh **free**mærker tahk
What's the postage for a letter to England?	**Hva er portoen for et brev til England?**	vah ær **poo**^{r}tooern for eht brāyv til **ehng**lahn
What's the postage for a postcard to the U.S.?	**Hva er portoen for et postkort til USA?**	vah ær **poo**^{r}tooern for eht **post**ko^{r}t til ēw-ehss-**aa**
Where's the letter box (mailbox)?	**Hvor er postkassen?**	voor ær **post**kahssern
I want to send this parcel.	**Jeg vil gjerne sende denne pakken.**	yæi vil **yæ**^{r}ner **seh**ner **deh**ner **pah**kern
I'd like to register this parcel.	**Jeg vil gjerne rekommandere denne pakken.**	yæi vil **yæ**^{r}ner rehkoomahn**dāy**rer **deh**ner **pah**kern
I'd like to send this by ...	**Jeg vil gjerne sende dette ...**	yæi vil **yæ**^{r}ner **seh**ner **deh**ter
airmail	**med fly**	meh(d) flēw
express mail	**ekspress**	ehks**prehss**
registered mail	**rekommandert**	rehkoomahn**dāy**^{r}**t**

I'd like some ..., please.	**Jeg vil gjerne ha noen ...**	yæi vil **yæ**[r]ner haa **noo**ern
aerogrammes	**aerogrammer**	ehroo**grah**merr
airmail labels	**luftpostetiketter**	**lewft**postehtikehterr
At which counter can I cash an international money order?	**I hvilken luke kan jeg løse inn en internasjonal postanvisning?**	ee **vil**kern **lew**ker kahn yæi **lur**sser in ehn inter[r]nahshoonaal **post**ahnveesning
Where's the poste restante (general delivery)?	**Hvor er poste-restanteluken?**	voor ær post-reh**stahngtlew**kern
Is there any post (mail) for me?	**Har det kommet noe post til meg?**	haar deh **kom**mert **noo**er post til mæi
My name is ...	**Mitt navn er ...**	mit nahvn ær

FRIMERKER	STAMPS
PAKKER	PARCELS
POSTANVISNINGER	MONEY ORDERS

Telegrams—Telex—Fax *Telegrammer – Telex – Telefax*

Where's the nearest telegraph office?	**Hvor er nærmeste telesenter?**	voor ær **nær**mehster **tay**lerssehnterr
I'd like to send a ...	**Jeg vil gjerne sende ...**	yæi vil **yæ**[r]ner **seh**ner
fax	**en telefax**	ehn **tay**lerfahkss
telegram	**et telegram**	eht tehler**grahm**
telex	**en telex**	ehn **tay**lehkss
May I have a form, please?	**Kan jeg få en blankett?**	kahn yæi faw ehn blahng**keht**
How much is it per word?	**Hva koster det pr. ord?**	vaa **kos**terr deh pær **oor**
How long will a telegram to Boston take?	**Hvor lang tid tar et telegram til Boston?**	voor lahng teed taar eht tehler**grahm** til **bos**ton
How much will this telex cost?	**Hvor mye vil denne telexen komme på?**	voor **mew**er vil **deh**ner **tay**lehksern **kom**mer paw

Telephone *Telefon*

International and long-distance calls can be made from phone booths, but if you need help in making a call, go to a telegraph office. Dialling instructions in English are posted inside the booth and can be found at the front of the telephone directory.

For direct calls abroad, dial 095, then the country code (Britain, 44, U.S.A. and Canada, 1), the national dialling (area) code (minus the initial "0") and the local telephone number.

Where's the telephone?	**Hvor er telefonen?**	voor ær tehler**fōōn**ern
Where's the nearest telephone booth?	**Hvor er nærmeste telefonkiosk?**	voor ær **nær**mehster tehler**fōōn**khyosk
May I use your phone?	**Kan jeg få låne telefonen?**	kahn yæi faw **law**ner tehler**fōōn**ern
Do you have a telephone directory for Bergen?	**Har du en telefonkatalog for Bergen?**	haar dew ehn tehler**fōōn**-kahtahlawg for **bær**gern
I'd like to call someone in England.	**Jeg vil gjerne ringe til England.**	yæi vil **yæ^{r}**ner **ring**er til **ehng**lahn
What's the dialling (area) code for ...?	**Hva er retningsnummeret til ...?**	vah ær **reht**nings-noommerrer til
How do I get the international operator?	**På hvilket nummer kan jeg få hjelp med fjernvalg til utlandet?**	paw **vil**kert **noom**merr kahn yæi faw yehlp meh(d) **fyæ^{r}n**vahlg til **ēwt**lahner

Operator *Telefonist*

Could you give me the number of ...?	**Kan du gi meg nummeret til ...?**	kahn dew yee mæi **noom**merrer til
Can you help me get this number?	**Kan du hjelpe meg å komme til dette nummeret?**	kahn dew **yehl**per mæi aw **kom**mer til **deh**ter **noom**merrer
I'd like to place a personal (person-to-person) call.	**Jeg vil gjerne bestille en personlig samtale.**	yæi vil **yæ^{r}**ner ber**stil**ler ehn pæ**shōōn**li **sahm**taaler

NUMBERS, see page 147

I'd like to reverse the charges (call collect).	**Jeg vil gjerne bestille en noteringsoverføring.**	yæi vil **yæ^{r}**ner ber**stil**ler ehn noo**tay**ringsawverrfurring

Telephone alphabet	*Bokstavering*				
A	**Anna**	ahnah	P	**Petter**	pehterr
B	**Bernhard**	bæ^{r}nah^{r}t	Q	**Quintus**	kvintewss
C	**Cæsar**	sayssahr	R	**Rikard**	rikah^{r}t
D	**David**	daaveed	S	**Sigrid**	sigree
E	**Edith**	aydit	T	**Teodor**	tayoodoor
F	**Fredrik**	frehdrik	U	**Ulrik**	ewlrik
G	**Gustav**	gewstahv	V	**enkelt-V**	ehngkerlt-vay
H	**Harald**	hahrahl	W	**dobbelt-V**	dobberlt-vay
I	**Ivar**	eevahr	X	**Xerxes**	ksærksehss
J	**Johan**	yoohahn	Y	**Yngling**	ewngling
K	**Karin**	kaareen	Z	**Zakarias**	sahkahreeahss
L	**Ludvig**	lewdvik	Æ	**Ærlig**	æ^{r}li
M	**Martin**	mah^{r}tin	Ø	**Ørn**	ur^{r}n
N	**Nils**	nilss	Å	**Åse**	awsser
O	**Olivia**	ooleeveeah			

Speaking *Samtale*

Hello. This is ...	**Hallo. Dette er ...**	hahl**loo**. **deh**ter ær
I'd like to speak to ...	**Kan jeg få snakke med ...?**	kahn yæi faw **snah**ker meh(d)
Is ... there?	**Er ... til stede?**	ær ... til **stay**der
Extension ...	**Linje ...**	**lin**yer
Who's speaking?	**Hvem er det jeg snakker med?**	vehm ær deh yæi **snah**kerr meh(d)
Pardon?	**Unnskyld?**	**ewn**shewl
Can you speak louder/more slowly, please.	**Kan du snakke litt høyere/litt langsommere?**	kahn dew **snah**ker lit **hoy**errer/lit **lahng**sommerrer

Bad luck *Uheldig*

Operator, you gave me the wrong number.	**Jeg tror du ga meg feil nummer.**	yæi troor dew gaa mæi fæil **noom**merr
We were cut off.	**Vi ble avbrutt.**	vee bleh **aav**brewt

Not there *Ikke til stede*

When will he/she be back?	**Når kommer han/ hun tilbake?**	nor **kom**merr hahn/ hewn til**baa**ker
Will you tell him I called?	**Kan du si til ham at jeg har ringt?**	kahn dew see til hahm aht yæi haar ringt
My name is ...	**Mitt navn er ...**	mit nahvn ær
Would you ask her to phone me?	**Kan du be henne om å ringe meg?**	kahn dew ba̅y̅ **heh**ner om aw **ring**er mæi
My number is ...	**Mitt nummer er ...**	mit **noom**merr ær
Would you take a message?	**Kan du ta imot en beskjed?**	kahn dew taa ee**mo̅o̅t** ehn ber**sha̅y̅**
I'll call back later.	**Jeg ringer senere.**	yæi **ring**err **sa̅y̅**nerrer

Charges *Gebyr*

How much did the call cost?	**Hvor mye kostet samtalen?**	voor **me̅w̅**er **kos**tert **sahm**taalern
I'd like to pay for the call.	**Jeg vil gjerne betale samtalen.**	yæi vil **yæʳ**ner ber**taa**ler **sahm**taalern

Det er telefon til deg.	There's a telephone call for you.
Hvilket nummer ringer du?	What number are you calling?
Linjen er opptatt.	The line's engaged.
Det svarer ikke.	There's no answer.
Du har ringt feil.	You've got the wrong number.
Telefonen er i uorden.	The phone is out of order.
Et øyeblikk.	Hold on, please/Just a moment.
Han/Hun er ute for øyeblikket.	He's/She's out at the moment.
Han/Hun er tilbake klokken ...	He'll/She'll be back at ...
Kan du prøve igjen litt senere?	Would you try again later?

Doctor

British subjects are covered by a British-Norwegian health insurance agreement. For nationals of other countries it is advisable to take out health insurance covering the cost of illness or accident while on holiday.

General *Allment*

Can you get me a doctor?	**Kan du skaffe meg en lege?**	kahn dew **skah**fer mæi ehn **la̅y̅**ger
Is there a doctor here?	**Fins det en lege her?**	finss deh ehn **la̅y̅**ger hæ̅r̅
I need a doctor, quickly.	**Jeg trenger lege øyeblikkelig.**	yæi **trehng**err **la̅y̅**ger oyer**blik**kerli
Where can I find a doctor who speaks English?	**Hvor kan jeg få tak i en lege som snakker engelsk?**	voor kahn yæi faw taak ee ehn **la̅y̅**ger som **snah**kerr **ehng**erlsk
Where's the surgery (doctor's office)?	**Hvor er lege-kontoret?**	voor ær **la̅y̅**ger-koonto̅o̅rer
What are the surgery (office) hours?	**Når har legen kontortid?**	nor haar **la̅y̅**gern koon**to̅o̅r**teed
Could the doctor come to see me here?	**Kan legen komme hit å undersøke meg?**	kahn **la̅y̅**gern **kom**mer heet aw **ewn**ershu̅r̅ker mæi
What time can the doctor come?	**Når kan legen komme?**	nor kahn **la̅y̅**gern **kom**mer
Can you recommend a/an ...?	**Kan du anbefale en ...?**	kahn dew **ahn**berfaaler ehn
general practitioner	**allmennpraktiker**	**ahl**mehnprahktikkerr
children's doctor	**barnelege**	**baa**^{r}nerla̅y̅ger
eye specialist	**øyenlege**	**oy**ernla̅y̅ger
gynaecologist	**gynekolog**	gewnerkoo**lawg**
Can I have an appointment ...?	**Kan jeg få time ...?**	kahn yæi faw **tee**mer
immediately	**med én gang**	meh(d) a̅y̅n gahng
tomorrow	**i morgen**	ee **maw**er^{r}n
as soon as possible	**så snart som mulig**	saw snaa^{r}t som **me̅w̅**li

CHEMIST'S (DRUGSTORE), see page 108

Parts of the body *Kroppsdeler*

appendix	**blindtarmen**	**blin**tahrmern
arm	**armen**	**ahr**mern
artery	**pulsåren**	**pewls**awrern
back	**ryggen**	**rew**gern
bladder	**urinblæren**	ewr**een**blǣrern
bone	**benet (i kroppen)**	bāyner (ee **krop**pern)
bowel	**tarmen**	**tahr**mern
breast	**brystet**	**brew**ster
chest	**brystkassen**	**brewst**kahssern
ear	**øret**	**ūr**rer
face	**ansiktet**	**ahn**sikter
finger	**fingeren**	**fing**errern
foot	**foten**	**fōō**tern
genitals	**kjønnsorganene**	**khurns**orgaanerner
gland	**kjertelen**	**khæ^{r}**terlern
hand	**hånden**	**hon**ern
head	**hodet**	h**ōō**der
heart	**hjertet**	**yæ^{r}**ter
jaw	**kjeven**	**khāy**vern
joint	**leddet**	**leh**der
kidney	**nyren**	**nēw**rern
knee	**kneet**	**knāy**er
leg	**benet**	**bāy**ner
lip	**leppen**	**leh**pern
liver	**leveren**	**leh**verrern
lung	**lungen**	**loong**ern
mouth	**munnen**	**mew**nern
muscle	**muskelen**	**mews**kerlern
neck	**nakken**	**nah**kern
nerve	**nerven**	**nær**vern
nervous system	**nervesystemet**	**nær**versewstāymer
nose	**nesen**	**nāy**ssern
rib	**ribbenet**	**rib**bāyner
shoulder	**skulderen**	**skewl**derrern
skin	**huden**	**hewd**ern
spine	**ryggraden**	**rewg**raadern
stomach	**magen**	**maa**gern
tendon	**senen**	**sāy**nern
thigh	**låret**	**law**rer
throat	**halsen**	**hahl**sern
thumb	**tommelen**	**tom**merlern
toe	**tåen**	**taw**ern
tongue	**tungen**	**toong**ern
tonsils	**mandlene**	**mahn**dlerner
vein	**venen / åren**	**vāy**nern / **aw**rern

Accident—Injury *Ulykke – Skade*

There's been an accident.	**Det har skjedd en ulykke.**	deh haar shehd ehn **ew**lewker
My child has had a fall.	**Barnet mitt har falt og slått seg.**	**baa^{r}ner** mit haar fahlt o(g) shlot sæi
He/She has hurt his/her head.	**Han/Hun har slått seg i hodet.**	hahn/hewn haar shlot sæi ee **hoo**der
He's/She's unconscious.	**Han/Hun er bevisstløs.**	hahn/hewn ær ber**vist**lurss
He's/She's bleeding (heavily).	**Han/Hun blør (kraftig).**	hahn/hewn blurr (**krahf**ti)
He's/She's (seriously) injured.	**Han/Hun er (alvorlig) skadet.**	hahn/hewn ær (ahl**vaw^{r}**li) **skaa**dert
His/Her ankle is swollen.	**Han/Hun har en hoven ankel.**	hahn/huhn haar ehn **haw**vern **ahng**kerl
I've broken my arm.	**Jeg har brukket armen.**	yæi haar **brook**kert **ahr**mern
I've been stung.	**Jeg er blitt bitt.**	yæi ær blit bit
I've got something in my eye.	**Jeg har fått noe i øyet.**	yæi haar fawt **noo**er ee **oy**er
I've been bitten by a dog.	**Jeg er blitt bitt av en hund.**	yæi ær blit bit ahv ehn hewn
I've got a/an ...	**Jeg har fått ...**	yæi haar fot
blister	**en blemme**	ehn **bleh**mer
boil	**en byll**	ehn bewl
bruise	**et blått merke**	eht blot **mær**ker
bump	**en kul**	ehn kewl
burn	**et brannsår**	eht **brahn**sawr
cut	**et kutt**	eht kewt
graze	**et skrubbsår**	eht **skrewb**sawr
rash	**et utslett**	eht **ewt**shleht
sting	**et stikk**	eht stik
swelling	**en hevelse**	ehn **hay**verlser
wound	**et sår**	eht sawr
Could you have a look at it?	**Kan du undersøke det?**	kahn dew **ewn**ershurker deh
I can't move my ...	**Jeg kan ikke bevege ...**	yæi kahn **ik**ker ber**vay**ger
It hurts.	**Det gjør vondt.**	deh yurr voont

Hvor gjør det vondt?	Where does it hurt?
Hva slags smerte er det?	What kind of pain is it?
dump/skarp **pulserende/konstant** **kommer og går**	dull/sharp throbbing/constant on and off
Det er ...	It's ...
brukket/vrikket/ute av ledd	broken/sprained/dislocated
Du har et avslitt leddbånd.	You have a torn ligament.
Det bør røntgenfotograferes.	I'd like you to have an X-ray.
Det må gipses.	We'll have to put it in plaster.
Det er infisert.	It's infected.
Er du vaksinert mot stivkrampe?	Have you been vaccinated against tetanus?
Jeg skal gi deg noe smertestillende.	I'll give you a painkiller.
Har du noen allergier?	Do you have any allergies?

Illness *Sykdom*

I'm not feeling well.	**Jeg føler meg ikke bra.**	yæi **fur**lerr mæi **ik**ker braa
I'm ill.	**Jeg er syk.**	yæi ær sewk
I feel ...	**Jeg føler meg ...**	yæi **fur**ler mæi
dizzy/nauseous/ weak	**svimmel/kvalm/ svak**	**svim**merl/kvahlm/ svaak
I feel shivery.	**Jeg har kulde-gysninger.**	yæi haar **kew**ler-yewsningerr
I have a temperature (fever).	**Jeg har feber.**	yæi haar **fay**berr
I've been vomiting.	**Jeg har kastet opp.**	yæi haar **kah**stert op
I'm constipated.	**Jeg har forstoppelse.**	yæi haar fo**shtop**perlser
I've got diarrhoea.	**Jeg har diarré.**	yæi haar deeah**ray**
My ... hurt(s).	**Jeg har vondt i ...**	yæi haar voont ee

I've got (a/an) ...	**Jeg har ...**	yæi haar
asthma	**astma**	**ahst**mah
backache	**ryggsmerter**	**rewg**smæ^{r}terr
cough	**hoste**	**hoo**ster
cramps	**krampe**	**krahm**per
earache	**øreverk**	**ur**rerværk
hay fever	**høysnue**	**hoy**snewer
headache	**hodepine**	**hoo**derpeener
indigestion	**fordøyelsesbesvær**	fo^{r}**doy**erlsersbersvær
nosebleed	**neseblødning**	**nay**sserblurdning
palpitations	**hjerteklapp**	**yæ^{r}**terklahp
rheumatism	**reumatisme**	rehvmah**tis**mer
sore throat	**sår hals**	sawr hahlss
stiff neck	**stiv nakke**	steev **nah**ker
stomach ache	**magesmerter**	**maa**gersmæ^{r}terr
sunburn	**solforbrenning**	**sool**forbrehning
I've got a cold.	**Jeg er forkjølet.**	yæi ær fo^{r}**khur**lert
I have difficulties breathing.	**Jeg har vanskeligheter med å puste.**	yæi haar **vahn**skerlihehter meh(d) aw **pew**ster
I have chest pains.	**Jeg har vondt i brystet.**	yæi haar voont ee **brew**ster
I had a heart attack ... years ago.	**Jeg hadde et hjerteslag for ... år siden.**	yæi **hah**der eht **yæ^{r}**tershlaag for ... awr **see**dern
My blood pressure is too high/too low.	**Jeg har for høyt/ for lavt blodtrykk.**	yæi haar for hoyt/ for laavt **bloo**trewk
I'm allergic to ...	**Jeg er allergisk mot ...**	yæi ær ah**lær**gisk moot
I'm diabetic.	**Jeg er diabetiker.**	yæi ær deeah**bay**tikkerr

At the gynaecologist's *Hos gynekologen*

I have period (menstrual) pains.	**Jeg har menstruasjonssmerter.**	yæi haar mehnstrewah**shoons**smæ^{r}terr
I have a vaginal infection.	**Jeg har underlivsbetennelse.**	yæi haar **ewn**errleevsbertehnerlser
I'm on the pill.	**Jeg tar p-piller.**	yæi taar **pay**-pillerr
I haven't had a period for 2 months.	**Jeg har ikke hatt menstruasjon på 2 måneder.**	yæi haar **ik**ker haht mehnstrewah**shoon** paw 2 **maw**nerderr
I'm pregnant.	**Jeg er gravid.**	yæi ær grah**veed**

Hvor lenge har du følt deg slik?	How long have you been feeling like this?
Har du hatt dette før?	Have you had this before?
Jeg skal ta temperaturen/ måle blodtrykket.	I'll take your temperature/ blood pressure.
Vær snill å rulle opp ermet.	Roll up your sleeve, please.
Vær snill å ta av deg ...	Take off your ..., please.
Vær snill å kle av deg (på overkroppen).	Please undress (down to the waist).
Sett/Legg deg ned der borte.	Please sit/lie down over there.
Gap opp.	Open your mouth.
Pust dypt/Host.	Breathe deeply/Cough.
Hvor gjør det vondt?	Where does it hurt?
Du har ...	You've got (a/an) ...
en allergi	allergy
en betennelse i ...	inflammation of ...
blindtarmbetennelse	appendicitis
blærekatarr	cystitis
gulsott	jaundice
influensa	flu
en kjønnssykdom	venereal disease
lungebetennelse	pneumonia
magekatarr	gastritis
en matforgiftning	food poisoning
meslinger	measles
Det er (ikke) smittsomt.	It's (not) contagious.
Jeg skal gi deg en sprøyte.	I'll give you an injection.
Jeg vil ha en blodprøve/ avføringsprøve/urinprøve.	I want a specimen of your blood/stools/urine.
Du bør holde sengen i ... dager.	You must stay in bed for ... days.
Du bør oppsøke en spesialist.	I want you to see a specialist.
Du bør få foretatt en allmenn undersøkelse på sykehuset.	I want you to go to the hospital for a general check-up.

Prescription—Treatment *Resept – Behandling*

This is my usual medicine.	**Dette er min vanlige medisin.**	**deh**ter ær meen **vaan**leeyer mehdi**sseen**
Can you give me a prescription for this?	**Kan du gi meg en resept på dette?**	kahn dew yee mæi ehn reh**sehpt** paw **deh**ter
Can you prescribe a/an/some ...?	**Kan du skrive ut ...?**	kahn dew **skree**ver e͞wt
antidepressant	**et middel mot depresjoner**	eht **mid**derl mo͞ot dehprer**sho͞o**nerr
sleeping pills	**noen sovetabletter**	**no͞o**ern **saw**vertahblehterr
tranquillizer	**et beroligende middel**	eht berr**o͞o**leeyerner **mid**derl
I'm allergic to certain antibiotics/penicillin.	**Jeg er allergisk mot visse antibiotika/penicillin.**	yæi ær ahl**ær**gisk mo͞ot **vis**ser ahntibee**o͞o**tikkah/pehnissi**leen**
I don't want anything too strong.	**Jeg vil ikke ha noe som er for sterkt.**	yæi vil **ik**ker haa **no͞o**er som ær for stærkt
How many times a day should I take it?	**Hvor mange ganger om dagen skal jeg ta det?**	voor **mahn**ger **gahng**err om **daa**gern skahl yæi taa deh
Must I swallow the tablets whole?	**Må jeg svelge tablettene hele?**	maw yæi **svehl**ger tah**bleh**terner **ha͞y**ler

Hva slags behandling får du?	What treatment are you having?
Hvilken medisin tar du?	What medicine are you taking?
Tar du noen andre medisiner?	Are you taking any other medicines?
Intravenøst eller oralt?	By injection or orally?
Ta 2 teskjeer/1 tablett ...	Take 2 teaspoons/1 tablet ...
hver ... time	every ... hour(s)
... ganger om dagen	... times a day
før/etter hvert måltid	before/after every meal
om morgenen/om kvelden	in the morning/at night
i ... dager	for ... days
ved smerter	if there is any pain

CHEMIST'S (DRUGSTORE), see page 108

Fee *Honorar*

How much do I owe you?	**Hvor mye skylder jeg?**	voor **mew**er **shew**lerr yæi
May I have a receipt for my health insurance?	**Kan jeg få en kvittering for sykeforsikringen?**	kahn yæi faw ehn kvit**tay**ring for **sew**kerfoshikringern
Can I have a medical certificate?	**Kan jeg få en legeattest?**	kahn yæi faw ehn **lay**gerahtehst
Would you fill in this health insurance form, please?	**Kan du fylle ut dette sykeforsikringsskjemaet?**	kahn dew **few**ler ewt **deh**ter **sew**kerfoshikringsshaymaher

Hospital *Sykehus*

Please notify my family.	**Vær snill å underrette familien min.**	vær snil aw **ewn**errrehter fah**meel**yern meen
What are the visiting hours?	**Når er det besøkstid?**	nor ær deh ber**surks**teed
How long do I have to stay in bed?	**Hvor lenge må jeg ligge til sengs?**	voor **lehng**er maw yæi **lig**ger til sehngss
When can I get up?	**Når kan jeg stå opp?**	nor kahn yæi staw op
When will the doctor come?	**Når kommer legen?**	nor **kom**merr **lay**gern
I am in pain.	**Jeg har smerter.**	yæi haar **smær**terr
I can't eat.	**Jeg kan ikke spise.**	yæi kahn **ik**ker **spee**sser
I can't sleep.	**Jeg får ikke sove.**	yæi fawr **ik**ker **saw**ver
Where is the bell?	**Hvor er ringeklokken?**	voor ær **ring**erklokkern

nurse	**en sykepleier**	ehn **sew**kerplæierr
patient	**en pasient**	ehn pahsseey**ehnt**
anaesthetic	**en narkose**	ehn nahr**koo**sser
blood transfusion	**en blodoverføring**	ehn **bloo(d)**awverr**fur**ring
injection	**en sprøyte**	ehn **sproy**ter
operation	**en operasjon**	ehn operrah**shoon**
bed	**en seng**	ehn sehng
bedpan	**et stikkbekken**	eht **stik**behkern
thermometer	**et termometer**	eht tærmoo**may**terr

Dentist *Tannlege*

Can you recommend a good dentist?	**Kan du anbefale en god tannlege?**	kahn dew **ahn**berfaaler ehn goo(d) **tahnlay**ger
Can I make an (urgent) appointment to see Dr. ...?	**Kan jeg få time (så snart som mulig) hos dr. ...**	kahn yæi faw **tee**mer (saw snaa^{r}t som **mew**li) hooss **dok**toor
Couldn't you make it earlier?	**Er det ikke mulig å få time tidligere?**	ær deh **ik**ker **mew**li aw faw **tee**mer **tee**leeyerrer
I have a broken tooth.	**Jeg har brukket en tann.**	yæi haar **brook**kert ehn tahn
I have a loose tooth.	**Jeg har en løs tann.**	yæi har ehn lurss tahn
I have toothache.	**Jeg har tannpine.**	yæi haar **tahn**peener
Is it an abscess?	**Er det en byll?**	ær deh ehn bewl
This tooth hurts.	**Denne tannen verker.**	**deh**ner **tah**nern **vær**kerr
at the top	**her oppe**	hær **op**per
at the bottom	**her nede**	hær **nay**der
at the front	**her foran**	hær **for**ahn
at the back	**her bak**	hær baak
Can you fix it temporarily?	**Kan du foreta en provisorisk behandling?**	kahn dew **faw**rertah ehn prooveess**oo**risk ber**hahnd**ling
I don't want it taken out.	**Jeg vil ikke ha den trukket.**	yæi vil **ik**ker haa dehn **trook**kert
Could you give me an anaesthetic?	**Kan jeg få bedøvelse?**	kahn yæi faw ber**dur**verlser
I've lost a filling.	**Jeg har mistet en plombe.**	yæi haar **mis**tert ehn **ploom**ber
My gums are bleeding/sore.	**Tannkjøttet blør/er sårt.**	**tahn**khurter blurr/ær saw^{r}t
I've broken my dentures.	**Jeg har brukket gebisset.**	yæi haar **brook**kert ger**bis**ser
Can you repair my dentures?	**Kan du reparere gebisset?**	kahn dew rehpah**ray**rer ger**bis**ser
When will they be ready?	**Når blir det ferdig?**	nor bleer deh **fæ**^{r}di

Reference section

Where do you come from? *Hvor kommer du fra?*

I'm from ...	**Jeg er fra ...**	yæi ær fraa
Africa	**Afrika**	**aa**freekah
Asia	**Asia**	**aa**sseeah
Australia	**Australia**	ou**straa**leeah
Europe	**Europa**	ou**ro̅o̅**pah
North America	**Nord-Amerika**	**no̅o̅r**-ahma̅y̅reekah
South America	**Sør-Amerika**	**su̅r̅r**-ahma̅y̅reekah
Austria	**Østerrike**	**urs**terreeker
Belgium	**Belgia**	**behl**geeah
Canada	**Kanada**	**kah**nahdah
China	**Kina**	**khee**nah
Czechoslovakia	**Tsjekkoslovakia**	tshehkooshloo**vaa**keeah
Denmark	**Danmark**	**dahn**mahrk
England	**England**	**ehng**lahn
Finland	**Finland**	**fin**lahn
France	**Frankrike**	**frahngk**reeker
Germany	**Tyskland**	**tewsk**lahn
Great Britain	**Storbritannia**	**stoor**brittahneeah
Greece	**Hellas**	**heh**lahss
Hungary	**Ungarn**	**oong**gah[r]n
Iceland	**Island**	**ees**lahn
India	**India**	**in**deeah
Ireland	**Irland**	**eer**lahn
Israel	**Israel**	**ees**rahehl
Italy	**Italia**	ee**taa**leeah
Japan	**Japan**	**yaa**pahn
Luxembourg	**Luxembourg**	**lew**ksermbewrg
Netherlands	**Nederland**	**na̅y̅**derlahn
New Zealand	**Ny-Zealand**	ne̅w̅-**sa̅y̅**lahn
Norway	**Norge**	**nor**gger
Poland	**Polen**	**po̅o̅**lern
Portugal	**Portugal**	**poo**[r]tewgahl
Scotland	**Skottland**	**skot**lahn
South Africa	**Sør-Afrika**	**su̅r̅r**-aafreekah
Soviet Union	**Sovjetunionen**	sov**yeh**tewneeoonern
Spain	**Spania**	**spaa**neeah
Sweden	**Sverige**	**svær**yer
Switzerland	**Sveits**	svæitss
Turkey	**Tyrkia**	**tewr**keeah
United States	**USA**	e̅w̅-ehss-**aa**
Wales	**Wales**	væilss
Yugoslavia	**Jugoslavia**	yewgoo**shlaa**veeah

Numbers *Tall*

0	**null**	newl
1	**en**	ayn
2	**to**	too
3	**tre**	tray
4	**fire**	**fee**rer
5	**fem**	fehm
6	**seks**	sehkss
7	**sju**	shew
8	**åtte**	**ot**ter
9	**ni**	nee
10	**ti**	tee
11	**elleve**	**ehl**ver
12	**tolv**	tol
13	**tretten**	**treh**tern
14	**fjorten**	**fyoo**^{r}tern
15	**femten**	**fehm**tern
16	**seksten**	**sæi**stern
17	**sytten**	**sur**tern
18	**atten**	**ah**tern
19	**nitten**	**nit**tern
20	**tjue**	**khew**er
21	**tjueen**	khewer**ayn**
22	**tjueto**	khewer**too**
23	**tjuetre**	khewer**tray**
24	**tjuefire**	khewer**fee**rer
25	**tjuefem**	khewer**fehm**
26	**tjueseks**	khewer**sehkss**
27	**tjuesju**	khewer**shew**
28	**tjueåtte**	khewer**ot**ter
29	**tjueni**	khewer**nee**
30	**tretti**	**treh**ti
31	**trettien**	trehti**ayn**
32	**trettito**	trehti**too**
33	**trettitre**	trehti**tray**
40	**førti**	**fur**^{r}ti
50	**femti**	**fehm**ti
60	**seksti**	**sehk**sti
70	**sytti**	**sur**ti
80	**åtti**	**ot**ti
90	**nitti**	**nit**ti
100	**hundre**	**hewn**drer
101	**hundreogen**	hewndrero(g)**ayn**
102	**hundreogto**	hewndrero(g)**too**
110	**hundreogti**	hewndrero(g)**tee**
120	**hundreogtjue**	hewndrero(g)**khew**er

200	**to hundre**	tōō **hewn**drer
300	**tre hundre**	trāy **hewn**drer
400	**fire hundre**	**fee**rer **hewn**drer
500	**fem hundre**	fehm **hewn**drer
600	**seks hundre**	sehkss **hewn**drer
700	**sju hundre**	shēw **hewn**drer
800	**åtte hundre**	**ot**ter **hewn**drer
900	**ni hundre**	nee **hewn**drer
1,000	**tusen**	**tēw**ssern
1,100	**et tusen et hundre**	eht **tēw**ssern eht **hewn**drer
1,200	**et tusen to hundre**	eht **tēw**ssern tōō **hewn**drer
2,000	**to tusen**	tōō **tēw**ssern
10,000	**ti tusen**	tee **tēw**ssern
50,000	**femti tusen**	**fehm**ti **tēw**ssern
100,000	**hundre tusen**	**hewn**drer **tēw**ssern
1,000,000	**en million**	ehn mil**yōōn**
1,000,000,000	**en milliard**	ehn mil**yahrd**
first	**første**	**fursh**ter
second	**annen/andre**	**aa**ern/**ahn**drer
third	**tredje**	**trāyd**yer
fourth	**fjerde**	**fyǣ**rer
fifth	**femte**	**fehm**ter
sixth	**sjette**	**sheh**ter
seventh	**sjuende**	**shew**erner
eighth	**åttende**	**ot**terner
ninth	**niende**	**nee**erner
tenth	**tiende**	**tee**erner
once/twice	**en gang/to ganger**	ehn gahng/tōō **gahng**err
three times	**tre ganger**	trāy **gahng**err
a half	**en halv**	ehn hahl
half a ...	**en halv ...**	ehn hahl
half of ...	**halvparten av ...**	**hahl**pahʳtern ahv
half (adj.)	**halv**	hahl
a quarter	**en fjerdedel**	ehn **fyǣ**rerdāyl
three quarters	**tre fjerdedeler**	trāy **fyǣ**rerdāylerr
a third	**en tredjedel**	ehn **trāyd**yerdāyl
two thirds	**to tredjedeler**	tōō **trāyd**yerdāylerr
a pair of	**et par**	eht pahr
a dozen	**et dusin**	eht dew**sseen**
3.4%	**3,4%**	trāy **kom**mah **fee**rer proo**ssehnt**
1981	**nitten åttien**	**nit**tern otti**āyn**
1992	**nitten nittito**	**nit**tern nitti**tōō**
2003	**to tusen og tre**	tōō **tēw**ssern o(g) trāy

Year and age *År og alder*

year	**et år**	eht awr
leap year	**et skuddår**	eht **skewd**awr
decade	**et tiår**	eht **tee**awr
century	**et århundre**	eht **awr**hewndrer
this year	**i år**	ee awr
last year	**i fjor**	ee fyoor
next year	**neste år**	**neh**ster awr
each year	**hvert år**	vær^{r}t awr
2 years ago	**for 2 år siden**	for 2 awr **see**dern
in one year	**om et år**	om eht awr
in the eighties	**på 80-tallet/ i 80-årene**	paw **otti**tahler/ ee **otti**awrerner
the 17th century	**17. århundre/ 1600-tallet**	**sur**terner **awr**hewndrer/ **sæis**tern-hewndrertahler
in the 20th century	**i 20. århundre**	ee **khew**erner **awr**hewndrer
in the 21st century	**i 21. århundre**	ee khewer**furshter** **awr**hewndrer
old/young	**gammel/ung**	**gah**merl/oong
old/new	**gammel/ny**	**gah**merl/new
How old are you?	**Hvor gammel er du?**	voor **gah**merl ær dew
I'm 30 years old.	**Jeg er 30 år.**	yæi ær 30 awr
At my age ...	**I min alder ...**	ee meen **ahl**derr
He/She was born in 1980.	**Han/Hun ble født i 1980.**	hahn/hewn bleh furt ee **nit**tern **otti**
He/She is under 4.	**Han/Hun er under 4 år.**	hahn/hewn ær **ew**nerr **fee**rer awr

Seasons *Årstider*

spring	**vår**	vawr
summer	**sommer**	**som**merr
autumn	**høst**	hurst
winter	**vinter**	**vin**terr
in spring	**om våren**	om **vaw**rern
during the summer	**i løpet av sommeren**	ee **lur**per(t) ahv **som**merrern
in autumn	**om høsten**	om **hur**stern
during the winter	**i løpet av vinteren**	ee **lur**per(t) ahv **vin**terrern
high season	**høysesong**	**hoy**sehssong
low season	**lavsesong**	**laav**sehssong

Months *Måneder*

January	**januar** *	yahnew**aar**
February	**februar**	fehbrew**aar**
March	**mars**	mahsh
April	**april**	ah**preel**
May	**mai**	maay
June	**juni**	**yew**nee
July	**juli**	**yew**lee
August	**august**	ou**gewst**
September	**september**	sehp**tehm**berr
October	**oktober**	ok**taw**berr
November	**november**	noo**vehm**berr
December	**desember**	deh**ssehm**berr
after June	**etter juni**	**eh**terr **jew**nee
before July	**før juli**	furr **yew**lee
during the month of August	**i løpet av august**	ee **lur**per(t) ahv ou**gewst**
in September	**i september**	ee sehp**tehm**berr
until October	**til oktober**	til ok**taw**berr
not until November	**ikke før november**	**ik**ker **furr** noo**vehm**berr
since December	**siden desember**	**see**dern deh**ssehm**berr
last month	**forrige måned**	**for**yer **maw**nerd
next month	**neste måned**	**neh**ster **maw**nerd
the month before	**måneden før**	**maw**nerdern **furr**
the month after	**måneden etter**	**maw**nerdern **eh**terr
the beginning of January	**begynnelsen av januar**	ber**yew**nerlsern ahv yahnew**aar**
the middle of February	**midten av februar**	**mit**tern ahv fehbrew**aar**
the end of March	**slutten av mars**	**shlew**tern ahv mahsh

Days and date *Dager og dato*

What day is it today?	**Hvilken dag er det i dag?**	**vil**kern daag ær deh ee daag
Monday	**mandag** *	**mahn**dah(g)
Tuesday	**tirsdag**	**teesh**dah(g)
Wednesday	**onsdag**	**oons**dah(g)
Thursday	**torsdag**	**tawsh**dah(g)
Friday	**fredag**	**fray**dah(g)
Saturday	**lørdag**	**lur**[r]dah(g)
Sunday	**søndag**	**surn**dah(g)

* The names of months and days aren't capitalized in Norwegian.

What's the date today?	**Hvilken dato er det i dag?**	vilkern **daa**too ær deh ee daag
It's ...	**Det er ...**	deh ær
July 1	**1. juli**	**fur**shter **yew**lee
March 31	**31. mars**	trehtifurshter mahsh
When's your birthday?	**Når har du fødselsdag?**	nor haar dew **furt**serlsdaag
May 17th.	**17. mai.**	**sur**terner maay
in the morning	**om morgenen**	om **maw^r**nern
during the day	**om dagen/i løpet av dagen**	om **daa**gern/ee **lur**per(t) ahv **daa**gern
in the afternoon	**om ettermiddagen**	om **eh**terrmiddaagern
in the evening	**om kvelden**	om **kveh**lern
at night	**om natten**	om **nah**tern
the day before yesterday	**i forgårs**	ee **for**gosh
yesterday	**i går**	ee gawr
today	**i dag**	ee daag
tomorrow	**i morgen**	ee **maw**er^{r}n
the day after tomorrow	**i overmorgen**	ee **aw**verrmawer^{r}n
the day before	**dagen før**	**daa**gern furr
the next day	**neste dag**	**neh**ster daag
two days ago	**for to dager siden**	for too **daa**gerr **see**dern
in a few days	**om et par dager**	om eht pahr **daa**gerr
in three days' time	**om tre dager**	om tray **daa**gerr
the other day	**forleden dag**	fo^r**lay**dern daag
all day long	**hele dagen**	**hay**ler **daa**gern
day by day	**dag for dag**	daag for daag
Monday to (through) Friday	**mandag til fredag**	**mahn**dah(g) til **fray**dah(g)
nowadays	**i våre dager**	ee **vaw**rer **daa**gerr
day off	**fridag**	**free**daag
holiday	**helligdag**	**heh**lidaag
holidays/vacation	**ferie**	**fay**ryer
school holidays	**skoleferie**	**skoo**lerfayryer
week	**uke**	**ew**ker
last week	**forrige uke**	foryer **ew**ker
next week	**neste uke**	**neh**ster **ew**ker
for a fortnight (two weeks)	**i fjorten dager**	ee **fyoo**^{r}tern **daa**gerr
weekday	**hverdag**	**vær**^{r}daag
weekend	**weekend**	**vee**kehnd
working day	**arbeidsdag**	**ahr**bæidsdaag

Greetings and wishes *Hilsener og gratulasjoner*

Merry Christmas!	**God jul!**	goo(d) y̅e̅w̅l̅
Happy New Year!	**Godt nytt år!**	got newt awr
Happy Easter!	**God påske!**	goo(d) **paw**sker
Happy birthday!	**Gratulerer med dagen!**	grahtew**la̅y̅**rerr meh(d) **daa**gern
Best wishes for a Happy New Year!	**De beste ønsker om et godt nytt år!**	dee **behs**ter **urns**kerr om eht got newt awr
Many happy returns of the day!	**Til lykke med dagen!**	til **lew**ker meh(d) **daa**gern
Congratulations!	**Gratulerer!**	grahtew**la̅y̅**rerr
Good luck/All the best!	**Lykke til!**	**lew**ker til
Have a good trip!	**God reise!**	goo(d) **ræi**sser
Have a good holiday (vacation)!	**God ferie!**	goo(d) **fa̅y̅**ryer
Regards from ...	**Jeg skal hilse fra ...**	yæi skahl **hil**ser fraa
My regards to ...	**Hils til ...**	hilss til

Public (Legal) holidays *Offentlige høytidsdager*

Offices, banks, post offices and shops close early on Christmas Eve and New Year's Eve.

January 1	**Første nyttårsdag**	New Year's Day
May 1	**Første mai**	May Day (Labor Day)
May 17	**Grunnlovsdagen**	Constitution Day
December 25	**Første juledag**	Christmas Day
December 26	**Annen juledag**	Boxing Day
Movable Dates:	**Skjærtorsdag**	Maundy Thursday
	Langfredag	Good Friday
	Annen påskedag	Easter Monday
	Kristi himmelfartsdag	Ascension Day
	Annen pinsedag	Whit Monday

What time is it? *Hvor mange er klokken?*

Excuse me. Can you tell me the time?	**Unnskyld, men kan du si meg hvor mange klokken er?**	**ewn**shewl mehn kahn dew see mæi voor **mahng**er **klok**kern ær
It's ...	**Den er ...**	dehn ær
five past one	**fem over ett***	fehm **aw**verr eht
ten past two	**ti over to**	tee **aw**verr too
a quarter past three	**kvart over tre**	kvah^{r}t **aw**verr tray
twenty past four	**tjue over fire/ ti på halv fem**	**khew**er **aw**verr **fee**rer/ tee paw hahl fehm
twenty-five past five	**fem på halv seks**	fehm paw hahl sehkss
half past six	**halv sju**	hahl shew
twenty-five to seven	**fem over halv sju**	fehm **aw**verr hahl shew
twenty to eight	**ti over halv åtte/ tjue på åtte**	tee **aw**ver hahl **ot**ter/ **khew**er paw **ot**ter
a quarter to nine	**kvart på ni**	kvah^{r}t paw nee
ten to ten	**ti på ti**	tee paw tee
five to eleven	**fem på elleve**	fehm paw **ehl**ver
twelve o'clock	**tolv**	tol
noon	**klokken tolv (om dagen)**	**klok**kern tol (om **daa**gern)
midnight	**midnatt**	**mid**naht
in the morning	**om morgenen**	om **maw**^{r}nern
in the afternoon	**om ettermiddagen**	om **eh**terrmiddaagern
in the evening	**om kvelden**	om **kveh**lern
What time does the train leave?	**Når går toget?**	nor gawr **taw**ger
It leaves at ...	**Det går kl. ...**	deh gawr **klok**kern
13.04 (1.04 p.m.)	**13.04**	**treh**tern newl **fee**rer
00.40 (00.40 a.m.)	**00.40**	newl **fur**^{r}ti
in five minutes	**om fem minutter**	om fehm min**new**terr
in a quarter of an hour	**om et kvarter**	om eht kvah^{r}**tayr**
half an hour ago	**for en halvtime siden**	for ehn **hahl**teemer **see**dern
about two hours	**ca. to timer**	**sirr**kah too **tee**merr
a few seconds	**et par sekunder**	eht pahr seh**kew**nerr
The clock is fast/ slow.	**Klokken går for fort/sakte.**	**klok**kern gawr for foo^{r}t/**sahk**ter

---

* In everyday conversation, time is expressed as shown here. However, official time uses a 24-hour clock, which means that after noon hours are counted from 13 to 24.

Common abbreviations *Vanlige forkortelser*

A/S	**aksjeselskap**	Ltd./Inc.
ca.	**cirka**	around
e.Kr.	**etter Kristus**	A.D.
EM	**europamesterskap**	European Championship
ent.	**entall**	singular
et.	**etasje**	floor
f.Kr.	**før Kristus**	B.C.
fl.	**flertall**	plural
f.m.	**forrige måned**	last month
FN	**De forente nasjoner**	United Nations
g	**gram**	gram
gt.	**gate**	street
hg	**hekto(gram)**	hectogram
hk	**hestekrefter**	horsepower
H.M.	**Hans Majestet**	His Majesty
kg	**kilo(gram)**	kilogram
kl.	**klokken**	o'clock
km	**kilometer**	kilometre
KNA	**Kongelig Norsk Automobilklub**	Royal Norwegian Automobile Club
kr/kr.	**kroner**	kroner
l	**liter**	litre
md.	**måned(er)**	month(s)
moms	**merverdiavgift**	VAT/sales tax
NAF	**Norges Automobil-Forbund**	Norwegian Automobile Association
nr.	**nummer**	number
NRK	**Norsk rikskringkasting**	Norwegian Broadcasting System
NSB	**Norges Statsbaner**	Norwegian State Railways
NTB	**Norsk Telegrambyrå**	Norwegian News Agency
NTH	**Norges tekniske høgskole**	Norwegian Technical University
osv.	**og så videre**	etc.
pk.	**pakke**	packet, parcel
pr. stk.	**per stykk**	per item
str.	**størrelse**	size
s.u.	**svar utbes**	R.S.V.P.
tlf.	**telefon**	telephone
t.v.	**til venstre**	to the left
UD	**Utenriksdepartementet**	Ministry for Foreign Affairs
veil. pris	**veiledende pris**	recommended price
VM	**verdensmesterskap**	World Championship

Signs and notices *Skilt og oppslag*

Adgang forbudt (for uvedkommende)	No trespassing, No entrance
Damer	Ladies
Fare	Danger
Forsiktig	Caution
Forsiktig, trapp	Mind the step
Gangbro/Gangbru	Footbridge
Gratis adgang	Admission free
Gågate	Pedestrian zone
Heis	Lift (Elevator)
Herrer	Gentlemen
Høgspenning	High voltage
Inngang	Entrance
I uorden	Out of order
Kaldt	Cold
Kasse	Cash desk (Cashier)
Ledig	Free/Vacant
Livsfare	Danger of death
Ned	Down
Nymalt	Wet paint
Nødutgang	Emergency exit
Opp	Up
Opptatt	Occupied
Privat	Private
Privat vei/veg	Private road
Reservert	Reserved
Røyking forbudt	No smoking
Røyking (ikke) tillatt	(Non)Smoker
Stengt	Closed
Skyv	Push
Til leie	For hire (rent), To let
Til salgs	For sale
Trekk	Pull
Trykk	Press
Tråkk ikke på gresset	Keep of the grass
Underetasje	Lower ground floor
Utgang	Exit
Utsalg	Sales
Utsolgt	Sold out
Vareheis	Goods lift (Freight elevator)
Varmt	Hot
Vokt deg/Dem for hunden	Beware of the dog
Åpent	Open
Åpningstider	Opening hours

Emergency *Nødsfall*

Call the police	**Ring til politiet**	ring til poo**litteeyer**
Consulate	**Konsulat**	koonsew**laat**
DANGER	**FARE**	**faa**rer
Embassy	**Ambassade**	ahmbahs**saa**der
FIRE	**BRANN**	brahn
Gas	**Gass**	gahss
Get a doctor	**Hent en lege**	hehnt ehn **lāy**ger
Go away	**Gå vekk**	gaw vehk
HELP	**HJELP**	yehlp
Get help quickly	**Hent hjelp øyeblikkelig**	hehnt yehlp oyer**blikk**erli
I'm ill	**Jeg er syk**	yæi ær sēwk
I'm lost	**Jeg har gått meg bort**	yæi haar got mæi boo^rt
Leave me alone	**La meg være i fred**	lah mæi **væ**rer ee frāy(d)
LOOK OUT	**SE OPP**	sāy op
Poison	**Gift**	yift
POLICE	**POLITI**	poo**littee**
Stop that man/woman	**Stopp den mannen/kvinnen**	stop dehn **mah**nern/**kvin**nern
STOP THIEF	**STOPP TYVEN**	stop **tēw**vern

Emergency telephone numbers *Nødnummere*

In Oslo or Bergen:		
	Fire	**001**
	Police	**002**
	Ambulance	**003**

Lost property—Theft *Hittegods – Tyveri*

Where's the ...	**Hvor er ...**	voor ær
lost property (lost and found) office	**hittegodskontoret**	**hit**tergoodskoontōōrer
police station	**politistasjonen**	poo**littee**stahshōōnern
I want to report a theft.	**Jeg vil anmelde et tyveri.**	yæi vil **ahn**mehler eht tewver**ree**
My ... has been stolen.	**... er blitt stjålet.**	... ær blit **styaw**lert
I've lost my ...	**Jeg har mistet ...**	yæi haar **mis**tert
handbag/passport/wallet	**håndvesken/passet lommeboken**	**hon**vehskern/**pah**sser/**loom**merbōōkern

CAR ACCIDENTS, see page 78

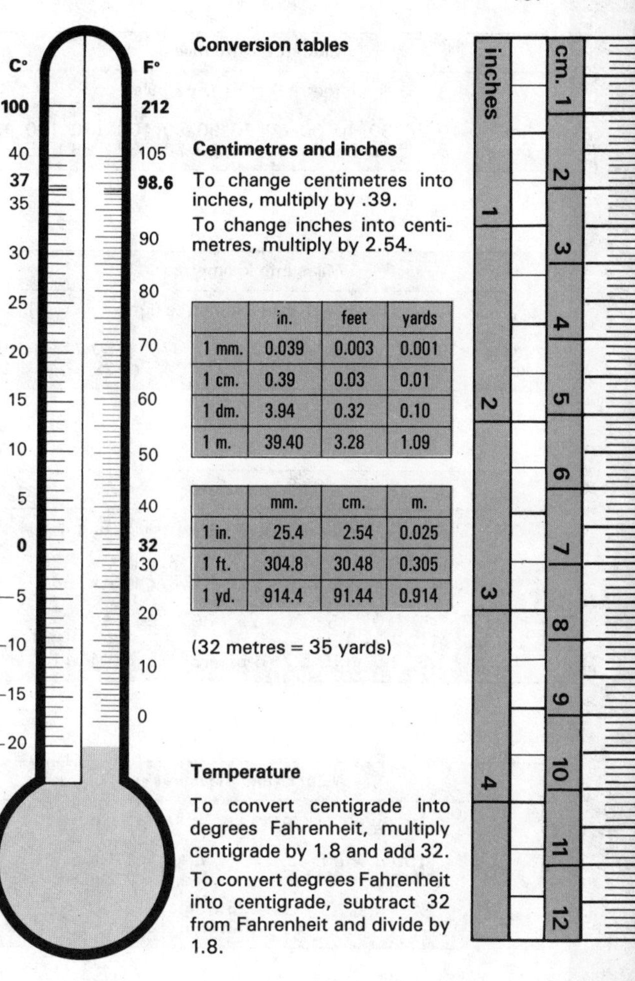

Conversion tables

Centimetres and inches

To change centimetres into inches, multiply by .39.

To change inches into centimetres, multiply by 2.54.

	in.	feet	yards
1 mm.	0.039	0.003	0.001
1 cm.	0.39	0.03	0.01
1 dm.	3.94	0.32	0.10
1 m.	39.40	3.28	1.09

	mm.	cm.	m.
1 in.	25.4	2.54	0.025
1 ft.	304.8	30.48	0.305
1 yd.	914.4	91.44	0.914

(32 metres = 35 yards)

Temperature

To convert centigrade into degrees Fahrenheit, multiply centigrade by 1.8 and add 32.

To convert degrees Fahrenheit into centigrade, subtract 32 from Fahrenheit and divide by 1.8.

Kilometres into miles

1 kilometre (km.) = 0.62 miles

km.	10	20	30	40	50	60	70	80	90	100	110	120	130
miles	6	12	19	25	31	37	44	50	56	62	68	75	81

Miles into kilometres

1 mile = 1.609 kilometres (km.)

miles	10	20	30	40	50	60	70	80	90	100
km.	16	32	48	64	80	97	113	129	145	161

Fluid measures

1 litre (l.) = 0.88 imp. quart or = 1.06 U.S. quart

1 imp. quart = 1.14 l.
1 imp. gallon = 4.55 l.

1 U.S. quart = 0.95 l.
1 U.S. gallon = 3.8 l.

litres	5	10	15	20	25	30	35	40	45	50
imp. gal.	1.1	2.2	3.3	4.4	5.5	6.6	7.7	8.8	9.9	11.0
U.S. gal.	1.3	2.6	3.9	5.2	6.5	7.8	9.1	10.4	11.7	13.0

Weights and measures

1 kilogram or kilo (kg.) = 1000 grams (g.)

100 g. = 3.5 oz.
200 g. = 7.0 oz.

½ kg. = 1.1 lb.
1 kg. = 2.2 lb.

1 oz. = 28.35 g.
1 lb. = 453.60 g.

CLOTHING SIZES, see page 115/YARDS AND INCHES, see page 11

Basic grammar

Norway has two official written, mutually comprehensible languages, *bokmål* and *nynorsk.* A traveller in Norway must expect to see and hear both, but *bokmål*—the most common—is used throughout this book.

Articles

The article shows the gender of Norwegian nouns, that are either common (masculine), feminine or neuter. The majority of feminine* nouns also have a common form, so we have chosen to simplify matters by using only the two most frequently met genders: the common and the neuter.

1. Indefinite article (a/an)

common:	***en* bil**	*a* car
neuter:	***et* eple**	*an* apple

2. Definite article (the)

Where we, in English say "the house", Norwegians tag the definite article onto the end of the noun and say "house-the". In common nouns "the" is **-(e)n**, in neuter nouns **-(e)t**.

common:	**bil*en***	*the* car
neuter:	**eple*t***	*the* apple

Nouns

1. There are no easy rules for determining the gender. Learn each new word with its accompanying article.

2. The plural of most nouns is formed by an **-(e)r** ending (indefinite plural) and an **-(e)ne** ending (definite plural).

common:	**bil*er***	car*s*	**bil*ene***	*the* cars
neuter:	**epl*er***	apple*s*	**epl*ene***	*the* apples

* In the feminine form "a night, the night" would be *ei* natt, natt*a*; the common form is *en* natt, natt*en*.

Many monosyllabic nouns have irregular plurals.

en mann	a man	**menn**	men	**mennene**	the men
en sko	a shoe	**sko**	shoes	**skoene**	the shoes
et hus	a house	**hus**	houses	**husene**	the houses
et barn	a child	**barn**	children	**barna**	the children

3. Possession is shown by adding **-s** (singular and plural). Note that there is no apostrophe.

Johns bror	John's brother
hotellets eier	the owner of the hotel
barnas far	the children's father

Adjectives

1. Adjectives agree with the noun in gender and number. For the indefinite form, the neuter is generally formed by adding **-t**, the plural by adding **-e**.

(en) stor hund	(a) big dog	**stor*e* hunder**	big dogs
(et) stor*t* hus	(a) big house	**stor*e* hus**	big houses

2. For the definite declension of the adjective, add the ending **-e** (common, neuter and plural). This form is used when the adjective is preceded by **den**, **det**, **de** (the definite article used with adjectives) or by a demonstrative or a possessive adjective.

den stor*e* hunden	the big dog
de stor*e* hundene	the big dogs
det stor*e* huset	the big house
de stor*e* husene	the big houses

3. Comparative and superlative

The comparative and superlative are normally formed either by adding the endings **-(e)re** and **-(e)st**, respectively, to the adjective or by putting **mer** (more) and **mest** (most) before the adjective.

stor/stør*re*/stør*st*	big/bigger/biggest
lett/lett*ere*/lett*est*	easy/easier/easiest
imponerende/*mer* imponerende/*mest* imponerende	impressive/more impressive/the most impressive

4. Demonstrative adjectives:

	common	neuter	plural
this/these	**denne**	**dette**	**disse**
that/those	**den**	**det**	**de**

5. Possessive adjectives agree in number and gender with the noun they modify, i.e. with the thing possessed and not the possessor.

	common	neuter	plural
my	**min**	**mitt**	**mine**
your	**din**	**ditt**	**dine**
his	**sin, hans**	**sitt, hans**	**sine, hans**
her	**sin, hennes**	**sitt, hennes**	**sine, hennes**
its	**sin, dens/dets***	**sitt, dens/dets**	**sine, dens/dets**
our	**vår**	**vårt**	**våre**
their	**sin, deres**	**sitt, deres**	**sine, deres**

The forms **sin, sitt, sine** always refer back to the subject, but cannot be used to modify a subject.

Han har mistet broken sin. He has lost his (own) book.
De har mistet bøkene sine. They have lost their (own) books.

but:

Boken hans er blitt borte. His book has disappeared.

The forms **hans, hennes, dens/dets, deres** are actually the genitive of the personal pronouns (see page 162). These forms can qualify the subject, as shown above, as well as the object. However, qualifying the latter, they indicate that the subject and the possessor of the object are two different people.

Han har misted boken hans. He has lost his (John's) book.
De har mistet bøkene deres. They have lost their (John and Mary's) books.

---

* Use **dens** if "it" is of common gender and **dets** if "it" is neuter.

Adverbs

Adverbs are often formed by adding **-t** to the corresponding adjective.

rask/raskt	quick/quickly
langsom/langsomt	slow/slowly

Personal pronouns

	subject	object	genitive
I	**jeg**	**meg**	–
you	**du**	**deg**	–
he	**han**	**ham/han**	**hans**
she	**hun**	**henne**	**hennes**
it	**den/det**	**den/det**	**dens/dets**
we	**vi**	**oss**	–
you (plural)	**dere**	**dere**	–
they	**de**	**dem**	**deres**

Norwegian has two forms for "you", an informal one (**du**) and a formal one (**De**). However, today the use of the formal **De** has practically disappeared from the language.

Verbs

Here we are concerned only with the infinitive, imperative and present tense. The present tense is simple, because it has the same form for all persons. The infinitive of most Norwegian verbs ends in **-e** (some compound and monosyllabic end in other vowels). Here are three useful auxiliary verbs:

	to be	to have	to be able to
Infinitive	**å være**	**å ha**	**å kunne**
Present tense (same form for all persons)	**er**	**har**	**kan**
Imperative	**vær**	**ha**	–

The present tense of most Norwegian verbs ends in **-r**:

	to ask	to buy	to go	to do
Infinitive	**å spørre**	**å kjøpe**	**å gå**	**å gjøre**
Present tense (same form for all persons)	**spør**	**kjøper**	**går**	**gjør**
Imperative	**spør**	**kjøp**	**gå**	**gjør**

There is no equivalent to the English present continuous tense. Thus:

Jeg reiser. I travel/I am travelling.

Negatives

Negation is expressed by using the adverb **ikke** (not). It is usually placed immediately after the verb in a main clause. In compound tenses, **ikke** appears between the auxiliary and the main verb.

Jeg snakker norsk. I speak Norwegian.
Jeg snakker ikke norsk. I do not speak Norwegian.

Questions

Questions are formed by reversing the order of the subject and the verb:

Bussen stanser her. The bus stops here.
Stanser bussen her? Does the bus stop here?

Jeg kommer i kveld. I am coming tonight.
Kommer du i kveld? Are you coming tonight?

DICTIONARY

Dictionary
and alphabetical index

English–Norwegian

c common *nt* neuter *pl* plural

a en 159; et 159
abbreviation forkortelse *c* 154
able, to be kunne 162
about *(approximately)* ca./cirka 79, 153
above ovenfor 62; over 15
abscess byll *c* 145
absorbent cotton bomull *c* 109
accept, to *(take)* ta 61, 102
accessories tilbehør *nt* 116, 125
accident ulykke *c* 79, 139
accommodation service innkvarteringsservice *c* 22
account konto *c* 130
adaptor adapter *c* 119
address adresse *c* 21, 31, 76, 79, 102
adhesive tape limbånd *nt* 104
admission adgang *c* 82, 155; *(fee)* inngangsbillett *c* 89
adult voksen *c* 82
aerogramme aerogram *nt* 133
Africa Afrika 146
after etter 15, 77, 150
afternoon ettermiddag *c* 151, 153
after-shave lotion etterbarberingsvann *nt* 110
age alder *c* 149
ago for ... siden 149, 153
air bed luftmadrass *c* 106
airmail med fly 132
airmail label luftpostetikett *c* 133
air mattress luftmadrass *c* 106
airplane fly *nt* 65
airport flyplass *c* 16, 21, 65
alarm clock vekkeklokke *c* 121
alcohol alkohol *c* 37, 59
alcoholic alkoholholdig 58
all alt 103
allergic allergisk 141, 143
allergy allergi *c* 140
allowed tillatt 155
almond mandel *c* 54
alphabet alfabet *nt* 9, 135
also også 15
alter, to endre 116
amazing praktfull 84
ambulance sykebil *c* 79, 156
American amerikansk 105
American amerikaner *c* 93
American plan helpensjon *c* 24
amount beløp *nt* 61, 131
amplifier forsterker *c* 119
amusement park fornøyelsespark *c* 81
anaesthetic bedøvelse *c* 145; narkose *c* 144
analgesic analgetikum *nt* 109
analogue analog 122
and og 15
animal dyr *nt* 85
ankle ankel *c* 139
anorak anorakk *c* 116
answer, to svare 136
antibiotic antibiotikum *nt* 143
antidepressant middel mot depresjoner *nt* 143
antique antikvitet *c* 83
antique shop antikvitetsforretning *c* 98
antiseptic antiseptisk 109
any noe 15
anyone noen 12
anything noe 17, 101, 103, 113, 143
anywhere noe sted 89
aperitif aperitiff *c* 58
appendicitis blindtarmbetennelse *c* 142
appendix blindtarm *c* 138
appetizer forrett *c* 43
apple eple *nt* 54, 64
apple juice eplesaft *c* 59

Ordliste

apple pie eplekake *c* 55, 63
appointment avtalt møte *nt* 131; time *c* 30, 137, 145
April april *(c)* 150
aquarium akvarium *nt* 81
aquavit akevitt *c* 56
archaeology arkeologi *c* 83
architect arkitekt *c* 83
area *(of town)* strøk *nt* 81
area code retningsnummer *nt* 134
arm arm *c* 138, 139
around *(approximately)* ca./cirka 154; *(nearby)* i nærheten 35
arrival ankomst *c* 16, 25, 65
arrive, to være fremme 65, 68
art kunst *c* 83
artery pulsåre *c* 138
art gallery kunstgalleri *nt* 98
artificial kunstig 124
artificial sweetener søtningsmiddel *nt* 37
artist kunstner *c* 83
art museum kunstmuseum *nt* 81
ashtray askebeger *nt* 36
Asia Asia 146
ask, to spørre 76, 163; *(beg)* be 136
ask for, to be om 25, 60
asparagus asparges *c* 51
aspirin aspirin *c* 109
asthma astma *c* 141
at ved 15
athletics meeting friidrettsstevne *nt* 89
athletic shoe turnsko *c* 118
at least minst 24
at once med én gang 31
August august *(c)* 150
aunt tante *c* 93
Australia Australia 146
automatic automatisk 122, 124; *(car)* med automatgir 20
auto repair shop bilverksted *nt* 78
autumn høst *c* 149
average middels(god) 91
awful forferdelig 84, 94

B

baby baby *c* 24, 111
baby food barnemat *c* 111
babysitter barnevakt *c* 27
back rygg *c* 138
backache ryggsmerte *c* 141
backpack ryggsekk *c* 106
bacon bacon *nt* 38
bacon and eggs egg og bacon 38
bad dårlig 14, 95
bag bag *c* 17, 18; *(carrier)* bærepose *c* 103
baggage bagasje *c* 18, 26, 31, 71
baggage cart bagasjetralle *c* 18, 71
baggage checking reisegodsekspedisjon *c* 71
baggage locker oppbevaringsboks *c* 18, 67, 71
baked bakt 52
baker's bakeri *nt* 98
balance *(finance)* balanse *c* 131
balcony balkong *c* 23
ball *(inflated)* ball *c* 128
ballet ballett *c* 88
ball-point pen kulepenn *c* 104
banana banan *c* 54, 64
bandage bandasje *c* 109
Band-Aid plaster *nt* 109
bangle armring *c* 121
bank *(finance)* bank *c* 98, 129, 130
banknote seddel *c* 130
bar *(room)* bar *c* 33; *(chocolate)* plate *c* 64
barber's herrefrisør *c* 30, 98
barrette hårspenne *c* 111
bath bad *nt* 23, 25, 27
bathing cap badehette *c* 116
bathing hut badehus *nt* 91
bathrobe badekåpe *c* 116
bathroom bad *nt* 27
bath salts badesalt *nt* 110
bath towel badehåndkle *nt* 27
battery batteri *nt* 75, 78, 119, 125
battery-powered batteridrevet 128
be, to være 162
beach strand *c* 90
beach ball badeball *c* 128
bean bønne *c* 51
beard skjegg *nt* 31
beautiful pen 14; vakker 84
beauty salon skjønnhetssalong *c* 30, 98
bed seng *c* 24, 144
bed and breakfast rom med frokost 24
bedpan stikkbekken *nt* 144
beef oksekjøtt *nt* 47; okse- 48
beefsteak biff *c* 47, 49
beer øl *nt* 56, 64
before før 15, 143, 150
begin, to begynne 87, 88
beginner begynner *c* 91
beginning begynnelse *c* 150
behind bak 15, 77

bell *(electric)* ringeklokke *c* 144
bell captain portier *c* 26
bellman bærer *c* 26
below nedenfor 62; under 15
belt belte *nt* 117
berth køye *c* 69, 71
better bedre 14, 25, 101
between mellom 15
bicycle sykkel *c* 74
bicycle racing sykkelløp *nt* 89
bidet bidet *nt* 28
big stor 14, 25, 101, 118
bilberry blåbær *nt* 54
bill regning *c* 31, 61, 102; *(banknote)* seddel *c* 130
billion *(Am.)* milliard *c* 148
binoculars kikkert *c* 123
bird fugl *c* 85
birthday fødselsdag *c* 151
biscuit *(Br.)* småkake *c* 63
bite, to bite 139
bitter besk 60
black svart 113
black and white svart-hvitt 124, 125
blackberry bjørnebær *nt* 54
blackcurrant solbær *nt* 54
bladder urinblære *c* 138
blanket ullteppe *nt* 27
bleed, to blø 139, 145
blind *(window shade)* rullegardin *c* 29
blister blemme *c* 139
blood blod *nt* 141, 142
blood pressure blodtrykk *nt* 141, 142
blood transfusion blodoverføring *c* 144
blotting paper trekkpapir *nt* 104
blouse bluse *c* 116
blow-dry, to føne 30
blue blå 113
blueberry blåbær *nt* 54
blusher rouge *c* 110
boat båt *c* 73, 74
bobby pin hårklemme *c* 111
body kropp *c* 138
boil byll *c* 139
boiled kokt 49, 51, 52
bone ben *nt* 138
book bok *c* 12, 104
booking office billettkontor *nt* 19, 67
booklet of tickets billetthefte *nt* 72
bookshop bokhandel *c* 98, 104
boot støvel *c* 118
born født 149
botanical gardens botanisk hage *c* 81
botany botanikk *c* 83
bottle flaske *c* 17, 56, 57
bottle-opener flaskeåpner *c* 106
bowel tarm *c* 138
bowl *(container)* bolle *c* 127; skål *c* 107
bow tie flue *c* 116
box eske *c* 120
boy gutt *c* 112
boyfriend venn *c* 93
bra behå *c* 116
bracelet armbånd *nt* 121
braces *(suspenders)* (bukse)seler *c/pl* 116
braised braisert 49
brake brems *c* 78
brake fluid bremsevæske *c* 75
brandy brandy *c* 58
brass messing *c* 122
bread brød *nt* 36, 38, 64, 120
break, to brekke 139
break down, to få motorstopp 78
breakdown motorstopp *c* 78
breakdown van kranbil *c* 78
breakfast frokost *c* 24, 34, 38
breast bryst *nt* 138
breathe, to puste 141, 142
bridge bro *c* 81
bring, to gi 13; ta med 95
bring down, to bære ned 31
British brite *c* 93
broiled *(Am.)* grillstekt 49
broken brukket 140; gått i stykker 29, 119, 123
bronze bronse *c* 122
brooch brosje *c* 121
brother bror *c* 93
brown brun 113
bruise blått merke *nt* 139
brush børste *c* 111
Brussels sprouts rosenkål *c/pl* 51
bubble bath skumbad *nt* 110
bucket bøtte *c* 106; spann *nt* 128
buckle spenne *c* 117
buffet car kafeteriavogn *c* 70
build, to bygge 83
building bygning *c* 81, 83
building blocks/bricks byggeklosser *c/pl* 128
bulb *(light)* lyspære *c* 28, 75, 119
bump *(lump)* kul *c* 139

bun bolle *c* 63
burn brannsår *nt* 139
burned out *(bulb)* gått 28
bus buss *c* 18, 19, 65, 66, 72, 80
business forretning *c* 16, 131
business district forretningskvarter *nt* 81
business trip forretningsreise *c* 93
bus stop bussholdeplass *c* 72
busy opptatt 96
but men 15
butane gas butangass *c* 32, 106
butcher's slakter *c* 98
butter smør *nt* 36, 38, 64
button knapp *c* 29, 117
buy, to kjøpe 100, 104, 123, 163

C

cabana badehus *nt* 91
cabbage kål *c* 51
cabin *(camping)* hytte *c* 32; *(ship)* lugar *c* 74
cabin luggage håndbagasje *c* 65
cable car taubane *c* 74
cable release snorutløser *c* 125
café kafé *c* 33
cafeteria kafeteria *c* 32, 33, 67
cake kake *c* 55, 63, 64
cake shop konditori *nt* 98
calculator kalkulator *c* 105
calendar kalender *c* 104
call *(phone)* samtale *c* 134, 135, 136
call, to *(give name)* hete 11; *(phone)* ringe 79, 134, 136, 156
camera fotoapparat *nt* 124, 125
camera case kameraveske *c* 125
camera shop fotoforretning *c* 98
camp, to campe 32
camp bed campingseng *c* 106
camping camping *c* 32
camping equipment camping-utstyr *nt* 106
camp site campingplass *c* 32
can *(container)* boks *c* 120
can *(be able to)* kunne 12, 162
Canada Kanada 146
Canadian kanadier *c* 93
cancel, to annullere 65
candle stearinlys *nt* 106
candlestick lysestake *c* 127
candy godter *nt/pl* 126
candy store godtebutikk *c* 98
canoe kano *c* 74
can opener boksåpner *c* 106
cap lue *c* 116
capital *(finance)* kapital *c* 131
capsule *(medical)* kapsel *c* 109
car bil *c* 19, 20, 32, 75, 76, 78; (train) vogn *c* 70, 71
carafe karaffel *c* 57
carat karat *c* 121
caravan campingvogn *c* 32
caraway seed karve *c* 53
carbon paper blåpapir *nt* 104
carburettor forgasser *c* 78
card kort *nt* 93, 131
cardboard papp *c* 107
card game kortspill *nt* 128
cardigan golfjakke *c* 116; lusekofte *c* 127
car ferry *c* 74
car hire bilutleie *c* 20
car park parkeringsplass *c* 77; *(multistorey)* parkeringshus *nt* 77
car racing billøp *nt* 89
car rental bilutleie *c* 20
carrot gulrot *c* 51
carry, to bære 21
cart tralle *c* 18, 71
carton kartong *c* 17, 126
cartridge *(camera)* kassett *c* 124
car wash bilvask *c* 76
case futteral *nt* 123; veske *c* 125; *(cigarette)* etui *nt* 121, 126
cash, to løse inn 130, 133
cash desk kasse *c* 103, 155
cassette kassett *c* 127
cassette player kassettspiller *c* 119
cassette recorder kassettopptaker *c* 119
castle slott *nt* 81
catalogue katalog *c* 82
cathedral domkirke *c* 81
Catholic katolsk 84
cauliflower blomkål *c* 51
caution forsiktig 155
cave hule *c* 81
celery selleri *c* 51
cemetery gravlund *c* 81
centimetre centimeter *c* 112
centre sentrum *nt* 19, 21, 76, 81
century århundre *nt* 149
ceramics keramikk *c* 83
cereal frokostblanding *c* 38
chain *(jewellery)* kjede *nt* 121
chain bracelet armlenke *c* 121
chair stol *c* 36
chalk kritt *nt* 104

change *(money)* småpenger *c/pl* 130; vekslepenger *c/pl* 61, 77
change, to endre 65; *(replace)* bytte 60; skifte ut 123; *(money)* veksle 18, 130; *(trains)* bytte 68, 69, 73
changing room prøverom *nt* 115
chapel kapell *nt* 81
charcoal briquet trekullbrikett *c* 106
charcoal tablet kulltablett *c* 109
charge gebyr *nt* 136
charge, to koste 77
charm *(trinket)* berlokk *c* 121
charm bracelet berlokkarmbånd *nt* 121
cheap billig 14; *(inexpensive)* rimelig 24, 25, 101
check sjekk *c* 130; *(restaurant)* regning *c* 61
check, to kontrollere 75
check in, to *(airport)* sjekke inn 65
check out, to reise 31
checkroom *(railway)* bagasje-oppbevaring *c* 67, 71
check-up *(medical)* undersøkelse *c* 142
cheers! skål! 58
cheese ost *c* 38, 53, 62, 64
cheese shop osteforretning *c* 98
chef kjøkkensjef *c* 40
chemist's apotek *nt* 98, 108
cheque sjekk *c* 130
cherry kirsebær *nt* 54
chess sjakk *c* 93
chess set sjakkspill *nt* 128
chest bryst *nt* 141; brystkasse *c* 138
chewing gum tyggegummi *c* 126
chewing tobacco skråtobakk *c* 126
chicken kylling *c* 50
child barn *nt* 24, 60, 82, 90, 93, 139
children's ... barne- 116
children's doctor barnelege *c* 137
chilled avkjølt 58
China Kina 146
china shop glassmagasin *nt* 98
chips pommes frites *c/pl* 52, 62; *(Am.)* potetgull *nt* 52, 64
chives gressløk *c* 53
chocolate sjokolade *c* 38, 55, 59, 62
chocolate bar sjokoladeplate *c* 64, 126
cholesterol kolesterol *c* 37
chop *(meat)* kotelett *c* 48
Christmas jul *c* 152
chromium krom *c* 122
church kirke *c* 81, 84
cigar sigar *c* 126
cigarette sigarett *c* 17, 95, 126
cigarette case sigarettetui *nt* 126
cigarette holder sigarett-munnstykke *nt* 126
cigarette lighter lighter *c* 126
cinema kino *c* 86, 96
circle *(theatre)* balkong *c* 87
citadel festning *c* 81
city by *c* 81, 88
city centre sentrum *nt* 81
city hall rådhus *nt* 82
classical klassisk 128
clean ren 61
clean, to vaske 76
cleansing cream rensekrem *c* 110
cliff klippe *c* 85
cloakroom garderobe *c* 87
clock klokke *c* 121, 153
clock-radio klokkeradio *c* 119
close, to stenge 11, 82, 108, 132
closed stengt 155
cloth tøy *nt* 118
clothes klær *pl* 29, 116
clothes peg (pin) klesklype *c* 106
clothing klær *pl* 112
cloud sky *c* 94
coach *(bus)* ekspressbuss *c* 66; rutebil *c* 66
coach station busstasjon *c* 67
coast kyst *c* 85
coat *(man's)* frakk *c* 116; *(woman's)* kåpe *c* 116
coffee kaffe *c* 38, 59, 64
coffee shop konditori *nt* 33
cognac konjakk *c* 58
coin mynt *c* 83
cold kald 14, 25, 38, 60, 94, 155
cold *(illness)* forkjølelse *c* 108, 141
collar krage *c* 117
collect call noteringsoverføring *c* 135
colour farge *c* 112, 113, 124, 125
colour chart fargekart *nt* 30
colourfast fargeekte 114
colour rinse fargeskylling *c* 30
colour shampoo fargesjampo *c* 111
comb kam *c* 111
come, to komme 35, 92, 95 137
comedy komedie *c* 86
commission *(fee)* kommisjon *c* 130

compact disc CD-plate *c* 127
compartment *(train)* kupé *c* 71
compass kompass *nt* 106
complaint klage *c* 60
concert konsert *c* 88
concert hall konserthus *nt* 81, 88
condom kondom *nt* 109
conductor *(orchestra)* dirigent *c* 88
conference room konferanserom *nt* 23
confirm, to bekrefte 65
confirmation bekreftelse *c* 23
congratulation gratulasjon *c* 152
congress hall kongresshall *c* 81
connection *(transport)* forbindelse *c* 65, 68
consommé buljong *c* 44
constipation forstoppelse *c* 140
consulate konsulat *nt* 156
contact lens kontaktlinse *c* 123
contagious smittsom 142
contain, to inneholde 37
contraceptive prevensjonsmiddel *nt* 109
contract kontrakt *c* 131
control kontroll *c* 16
cookie småkake *c* 63
cool box kjøleboks *c* 106
cooler ice pack kjøleelement *nt* 106
copper kopper *nt* 122
corkscrew korketrekker *c* 106
corn *(Am.)* mais *c* 51; *(foot)* liktorn *c* 109
corner hjørne *nt* 21, 36
corn plaster liktornplaster *nt* 109
cosmetics kosmetikk *c* 110
cost kostnad *c* 131
cost, to koste 11, 24, 80, 136
cot barneseng *c* 24
cotton bomull *c* 114
cotton wool bomull *c* 109
couchette køye i liggevogn *c* 69
cough hoste *c* 108, 141
cough, to hoste 142
cough drops halspastiller *c/pl* 109
cough syrup hostesaft *c* 109
counter luke *c* 133
country land *nt* 92, 146
countryside land *nt* 85
court house tinghus *nt* 81
cousin *(male)* fetter *c* 93; *(female)* kusine *c* 93
crab krabbe *c* 43, 46
cramp krampe *c* 141
cranberry tyttebær *nt* 54
crayfish *(river)* kreps *c* 46
crayon fargeblyant *c* 104
cream fløte *c* 38, 55, 59; *(toiletry)* krem *c* 110; *(pharmaceutical)* salve *c* 109
crease resistant krøllfri 114
credit kreditt *c* 131
credit card kredittkort *nt* 20, 31, 61, 102, 130
crew-neck med rund hals 117
crispbread knekkebrød *nt* 120
crisps potetgull *nt* 52, 64
crockery servise *nt* 106, 107
cross kors *nt* 121
cross-country skiing langrenn *nt* 91
crossing *(maritime)* overfart *c* 73
crossroads (vei)kryss *nt* 77
cruise cruise *nt* 74
crystal krystall *nt* 122
cucumber agurk *c* 51
cuff link mansjettknapp *c* 121
cuisine kjøkken *nt* 34
cup kopp *c* 36, 59, 107
curler hårrull *c* 111
currant korint *c* 54
currency valuta *c* 18, 129
currency exchange office vekslingskontor *nt* 18, 67, 129
current strøm *c* 90
curry *(seasoning)* karri *c* 53
curtain gardin *c* 28
customs toll *c* 16, 79, 102
cut *(wound)* kutt *nt* 139
cut, to *(with scissors)* klippe 30
cut off, to avbryte 135
cut glass slepet glass *nt* 122
cuticle remover neglebåndsfjerner *c* 110
cutlery (spise)bestikk *nt* 107
cycling sykling *c* 90

D

dairy melkebutikk *c* 98
dance, to danse 88, 96
danger fare *c* 155, 156
dangerous farlig 90
Danish pastry wienerbrød *nt* 63
dark mørk 25, 101, 112, 113
date *(day)* dato *c* 25, 151; *(appointment)* stevnemøte *nt* 95; *(fruit)* daddel *c* 54
daughter datter *c* 93
day dag *c* 20, 24, 32, 80, 150, 151
daylight dagslys *nt* 124

day off fridag *c* 151
decade tiår *nt* 149
decaffeinated koffeinfri 38, 59
December desember *(c)* 150
decision avgjørelse *c* 102; beslutning *c* 25
deck *(ship)* dekk *nt* 74
deck chair fluktstol *c* 106
declare, to *(customs)* fortolle 17
deep dyp 90, 142
deep fried frityrstekt 46
deer hjort *c* 50
delicatessen delikatesseforretning *c* 98
delicious utsøkt 61
deliver, to levere 102
delivery levering *c* 102
Denmark Danmark 146
dentist tannlege *c* 98, 145
denture gebiss *nt* 145
deodorant deodorant *c* 110
department avdeling *c* 83, 100
department store stormagasin *nt* 98
departure avgang *c* 65
deposit *(down payment)* depositum *nt* 20; *(in bank)* innskudd *nt* 130
dessert dessert *c* 37, 55
detour *(traffic)* omkjøring *c* 79
diabetic diabetiker *c* 37, 141
dialling code retningsnummer *nt* 134
diamond diamant *c* 122
diaper bleie *c* 111
diarrhoea diarré *c* 140
dictionary ordbok *c* 104
diesel diesel *c* 75
diet diett *c* 37
difficult vanskelig 14
difficulty problem *nt* 102; vanskelighet *c* 28
dill dill *c* 53
dining car restaurantvogn *c* 68, 70
dining room spisesal *c* 27
dinner middag *c* 27, 34, 94
direct direkte 65
direct, to vise vei 13
direction retning *c* 76
directory *(phone)* telefonkatalog *c* 134
disabled bevegelseshemmet *c* 82
disc plate *c* 127
discotheque diskotek *nt* 88, 96
discount rabatt *c* 131
disease sykdom *c* 142
dish asjett *c* 127; fat *nt* 107; *(food)* rett *c* 37
dish detergent oppvaskmiddel *nt* 106
dish of the day dagens rett *c* 39, 40
disinfectant desinfeksjonsmiddel *nt* 109
dislocated ute av ledd 140
display case monter *c* 100
dissatisfied misfornøyd 103
district *(of town)* kvarter *nt* 81
dive, to dykke 90
diversion *(traffic)* omkjøring *c* 79
dizzy svimmel 140
do, to gjøre 163
doctor lege *c* 79, 98, 137, 144, 156; *(title)* dr./doktor 145
doctor's office legekontor *nt* 137
dog hund *c* 139, 155
doll dukke *c* 127, 128
dollar dollar *c* 18, 102, 130
double dobbel 74
double bed dobbeltseng *c* 23
double room dobbeltrom *nt* 19, 23
doughnut smultring *c* 63
down ned 15, 155
downhill skiing utforkjøring *c* 91
downstairs nede 15
downtown area sentrum *nt* 81
dozen dusin *nt* 148
draught beer fatøl *nt* 56
drawing pad tegneblokk *c* 104
drawing pin tegnestift *c* 104
dress kjole *c* 116
dressing gown morgenkåpe *c* 116
drink drikk *c* 58, 59; drikkevare *c* 56; drink *c* 60, 95
drink, to drikke 35, 36, 59
drinking water drikkevann *nt* 32
drip, to dryppe 28
drive, to kjøre 21, 76, 79
driving licence førerkort *nt* 20, 79
drop *(liquid)* dråpe *c* 109
drugstore apotek *nt* 98, 108
dry tørr 30, 58, 111
dry cleaner's rens *c* 29; renseri *nt* 98
dry shampoo tørrsjampo *c* 111
duck and *c* 50
dummy *(baby's)* narresmokk *c* 111
during i løpet av 15, 149, 151
duty *(customs)* toll *c* 17
duty-free shop tax-free-butikk *c* 19
dye, to farge 30

E

each hver 125, 149
ear øre *nt* 138
earache øreverk *c* 141
ear drops øredråper *c/pl* 109
early tidlig 14, 31
earring ørering *c* 121
east øst 77
Easter påske *c* 152
easy lett 14
eat, to spise 36, 37, 62, 144
eel ål *c* 43, 46
egg egg *nt* 38, 45, 62, 64
eight åtte 147
eighteen atten 147
eighty åtti 147
elastic elastisk 109
Elastoplast plaster *nt* 109
electric(al) elektrisk 119
electrical appliance elektrisk utstyr *nt* 119
electrical goods shop elektrisitetsforretning *c* 98
electricity elektrisitet *c* 32
electronic elektronisk 125, 128
elevator heis *c* 27, 100, 155
eleven elleve 147
elk elg *c* 50
embarkation point kai *c* 73
embassy ambassade *c* 156
emergency nødsfall *nt* 156
emergency exit nødutgang *c* 27, 99, 155
emery board sandpapirfil *c* 110
empty tom 14
enamel emalje *c* 122
end slutt *c* 150
engaged *(phone)* opptatt 136
engagement ring forlovelsesring *c* 122
engine *(car)* motor *c* 78
England England 146
English engelsk 12, 82, 84, 104
English englender *c* 93
engrave, to gravere 121
enjoyable hyggelig 31
enlarge, to forstørre 125
enough nok 15
enquiry forespørsel *c* 68
entrance inngang *c* 67, 99, 155; innkjørsel *c* 79
entrance fee inngangsbillett *c* 82
entree *(meal)* hovedrett *c* 40
envelope konvolutt *c* 104
equipment utstyr *nt* 91, 106
eraser viskelær *nt* 104
escalator rulletrapp *c* 100
estimate *(cost)* overslag *nt* 131
Europe Europa 146
evening kveld *c* 87, 95, 96, 151, 153
evening dress *(woman's)* aftenkjole *c* 116
event begivenhet *c* 80; *(sport)* stevne *nt* 89
everything alt 61
examine, to undersøke 137
exchange, to bytte 103
exchange rate vekslingskurs *c* 18, 130
excursion utflukt *c* 80
excuse, to unnskylde 10
exercise book skrivebok *c* 104
exhaust pipe eksosrør *nt* 78
exhibition utstilling *c* 81
exit utgang *c* 67, 99, 155; utkjørsel *c* 79
expect, to vente 130
expenses utgift *c* 131
expensive dyr 14, 19, 24, 101
exposure *(photography)* bilde *nt* 124
exposure counter telleverk *nt* 125
express ekspress 132
expressway motorvei *c* 76
extension *(phone)* linje *c* 135
extension cord/lead skjøteledning *c* 119
extra ekstra 27, 36
eye øye *nt* 139
eyebrow pencil øyenbrynsstift *c* 110
eye drops øyendråper *c/pl* 109
eye liner eyeliner *c* 110
eye shadow øyenskygge *c* 110
eyesight syn *nt* 123
eye specialist øyenlege *c* 137

F

fabric *(cloth)* (tøy)stoff *nt* 113
face ansikt *nt* 138
face flannel ansiktsklut *c* 110
face pack ansiktsmaske *c* 30
face powder pudder *nt* 110
facial tissue papirlommetørkle *nt* 111
factory fabrikk *c* 81
fair messe *c* 81
fall *(autumn)* høst *c* 149
fall, to falle 139
family familie *c* 93, 144

fan belt vifterem *c* 75
fantastic fantastisk 84
far fjern 14; langt 11, 100
fare takst *c* 69
farm bondegård *c* 85
fast hurtig 124
fat *(meat)* fett *nt* 37
father far *c* 93
faucet kran *c* 28
fax telefax *c* 133
February februar *(c)* 150
fee *(doctor's)* honorar *nt* 144
feeding bottle tåteflaske *c* 111
feel, to *(physical state)* føle seg 140, 142
felt filt *c* 114
felt-tip pen tusjpenn *c* 104
ferry ferge *c* 74; ferje *c* 74
fever feber *c* 140
few få 14; *(a few)* noen få 14
field jorde *nt* 85
fifteen femten 147
fifty femti 147
file *(tool)* fil *c* 110
fill in, to fylle ut 26, 144
filling *(tooth)* plombe *c* 145
filling station bensinstasjon *c* 75
film film *c* 86, 124, 125
film winder fremtrekker *c* 125
filter filter *nt* 125
filter-tipped med filter 126
find, to finne 11, 12, 100
fine *(OK)* bra 11, 25
finger finger *c* 138
finish, to slutte 87
Finland Finland 146
fire brann *c* 156
fire lighter tennvæske *c* 106
first første 68, 69, 148
first-aid kit førstehjelpsskrin *nt* 109
first class første klasse *c* 69
first name fornavn *nt* 25
fish fisk *c* 45
fish, to fiske 91
fishing fiske *nt* 90
fishing permit fiskekort *nt* 90
fishing tackle fiskeutstyr *nt* 106
fishmonger's fiskebutikk *c* 98
fit, to passe 115
five fem 147
fix, to reparere 75, 145
fizzy *(mineral water)* med kullsyre 59
fjord fjord *c* 85
flash *(photography)* blitz *c* 125
flashlight lommelykt *c* 106
flat *(shoe)* lavhælt 118
flat *(apartment)* leilighet *c* 19
flat tyre punktering *c* 75, 78
flatware (spise)bestikk *nt* 107
flea market loppemarked *nt* 81, 98
flight fly *nt* 65
flippers svømmeføtter *c/pl* 128
floor etasje *c* 23, 27, 154
floor show show *nt* 88
florist's blomsterbutikk *c* 98
flounder flyndre *c* 45
flour mel *nt* 37
flower blomst *c* 85
flu influensa *c* 142
fluid væske *c* 75, 123
foam rubber skumgummi *c* 106
fog tåke *c* 94
folding chair klappstol *c* 106
folding table klappbord *nt* 106
folk art folkekunst *c* 83
folk music folkemusikk *c* 128
follow, to følge 77
food mat *c* 37, 60, 111
food poisoning matforgiftning *c* 142
foot fot *c* 138
football fotball *c* 89
footbridge gangbro *c* 155
foot cream fotkrem *c* 110
footpath sti *c* 85
for for 15; *(time)* i 143, 151
forbid, to forby 155
forest skog *c* 85
forget, to glemme 60
fork gaffel *c* 36, 60, 107
form *(document)* blankett *c* 133; skjema *nt* 25, 26, 144
fortnight fjorten dager *c/pl* 151
fortress borg *c* 81
forty førti 147
foundation cream underlagskrem *c* 110
fountain fontene *c* 81
fountain pen fyllepenn *c* 104
four fire 147
fourteen fjorten 147
fowl fugl *c* 50
frame *(for glasses)* innfatning *c* 123
France Frankrike 146
free *(of charge)* gratis 155; *(vacant)* ledig 14, 71, 96, 155
French bean brekkbønne *c* 51
French fries pommes frites *c/pl* 52

fresh fersk 60; frisk 54
Friday fredag *c* 150
fried stekt 46, 49
fried egg speilegg *nt* 38, 45
friend venn *c* 93, 95
from fra 15
frost frost *c* 94
fruit frukt *c* 54, 55
fruit juice (frukt)juice *c* 37, 38
fruit salad fruktsalat *c* 54
frying pan stekepanne *c* 106
full full 14
full board helpensjon *c* 24
full insurance full forsikring *c* 20
fur coat pels *c* 116
furniture møbler *nt/pl* 83
furrier's pelsforretning *c* 98

G

gallery galleri *nt* 98
game spill *nt* 128; *(food)* vilt *nt* 50
gangway landgang *c* 74
garage *(parking)* garasje *c* 26; *(repairs)* bilverksted *nt* 78
garden(s) hage *c* 81, 85
garlic hvitløk *c* 52, 53
gas gass *c* 126, 156
gasoline bensin *c* 75
gastritis magekatarr *c* 142
gauze gasbind *nt* 109
gem edelsten *c* 121
general allmenn 27; vanlig 100
general delivery poste restante 133
general practitioner allmenn-praktiker *c* 137
genitals kjønnsorgan *nt* 138
gentleman herre *c* 155
genuine *(real)* ekte 118, 121
geology geologi *c* 83
Germany Tyskland 146
get, to *(obtain)* få 108; *(fetch)* skaffe 21, 31, 137; *(find)* få tak i 11, 19, 21, 32
get off, to gå av 72
get to, to komme til 11, 19, 70, 76
get up, to stå opp 144
gherkin sylteagurk *c* 51, 64
gift gave *c* 17
gin and tonic gin tonic *c* 58
girdle hofteholder *c* 116
girl pike *c* 112
girlfriend venninne *c* 93
give, to gi 13, 131, 135
gland kjertel *c* 138
glass glass *nt* 36, 57, 59, 60
glasses briller *c/pl* 123
glasses case brillefutteral *nt* 123
gloomy dyster 84
glove hanske *c* 116
glue lim *nt* 105
go, to gå 96, 163
go away! gå vekk! 156
gold gull *nt* 121, 122
golden gullfarget 113
gold plated gullbelagt 122
golf golf *c* 89
golf course golfbane *c* 89
good bra 14, 101; god 10
good afternoon god dag 10
goodbye adjø 10
good evening god aften 10
Good Friday langfredag *c* 152
good morning god morgen 10
good night god natt 10
goods vare *c* 16
goose gås *c* 50
gooseberry stikkelsbær *nt* 54
go, to gå 163
go out, to gå ut 96
gram gram *nt* 120
grammar book grammatikk *c* 105
grape drue *c* 54, 64
grapefruit grapefrukt *c* 54
grapefruit juice grapefruktjuice *c* 38, 59
gravel grus *c* 79
gravy brun saus *c* 52
gray grå 113
graze skrubbsår *nt* 139
greasy fet 30, 111
Great Britain Storbritannia 146
green grønn 113
green bean brekkbønne *c* 51
greengrocer's grønnsakhandel *c* 98
greeting hilsen *c* 152
grey grå 113
grilled grillstekt 46, 49
grocer's matvarehandel *c* 98, 120
grotto grotte *c* 81
groundsheet teltunderlag *nt* 106
group gruppe *c* 82
guesthouse pensjonat *nt* 19, 22
guide guide *c* 80
guidebook guidebok *c* 82; reise-håndbok *c* 104, 105
gum *(teeth)* tannkjøtt *nt* 145
gymnasium trimrom *nt* 23
gynaecologist gynekolog *c* 137, 141

H

habit vane *c* 34
hail hagl *nt* 94
hair hår *nt* 30, 111
hairbrush hårbørste *c* 111
haircut klipp *c* 30
hairdresser frisør *c* 98; frisørsalong *c* 27, 30
hair dryer hårføner *c* 119
hair dye hårfargingsmiddel *nt* 111
hair styling gel hårgelé *c* 111
hairgrip hårklemme *c* 111
hair lotion hårvann *nt* 111
hair mousse hårskum *nt* 111
hairpin hårnål *c* 111
hair slide hårspenne *c* 111
hair spray hårlakk *c* 30, 111
half halv 148
half halvpart *c* 148
half an hour halvtime *c* 153
half board halvpensjon *c* 24
half price halv pris *c* 69
hall porter portier *c* 26
ham skinke *c* 38, 48, 62, 64
ham and eggs egg og skinke 38
hamburger hamburger *c* 48
hammer hammer *c* 106
hammock hengekøye *c* 106
hand hånd *c* 138
handbag håndveske *c* 116, 156
hand cream håndkrem *c* 110
handicrafts kunsthåndverk *nt* 83, 127
handkerchief lommetørkle *nt* 116
handmade håndlaget 113
hanger (kles)henger *c* 27
happy god 152
harbour havn *c* 74, 81
hard hard 123
hard-boiled *(egg)* hardkokt 38
hardware store jernvarehandel *c* 98
hare hare *c* 50
hat hatt *c* 116
have, to ha 141, 162
hay fever høysnue *c* 108, 141
hazelnut hasselnøtt *c* 54
he han 162
head hode *nt* 138, 139
headache hodepine *c* 108, 141
headphones høretelefoner *c/pl* 119
head waiter hovmester *c* 61
health food shop helsekost-forretning *c* 99
health insurance sykeforsikring *c* 144
heart hjerte *nt* 138
heart attack hjerteslag *nt* 141
heated oppvarmet 90
heating varme *c* 23, 28
heavy tung 14, 101
heel hæl *c* 118
helicopter helikopter *nt* 74
hello hallo 10, 135
help hjelp *c* 156
help, to hjelpe 13, 21, 71, 100, 134; *(oneself)* ta selv 120
hen høne *c* 50
her hennes, sin, sitt (*pl* sine) 161
herb urt *c* 53
here her 14
herring sild *c* 41, 43, 46, 47
hi hei 10
high høy 85, 141
high season høysesong *c* 149
hike, to vandre 74
hill høyde *c* 85
hire utleie *c* 20
hire, to leie 19, 20, 74, 90, 91, 155
his hans, sin, sitt *(pl* sine) 161
history historie *c* 83
hitchhike, to haike 74
hold on! *(phone)* et øyeblikk! 136
hole hull *nt* 29
holiday helligdag *c* 151
holidays ferie *c* 16, 151, 152; *(school)* skoleferie *c* 151
home address hjemstedsadresse *c* 31
home town hjemsted *nt* 25
honey honning *c* 38
hope, to håpe 96
horseback riding ridning *c* 90
horse racing hesteveddeløp *nt* 89
horseradish pepperrot *c* 52
hospital sykehus *nt* 99, 144
hot varm 14, 25, 38, 59, 94, 155
hotel hotell *nt* 19, 21, 22
hotel directory/guide hotell-fortegnelse *c* 19
hotel reservation værelses-bestilling *c* 19
hot water varmt vann *nt* 23, 28
hot-water bottle varmeflaske *c* 27
hour time *c* 80, 90, 143, 153
house hus *nt* 83, 85
how hvordan 11
how far hvor langt 11, 76, 85
how long hvor lenge 11, 24

how many hvor mange 11
how much hvor mye 11, 24, 102
hundred hundre 147
hungry sulten 13, 35
hunting knife jaktkniv *c* 127
hurry *(to be in a)* ha det travelt 21
hurt, to gjøre vondt 139; ha vondt 140; verke 145; *(oneself)* slå seg 139
husband mann *c* 93
hydrofoil hydrofoil *c* 74

I
I jeg 162
ice is *c* 94
ice chest kjøleboks *c* 106
ice cream is(krem) *c* 55, 62
ice cube isbit *c* 27
iced tea iste *c* 59
ice hockey ishockey *c* 89
Iceland Island 146
ice pack kjøleelement *nt* 106
ignition tenning *c* 78
ill syk 140, 156
illness sykdom *c* 140
important viktig 13
imported importert 113
impressive imponerende 84
in i 15
include, to inkludere 24
included inkludert 20, 31, 40, 61, 80
India India 146
indicator *(car)* blinklys *nt* 78
indigestion fordøyelsesbesvær *nt* 141
indoor innendørs 90
inexpensive rimelig 35, 124
infected infisert 140
infection betennelse *c* 141
inflammation betennelse *c* 142
inflation inflasjon *c* 131
influenza influensa *c* 142
information informasjon *c* 67
information desk informasjonsskranke *c* 18
initial *(letter)* initial *c* 121
injection sprøyte *c* 142, 144
injure, to skade 139
injured skadet 79, 139
injury skade *c* 139
ink blekk *nt* 105
inlet vik *c* 85
inquiry forespørsel *c* 68
insect bite innsektstikk *nt* 108
insect killer insektgift *c* 106
insect repellent insektmiddel *nt* 109
insect spray insektgift *c* 106
inside inne 15
insole innleggssåle *c* 118
instant coffee pulverkaffe *c* 64
instead i stedet 37
insurance forsikring *c* 20, 71, 144
insurance company forsikringsselskap *nt* 79
interest *(finance)* rente *c* 131
interested, to be være interessert 83
interesting interessant 84
international internasjonal 133
interpreter tolk *c* 131
intersection (vei)kryss *nt* 77
introduce, to presentere 92
introduction *(social)* presentasjon *c* 92
investment investering *c* 131
invitation innbydelse *c* 94
invite to, to by på 94
invoice faktura *c* 131
iodine jod *c* 109
Ireland Irland 146
Irish irlender *c* 93
iron *(for laundry)* strykejern *nt* 119
iron, to stryke 29
ironmonger's jernvarehandel *c* 99
island øy *c* 85
Israel Israel 146
its dens/dets, sin, sitt (*pl* sine) 161

J
jack *(tool)* jekk *c* 78
jacket jakke *c* 116
jam *(preserves)* syltetøy *nt* 38, 63
jam, to sitte fast 28, 125
January januar *(c)* 150
Japan Japan 146
jar *(container)* glass *nt* 120
jaundice gulsott *c* 142
jaw kjeve *c* 138
jeans jeans *c/pl* 116
jerry can bensinkanne *c* 78
jetty brygge *c* 74
jewel box smykkeskrin *nt* 121
jeweller's gullsmed *c* 99, 121
jewellery smykke *nt* 121
joint ledd *nt* 138
juice juice *c* 37, 38, 59
July juli *(c)* 150
June juni *(c)* 150
just *(only)* bare 16, 37, 100

K

kayak kajakk *c* 74
keep, to beholde 61
kerosene parafin *c* 106
key nøkkel *c* 27
kidney nyre *c* 48, 138
kilo(gram) kilo *nt* 120
kilometre kilometer *c* 20, 79
kind snill 96
kind *(type)* slags *nt/pl* 47, 140
knee kne *nt* 138
kneesocks knestrømper *c/pl* 116
knife kniv *c* 36, 60, 107
know, to kjenne 114; vite 16, 24, 96
krone *(money)* krone *c* 18, 101, 129

L

label etikett *c* 105, 133
lace knipling *c* 114
lady dame *c* 155
lake (inn)sjø *c* 81, 90
lamb *(meat)* lammekjøtt *nt* 47; lamme- 48
lamp lampe *c* 29, 106, 119
landmark landemerke *nt* 85
language språk *nt* 104, 159
lantern lykt *c* 106
large stor 20, 101, 118, 130
last forrige 150, 151; siste 14, 68
last, to vare 87
late forsinket 69, 70; sen 14
later senere 136
laugh, to le 95
launderette selvbetjeningsvaskeri *nt* 99
laundry *(place)* vaskeri *nt* 99; *(clothes)* vask *c* 29
laundry service vaskeri-service *c* 23
laxative laksermiddel *nt* 109
lead *(metal)* bly *nt* 75
leap year skuddår *nt* 149
leather lær *nt* 114, 118
leave, to *(depart)* gå 68, 69, 74, 95; reise 31; *(deposit)* deponere 26; *(hand in)* levere inn 71; *(return)* levere tilbake 20
leave alone, to la være i fred 156
leek purre *c* 51
left venstre 21, 62, 69, 77
left-luggage office bagasje-oppbevaring *c* 67, 71
leg ben *nt* 138
legal holiday offentlig høytidsdag *c* 152
lemon sitron *c* 38, 54, 59
lemonade sitronbrus *c* 59
lend, to låne 78
lens *(for glasses)* glass *nt* 123; *(for camera)* objektiv *nt* 125
lens cap linsebeskytter *c* 125
lentil linse *c* 51
less mindre 14
lesson time *c* 90
let, to *(hire out)* til leie 155
letter brev *nt* 28, 132
letter box postkasse *c* 132
letter of credit kredittbrev *nt* 130
lettuce hodesalat *c* 51
library bibliotek *nt* 81, 99
licence *(driving)* førerkort *nt* 20, 79
lie down, to legge seg ned 142
life belt livbelte *nt* 74
life boat livbåt *c* 74
life jacket flytevest *c* 74
lift *(elevator)* heis *c* 27, 100, 155
ligament leddbånd *nt* 140
light *(weight)* lett 14, 55, 101; *(colour)* lys 101, 112, 113
light lys *nt* 28, 124; *(for cigarette)* fyr *c* 95
light bulb lyspære *c* 28, 75, 119
lighter lighter *c* 126
lighter fluid lighterbensin *c* 126
lighter gas lightergass *c* 126
light meter lysmåler *c* 125
lightning lyn *nt* 94
like, to like 25, 92, 102, 112; ha lyst på 96; *(want)* ville 20
line linje *c* 73
linen *(cloth)* lin *nt* 114
lip leppe *c* 138
lipsalve leppepomade *c* 110
lipstick leppestift *c* 110
liqueur likør *c* 58
liquid *(fluid)* væske *c* 123
liquor store vinmonopol *nt* 99
listen to, to høre på 128
litre liter *c* 75, 120
little *(a little)* lite 14
live, to leve 83; *(reside)* bo 83
liver lever *c* 48, 64, 138
loan lån *nt* 131
lobster hummer *c* 43, 45
local lokal 36
local train lokaltog *nt* 66, 69
long lang 116
long time lang tid 60, 76, 116; lenge 77, 92, 144
long-sighted langsynt 123

look, to se 100, 123
look for, to se etter 13
look out! se opp! 156
loose løs 145; *(clothes)* vid 116
lose, to miste 123, 156
loss tap *nt* 131
lost, to be gå seg bort 13, 156
lost and found office hittegods-kontor *nt* 67, 156
lost property office hittegods-kontor *nt* 67, 156
lot *(a lot)* mye 14
loud *(voice)* høy 135
lovely herlig 94
low lav 141
lower under- 69, 71
low season lavsesong *c* 149
luggage bagasje *c* 18, 26, 31, 71; *(registered)* reisegods *nt/pl* 71
luggage insurance reisegods-forsikring *c* 71
luggage locker oppbevaringsboks *c* 18, 67, 71
luggage trolley bagasjetralle *c* 18, 71
lunch lunsj *c* 27, 34, 80, 94
lung lunge *c* 138

M

machine maskin *c* 114
magazine ukeblad *nt* 105
magnificent storslagen 84
maid værelsespike *c* 26
mail post *c* 28, 132, 133
mail, to poste 28
mailbox postkasse *c* 132
main hoved- 80; størst 100
main course hovedrett *c* 40
make, to lage 113, 114
make up, to *(prepare)* gjøre i stand 71, 108
make-up bag sminkepung *c* 110
man mann *c* 115, 156; herre *c* 155
manager bestyrer *c* 61; direktør *c* 26
manicure manikyr *c* 30
man's ... herre- 116
many mange 11, 14
map kart *nt* 76, 105
March mars *(c)* 150
marinated marinert 46
maritime history sjøfartshistorie *c* 83
market torghandel c 81, 99
marmalade appelsinmarmelade *c* 38
married gift 93
marzipan marsipan *c* 63
mascara øyensverte *c* 110
mashed potatoes potetstappe *c* 52, 62
mass *(church)* messe *c* 84
match *(matchstick)* fyrstikk *c* 106, 126; *(sport)* kamp/match *c* 89
matinée matiné *c* 87
mattress madrass *c* 106
May mai *(c)* 150
may *(can)* kunne 12, 162
meadow eng *c* 85
meal måltid *nt* 24, 143
mean, to bety 11, 26
measles meslinger *c/pl* 142
measure, to ta mål av 114
meat kjøtt *nt* 47, 60
meatball frikadelle *c* 47; kjøttbolle *c* 48
mechanic mekaniker *c* 78
mechanical pencil skrublyant *c* 105, 121
medical certificate legeattest *c* 144
medicine medisin *c* 83, 143
medium *(meat)* medium stekt 49
medium-sized mellomstor 20
meet, to møtes 96; treffes 92; ses 96
melon melon *c* 54
memorial minnesmerke *nt* 81
mend, to lappe 29; reparere 75
menstrual pains menstruasjons-smerter *c/pl* 141
menthol mentol *c* 126
menu meny *c* 36, 37, 39; *(printed)* spisekart *nt* 36, 39, 40
message beskjed *c* 28, 136
metre meter *c* 112
mezzanine *(theatre)* balkong *c* 87
middle midten 69, 87, 150
midnight midnatt *c* 153
midnight sun midnattssol *c* 94
mild mild 126
mileage kjørelengde *c* 20
milk melk *c* 38, 59, 64
milkshake milkshake *c* 59
milliard milliard *c* 148
million million *c* 148
mineral water naturlig mineral vann *nt* 59

minister *(religion)* protestantisk prest *c* 84
minute minutt *nt* 21, 153
mirror speil *nt* 115, 123
miscellaneous forskjellig 127
Miss frøken *c* 92
miss, to mangle 18, 29, 60
mistake feil *c* 31, 61, 102; *(misunderstanding)* misforståelse *c* 60
modern moderne 83
modified American plan halvpensjon *c* 24
moisturizing cream fuktighetskrem *c* 110
moment øyeblikk *nt* 12, 136
monastery kloster *c* 81
Monday mandag *c* 150
money penger *c/pl* 129, 130
money order postanvisning *c* 133
month måned *c* 16, 150
monument monument *nt* 81
moon måne *c* 94
moped moped *c* 74
more mer 14
morning morgen *c* 31, 151, 153
mortgage hypotek *nt* 131
mosque moské *c* 84
mosquito net myggnett *nt* 106
mother mor *c* 93
motorbike motorsykkel *c* 74
motorboat motorbåt *c* 74
motorway motorvei *c* 76
mountain fjell *nt* 85
moustache bart *c* 31
mouth munn *c* 138
mouthwash munnvann *nt* 109
move, to bevege 139
movie film *c* 86
movies kino *c* 86, 96
Mr. herr *c* 92
Mrs. fru *c* 92
much mye 11, 14
mug krus *nt* 107
muscle muskel *c* 138
museum museum *nt* 81
mushroom sopp *c* 51
music musikk *c* 83, 128
musical musikal *c* 86
music box spilledåse *c* 121
mussel blåskjell *nt* 43, 45
must *(have to)* måtte 23, 31, 95
mustard sennep *c* 64
mutton fårekjøtt *nt* 42, 47, 49
my min, mitt (*pl* mine) 161

N

nail *(human)* negl *c* 110
nail brush neglebørste *c* 110
nail clippers negleklipper *c* 110
nail file neglefil *c* 110
nail polish neglelakk *c* 110
nail polish remover neglelakkfjerner *c* 110
nail scissors neglesaks *c* 110
name navn *nt* 23, 79, 133; *(surname)* etternavn *nt* 25
napkin serviett *c* 36, 105, 106
nappy bleie *c* 111
narrow trang 118
nationality nasjonalitet *c* 25, 92
natural history naturhistorie *c* 83
nauseous kvalm 140
near i nærheten av 19; nær 14
nearby i nærheten 77
nearest nærmeste 73, 75, 78, 132
neat *(drink)* bar 58
neck nakke *c* 30, 138
necklace halskjede *nt* 121
need, to trenge 29, 118, 137
needle nål *c* 27
negative negativ *nt* 124, 125
nephew nevø *c* 93
nerve nerve *c* 138
nervous system nervesystem *nt* 138
never aldri 15
new ny 14, 118, 149
newspaper avis *c* 104, 105
newsstand aviskiosk *c* 19, 67, 104
New Year nyttår *nt* 152
New Zealand Ny-Zealand 146
next neste 14, 65, 68, 73, 76, 149
next time neste gang 95
next to ved siden av 15, 77
nice *(beautiful)* pen 94
niece niese *c* 93
night natt *c* 10, 24, 151
nightclub nattklubb *c* 88
night cream nattkrem *c* 110
nightdress/-gown nattkjole *c* 116
nine ni 147
nineteen nitten 147
ninety nitti 147
no nei 10
noisy støyende 25
nonalcoholic alkoholfri 56, 57, 59
none ingen 15
nonsmoker ikke-røyker *c* 36
noodle nudel *c* 52
noon klokken tolv (om dagen) 153

normal normal 30
north nord 77
North America Nord-Amerika 146
Norway Norge 113, 146
Norwegian norsk 11, 12, 18, 95, 114, 127
nose nese *c* 138
nosebleed neseblødning *c* 141
nose drops nesedråper *c/pl* 109
not ikke 15, 163
note *(banknote)* seddel *c* 130
notebook notisbok *c* 105
note paper brevpapir *nt* 105
nothing ikke noe 15, 17; ingenting 15, 16
notice *(sign)* oppslag *nt* 155
notify, to underrette 144
November november *(c)* 150
now nå 15
number nummer *nt* 25, 134, 135, 136; tall *nt* 147
nurse sykepleier *c* 144
nut *(fruit)* nøtt *c* 54, 62

O

observatory observatorium *nt* 81
occupation *(profession)* yrke *nt* 25
occupied opptatt 14, 155
ocean hav *nt* 85
o'clock kl./klokken *c* 154
October oktober *(c)* 150
office kontor *nt* 22, 67, 80, 132
oil olje *c* 37, 75, 111
oily *(greasy)* fet 30, 111
ointment salve *c* 109
old gammel 14, 149
old town gamleby *c* 81
omelet omelett *c* 38, 45
on på 15
once en gang 148
one en 147
one-way ticket enkeltbillett *c* 65, 69
on foot til fots 76
onion løk *c* 51, 62
only bare 15, 24
on time i rute 68
open åpen 14, 82, 129, 155
open, to åpne 11, 17, 82, 108, 130
open-air utendørs 90
opening hours åpningstider *c/pl* 155
opera opera *c* 88
opera house operahus *nt* 81, 88
operation operasjon *c* 144
operator telefonist *c* 134
operetta operette *c* 88
opposite midt imot 77
opposite motsetning *c* 14
optician optiker *c* 99, 123
or eller 15
orange oransje 113
orange appelsin *c* 54, 64
orange juice appelsinjuice *c* 38, 59
orchestra orkester *nt* 88; *(seats)* parkett *c* 87
order, to *(goods, meal)* bestille 36, 60, 102, 103
ornithology ornitologi *c* 83
other andre 58, 74, 101
our vår, vårt (*pl* våre) 161
out of order i uorden 136
out of stock utsolgt 103
outlet *(electric)* stikkontakt *c* 27
outside ute 15, 36
oval oval 101
overalls overall *c* 116
overdone for mye stekt 60
overheat, to *(engine)* gå varm 78
overnight *(stay)* natten over 24
overtake, to kjøre forbi 79
owe, to skylde 144
oyster østers *c* 43, 46

P

pacifier *(baby's)* narresmokk *c* 111
packet pakke *c* 120, 126
pail spann *nt* 128
pain smerte *c* 140, 141, 143, 144
painkiller smertestillende middel *nt* 109
paint, to male 83
paintbox malerskrin *nt* 105
painter maler *c* 83
pair par *nt* 116, 118, 148
pajamas pyjamas *c* 117
palace slott *nt* 81
palpitation hjerteklapp *c* 141
pancake pannekake *c* 45
panties truser *c/pl* 116
pants *(trousers)* langbukser *c/pl* 117
panty hose strømpebukse *c* 117
paper papir *nt* 105
paperback pocketbok *c* 105
paperclip binders *c* 105
paper napkin papirserviett *c* 105
paper towel husholdningspapir *nt* 106
paraffin *(fuel)* parafin *c* 106

parcel pakke *c* 132
pardon unnskyld 10
parents foreldre *c/pl* 93
park park *c* 81
park, to parkere 26, 77
parka anorakk *c* 117
parking parkering *c* 77, 79
parking garage parkeringshus *nt* 77
parking lot parkeringsplass *c* 77
parking meter parkometer *nt* 77
parliament building storting *nt* 81
parsley persille *c* 53
part del *c* 138
partridge rapphøne *c* 50
party *(social gathering)* fest *c* 95
pass, to *(driving)* kjøre forbi 79
passport pass *nt* 16, 17, 25, 26, 156
passport photo passfoto *nt* 124
pass through, to være på gjennomreise 16
pastry bakverk *nt* 63
pastry shop konditori *nt* 99
path sti *c* 85
patient pasient *c* 144
pattern mønster *nt* 112
pay, to betale 31, 61, 100, 102
payment betaling *c* 131
pea ert *c* 51
peach fersken *c* 54
peak topp *c* 85
pear pære *c* 54
pearl perle *c* 122
pearl strand perlekjede *nt* 121
peg *(tent)* plugg *c* 107
pen penn *c* 105
pencil blyant *c* 105
pendant hengesmykke *nt* 121
penicillin penicillin *nt* 143
penknife lommekniv *c* 106
pensioner pensjonist *c* 82
people folk *nt/pl* 92
pepper pepper *c* 37, 38, 53, 64
per cent prosent *c* 148
percentage prosentsats *c* 131
per day pr. dag 20, 32, 90
perfume parfyme *c* 110
perfumery parfymeri *nt* 99
perhaps kanskje 15
per hour pr. time 77, 90
period *(monthly)* menstruasjon *c* 141
period pains menstruasjons-smerter *c/pl* 141
permanent wave permanent *c* 30
per night pr. natt 24
per person pr. person 32
person person *c* 32
personal personlig 17
personal call personlig samtale *c* 134
person-to-person call personlig samtale *c* 134
per week pr. uke 20, 24
petrol bensin *c* 75, 78
pewter tinn *nt* 122
pharmacy apotek *nt* 99, 108
pheasant fasan *c* 50
photo bilde *nt* 125; foto *nt* 124
photocopy fotokopi *c* 131
photograph, to fotografere 82
photographer fotograf *c* 99
photography fotografering *c* 124
phrase uttrykk *nt* 12
phrase book parlør *c* 105
pick up, to *(person)* hente 80, 96
pickled gherkin sylteagurk *c* 51, 64
picnic picnic *c* 64
picture bilde *nt* 83
picture-book billedbok *c* 105
piece stykke *nt* 63, 120
pier pir *c* 74
pill pille *c* 109; *(contraceptive)* p-pille *c* 141
pillow pute *c* 27
pin nål *c* 110, 111, 122
pineapple ananas *c* 54
pink rosa 113
pipe pipe *c* 126
pipe cleaner piperenser *c* 126
place sted *nt* 25, 76
place of birth fødested *nt* 25
plane fly *nt* 65
plaster, to put in gipse 140
plastic plast *c* 107
plastic bag plastpose *c* 107
plate asjett *c* 127; tallerken *c* 36, 60, 107
platform *(station)* perrong *c* 67, 68, 69, 70
play *(theatre)* stykke *nt* 86, 87
play, to spille 86, 88, 89, 93
playground lekeplass *c* 32
playing card spillkort *nt* 105
please vær (så) snill å ... 10; ... takk 10
pliers tang *c* 78, 107
plimsoll turnsko *c* 118
plug *(electric)* støpsel *nt* 29
plum plomme *c* 54

pneumonia lungebetennelse *c* 142
poached pochert 46; *(egg)* forlorent 45
pocket lomme *c* 117
pocket calculator lommekalkulator *c* 105
pocket dictionary lommeordbok *c* 104
pocketknife lommekniv *c* 107
pocket radio lommeradio *c* 119
pocket watch lommeur *nt* 121
point, to peke 12
poison gift *c* 109, 156
poisoning forgiftning *c* 142
pole *(ski)* stav *c* 91; *(tent)* stang *c* 107
police politi *nt* 79, 156
police station politistasjon *c* 99, 156
polo-neck høyhalset 117
pond dam *c* 85
pork svinekjøtt *nt* 47; svine- 48
porridge grøt *c* 38
port havn *c* 74; *(wine)* portvin *c* 58
portable bærbar 119
porter bærer *c* 18, 26, 71
portion porsjon *c* 37, 60
possible mulig 137
post *(mail)* post *c* 28, 133
post, to poste 28
postage porto *c* 132
postage stamp frimerke *nt* 28, 126, 132, 133
postcard postkort *nt* 105, 126, 132
poste restante poste restante 133
post office postkontor *nt* 99, 132
pot kanne *c* 59
potato potet *c* 52
pottery pottemakerkunst *c* 83
poultry fugl *c* 50
pound pund *nt (money)* 18, 102, 130, *(weight)* 120
powder pudder *nt* 110
powder compact pudderdåse *c* 121
prawn reke *c* 43, 46
prefer, to foretrekke 101
pregnant gravid 141
premium *(gasoline)* super 75
prescribe, to skrive ut 143
prescription resept *c* 108, 143
present presang *c* 121
press, to *(iron)* presse 29
press stud trykknapp *c* 117
pressure trykk *nt* 75, 141
pretty søt 84
price pris *c* 69, 124
priest katolsk prest *c* 84
primus stove primus *c* 107
print *(photo)* kopi *c* 125
private privat 80, 155
processing *(photo)* fremkalling *c* 124
profit utbytte *nt* 131
programme program *nt* 87
pronounce, to uttale 12
pronunciation uttale *c* 6
propelling pencil skrublyant *c* 105
propose, to anbefale 40
Protestant protestantisk 84
provide, to skaffe 131
prune sviske *c* 54
ptarmigan rype *c* 50
public holiday offentlig høytidsdag *c* 152
pull, to trekke 155
pullover genser *c* 117
pump pumpe *c* 107
puncture punktering *c* 75
purchase kjøp *nt* 131
pure ren 114
purple fiolett 113
push, to *(open)* skyve 155
put, to sette 24
pyjamas pyjamas *c* 117

Q

quail vaktel *c* 50
quality kvalitet *c* 113
quantity mengde *c* 14
quarter fjerdedel *c* 148; *(district of town)* kvarter *nt* 81
quarter of an hour kvarter *nt* 153
question spørsmål *nt* 11
quick rask 14
quickly øyeblikkelig 137, 156
quiet rolig 23, 25
quilt dyne *c* 27

R

rabbi rabbiner *c* 84
rabbit kanin *c* 50
race (vedde)løp *nt* 89
race course/track hesteveddeløpsbane *c* 89
racket *(sport)* racket *c* 90
radiator *(car)* kjøler *c* 78
radio radio *c* 23, 28, 119

radio cassette recorder radiokassettopptaker *c* 119
railway jernbane *c* 67, 154
railway station jernbanestasjon *c* 19, 21, 67
rain regn *nt* 94
rain, to regne 94
rainbow trout regnbueørret *c* 46
raincoat regnfrakk *c* 117
rainy regnfull 94
raisin rosin *c* 54, 63
rangefinder avstandsmåler *c* 125
rare *(meat)* blodig 60; råstekt 49
rash utslett *nt* 139
raspberry bringebær *nt* 54
rate *(of exchange)* kurs *c* 18, 130
razor barberhøvel *c* 110
razor blade barberblad *nt* 110
read, to lese 27
reading lamp leselampe *c* 27
ready ferdig 118, 123, 125, 145; klar 29, 31
real *(genuine)* ekte 118, 121
rear bak 69, 75
reason *(purpose)* hensikt *c* 25
receipt kvittering *c* 102, 103, 144
reception resepsjon *c* 23
receptionist resepsjonist *c* 26
recommend, to anbefale 35, 36, 80, 145; *(suggest)* foreslå 44
record *(disc)* plate *c* 127, 128
record player platespiller *c* 119
rectangular rektangulær 101
red rød 113
redcurrant rips *c* 54
reduction rabatt *c* 82; reduksjon *c* 24
refill *(pen)* refill *c* 105
refrigerator kjøleskap *nt* 28
refund, to get a få pengene tilbake 103
regards hilsen *c* 152
register, to *(luggage)* ekspedere 71; *(mail)* rekommandere 132
registered mail rekommandert 132
registration innskriving *c* 25
registration form meldeskjema *nt* 25
regular *(petrol)* normal 75
reindeer reinsdyr *nt* 50
reindeer skin reinsdyrskinn *nt* 127
religion religion *c* 83
religious service gudstjeneste *c* 84
rent, to leie 19, 20, 74, 90, 91, 155
rental utleie *c* 20
repair reparasjon *c* 125
repair, to reparere 29, 118, 119, 121, 123, 125, 145
repeat gjenta 12
report, to *(a theft)* anmelde 156
reservation bestilling *c* 19, 69; reservasjon *c* 65
reserve, to bestille 19, 23, 35, 87; reservere 69, 155
restaurant restaurant *c* 33, 35, 67
return ticket tur-returbillett *c* 65, 69
return, to *(come back)* være tilbake 21, 80; *(give back)* levere tilbake 103
reverse-charge call noteringsoverføring *c* 135
revue revy *c* 86
rheumatism reumatisme *c* 141
rib ribben *nt* 138
ribbon bånd *nt* 105
rice ris *c* 52
ridge ås *c* 85
right *(correct)* 14; *(direction)* høyre 21, 62, 69, 77
ring *(jewellery)* ring *c* 122
river elv *c* 85, 90
road vei *c* 76, 77
road assistance hjelp på veien *c* 78
road map veikart *nt* 105
road sign trafikkskilt *nt* 79
roast ovnsstekt 49
roast stek *c* 47, 48
roast beef oksestek *c* 48; roastbiff *c* 48
roll rull *c* 109; *(bread)* rundstykke *nt* 38, 64
roller skates rulleskøyter *c/pl* 128
roll film rullefilm *c* 124
romantic romantisk 84
room rom *nt* 19, 23, 24, 25; *(space)* plass *c* 32
room number romnummer *nt* 26
rope tau *nt* 107
rosé rosévin *c* 58
round rund 101
round *(golf)* runde *c* 90
round-trip ticket tur-returbillett *c* 65, 69
route vei *c* 85
rowing boat robåt *c* 74
royal kongelig 81
rubber *(eraser)* viskelær *nt* 105; *(material)* gummi *c* 118
rubber band gummistrikk *c* 105

rucksack ryggsekk *c* 107
ruin ruin *c* 82
ruler *(for measuring)* linjal *c* 105
rum rom *c* 58
running water rennende vann *nt* 23

S

safe *(free from danger)* trygg 90
safe safe *c* 26
safety pin sikkerhetsnål *c* 110
sailing boat seilbåt *c* 74
salad salat *c* 44, 51
sale salg *nt* 131; *(bargains)* (ut)salg *nt* 100, 155
sales tax moms *c* 24, 102, 154
salmon laks *c* 43, 46, 47
salt salt *nt* 37, 38, 53, 64
salty salt 60
same samme 118
sand sand *c* 90
sandal sandal *c* 118
sandwich smørbrød *nt* 41, 62
sanitary napkin/towel sanitetsbind *nt* 109
Saturday lørdag *c* 150
sauce saus *c* 52
saucepan kasserolle *c* 107
saucer skål (til kopp) *c* 107
sauna badstue *c* / sauna *c* 23, 32
sausage pølse *c* 48, 62, 64
Scandinavia Skandinavia 25
scarf skjerf *nt* 117
scenery *(landscape)* natur *c* 92
scenic naturskjønn 85
school skole *c* 151
school holidays skoleferie *c* 151
scissors saks *c* 107, 110
scooter scooter *c* 74
Scotland Skottland 146
scrambled egg eggerøre *c* 38
screwdriver skrutrekker *c* 107
sculptor billedhugger *c* 83
sculpture skulptur *c* 83
sea sjø *c* 85, 90
seafood skalldyr *nt/pl* 45
sealskin selskinn *nt* 127
search for, to lete etter 13
season årstid *c* 149
seasoning krydder *nt* 37
seat plass *c* 69, 70, 87
seat belt bilbelte *nt* 75
second andre 148; annen 148
second sekund *nt* 153
second class andre klasse *c* 69; annen klasse *c* 69
second hand sekundviser *c* 122
second-hand shop marsjandise-forretning *c* 99
secretary sekretær *c* 27, 131
see, to se 12, 80; *(examine)* undersøke 137
self-adhesive selvklebende 105
sell, to selge 100
send, to sende 78, 102, 132, 133
send up, to bringe opp 26
senior citizen pensjonist *c* 82
sentence setning *c* 12
September september *(c)* 150
serve, to servere 27, 40
service *(church)* gudstjeneste *c* 84
service charge service *c* 61
serviette serviett *c* 36
set menu meny *c* 36
setting lotion leggevann *nt* 30, 111
seven sju 147
seventeen sytten 147
seventy sytti 147
sew, to sy 29
shade *(colour)* nyanse *c* 112
shallow langgrunt 91
shampoo sjampo *c* 30, 111
shampoo and set vask og legg *c* 30
shape form *c* 103
share *(finance)* aksje *c* 131
shave barbering *c* 31
shaver barbermaskin *c* 27, 119
shaving cream barberkrem *c* 111
she hun 162
shellfish skalldyr *nt/pl* 45
sherbet sorbett *c* 55
ship skip *nt* 74
shirt skjorte *c* 117
shoe sko *c* 118
shoelace skolisse *c* 118
shoemaker's skomaker *c* 99
shoe polish skokrem *c* 118
shoe shop skoforretning *c* 99
shop butikk *c* / forretning *c* 98, 99
shopping shopping *c* 97
shopping area handlestrøk *nt* 82, 100
shopping centre butikksenter *nt* 99
shop window (utstillings)vindu *nt* 100, 112
short kort 30, 116
shorts shorts *c/pl* 117
short-sighted nærsynt 123

shoulder skulder *c* 138
shovel spade *c* 128
show show *nt* 88; *(theatre)* forestilling *c* 87
show, to vise 13, 76, 100, 101, 119
shower dusj *c* 23, 32
shrimp reke *c* 43, 46
shrink, to krympe 114
shut stengt 14
shutter *(camera)* lukker *c* 125
sick *(ill)* syk 140, 156
sickness *(illness)* sykdom *c* 140
side side *c* 31
sideboards/-burns kinnskjegg *nt* 31
side dish tilbehør *nt* 40
sightseeing sightseeing *c* 80
sightseeing tour sightseeingtur *c* 80
sign *(notice)* skilt *nt* 79, 155
sign, to undertegne 26, 130
signature underskrift *c* 25
signet ring signetring *c* 122
silk silke *c* 114
silver *(colour)* sølvfarget 113
silver sølv *nt* 121, 122
silver plate sølvplett *c* 122
silverware sølvtøy *nt* 122
simple enkel 124
since siden 15, 150
sing, to synge 88
single enkel 74; *(unmarried)* ugift 93
single room enkeltrom *nt* 19, 23
single ticket enkeltbillett *c* 65, 69
sink vask *c* 28
sister søster *c* 93
sit down, to sette seg 95, 142
six seks 147
sixteen seksten 147
sixty seksti 147
size *(clothes)* størrelse *c* 114, 115; *(film)* format *nt* 124; *(shoes)* nummer *nt* 118
skate skøyte *c* 91
skating rink skøytebane *c* 91
ski ski *c* 91
ski, to gå på ski 91
ski boot skistøvel *c* 91
ski jumping skihopping *c* 89
ski lift skiheis *c* 91
skin hud *c* 138
ski race skirenn *nt* 89
skirt skjørt *nt* 117
ski run skibakke *c* 91
ski track/trail skiløype *c* 91
sky himmel *c* 94
sleep, to sove 144
sleeping bag sovepose *c* 107
sleeping car sovevogn *c* 68, 71
sleeping pill sovetablett *c* 143
sleeve erme *nt* 116
slice skive *c* 62, 120
sliced oppskåret 120
slide *(photo)* lysbilde *nt* 124
slide film film for lysbilder *nt/p*124
slide projector lysbildeapparat *nt* 125
slip *(underwear)* underkjole *c* 117
slipper tøffel *c* 118, 127
slow sakte 14
slowly langsom 12, 135; sakte 21
small liten 14, 20, 25, 101, 118, 130
smoke, to røyke 95
smoked røkt 42, 43, 46, 49
smoker røyker *c* 36
smorgasbord koldtbord *nt* 41
snack småretter *c/pl* 62
snack bar snackbar *c* 67
snail snegle *c* 43
snap fastener trykknapp *c* 117
snorkel snorkel *c* 128
snow snø *c* 94
snow, to snø 94
snuff snus *c* 126
soap såpe *c* 27, 111
soccer fotball *c* 89
sock sokk *c* 117
socket *(electric)* stikkontakt *c* 27
soda water sodavann *nt* 58
soft myk 123
soft-boiled *(egg)* bløtkokt 38
soft drink leskedrikk 40, 59, 64
soft ice cream softis *c* 62
sold out utsolgt 87, 155
sole *(fish)* sjøtunge *c* 46; *(shoe)* såle *c* 118
soloist solist *c* 88
some litt15; noe 15
someone noen 95
something noe 29, 36, 55, 108
son sønn *c* 93
song sang *c* 128
soon snart 15, 137
sorbet sorbett *c* 55
sore *(painful)* sår 141, 145
sorry, to be beklage 10, 16, 103
sort *(kind)* slags *nt/pl* 86, 120
soup suppe *c* 44
south sør 77

South Africa Sør-Afrika 146
South America Sør-Amerika 146
souvenir suvenir *c* 127
souvenir shop suvenirbutikk *c* 99
Soviet Union Sovjetunionen 146
spade spade *c* 128
spanner skrunøkkel *c* 78
sparerib svineribbe *c* 48
spare tyre reservedekk *nt* 75
spark(ing) plug tennstift *c* 75
sparkling (spring water) med kullsyre 59; (wine) musserende 58
speak, to snakke 12, 135
speaker *(loudspeaker)* høyttaler *c* 119
special spesial- 20, 37; spesiell 80
specialist spesialist *c* 142
speciality spesialitet *c* 36, 40, 42
specimen *(medical)* prøve *c* 142
spell, to bokstavere 12
spend, to gi 101
spice krydder *nt* 53
spinach spinat *c* 51
spine ryggrad *c* 138
sponge svamp *c* 111
sponge bag toalettmappe *c* 111
spoon skje *c* 36, 60, 107
sport sport *c* 89
sporting event sportsstevne *nt* 89
sporting goods shop sportsforretning *c* 99
sportswear sportsklær *pl* 117
sprain, to vrikke 140
spring *(season)* vår *c* 149; *(water)* kilde *c* 85
spring water naturlig mineralvann *nt* 59
square firkantet 101
square plass *c* 82; torg *nt* 82
stadium stadion *nt* 82
staff *(personnel)* personale *nt* 26
stain flekk *c* 29
stainless steel rustfritt stål *nt* 107
stalls *(theatre)* parkett *c* 87
stamp *(postage)* frimerke *nt* 28, 126, 132, 133
staple heftestift *c* 105
stapler heftemaskin *c* 105
star stjerne *c* 94
start, to starte 78, 80
starter *(meal)* forrett *c* 43
station stasjon *c; (railway)* jernbanestasjon 19, 21, 67, 70; *(underground/subway)* T-banestasjon 73
stationer's papirhandel *c* 99, 104
statue statue *c* 82
stave church stavkirke *c* 82
stay opphold *nt* 31
stay, to bli 16, 24; *(reside)* bo 93
steak biff *c* 47
steal, to stjele 156
steamed dampkokt 46
steamer dampbåt *c* 74
steering *(car)* styring *c* 78
stew pot gryte *c* 107
stiff stiv 141
still *(mineral water)* uten kullsyre 59
sting stikk *nt* 139
sting, to bite 139
stitch, to sy sammen 29, 118
stock exchange børs *c* 82
stocking strømpe *c* 117
stomach mage *c* 138
stomach ache magesmerte *c* 141
stools avføring *c* 142
stop *(place)* holdeplass *c*, 72
stop, to stanse 21, 68, 72; stå 70
stop thief! stopp tyven! 156
store *(shop)* butikk *c* 98, 99; forretning *c* 98, 99
straight *(drink)* bar 58
straight ahead rett frem 21, 77
strange underlig 84
strawberry jordbær *nt* 54, 55
stream bekk *c* 85
street gate *c* 77
streetcar trikk *c* 72
street map kart *nt* 19, 105
string hyssing *c* 105; *(of pearls)* perlekjede *nt* 121
strong sterk 126, 143
student student *c* 82, 93
study, to studere 93
stuffed fylt 49, 51
sturdy robust 101; solid 101
styling gel hårgelé *c* 111
subway *(railway)* T-bane *c* 73
suede semsket skinn *nt* 114, 118
sugar sukker *nt* 37, 64
suit *(man's)* dress *c* 117; *(woman's)* drakt *c* 117
suitcase koffert *c* 18
summer sommer *c* 149
sun sol *c* 94
sunburn solforbrenning *c* 108, 141
Sunday søndag *c* 150
sunglasses solbriller *c/pl* 123
sunshade *(beach)* parasoll *c* 91

sun-tan cream solkrem *c* 110
sun-tan oil sololje *c* 111
super *(petrol)* super 75
superb ypperlig 84
supermarket supermarked *nt* 99
suppository stikkpille *c* 109
surgery *(consulting room)* legekontor *nt* 137
surname etternavn *nt* 25
suspenders *(Am.)* (bukse)seler *c/pl* 117
swallow, to svelge 143
sweater genser *c* 117
sweat suit treningsdrakt *c* 117
Sweden Sverige 146
sweet søt 58, 60
sweet *(confectionery)* godter *nt/pl* 126
sweet corn mais *c* 51
sweetener søtningsmiddel *nt* 37
sweet pepper paprika *c* 51
sweet shop godtebutikk *c* 99
swelling hevelse *c* 139
swim, to bade 90; svømme 90
swimming svømming *c* 90
swimming pool badebasseng *nt* 32; svømmebasseng *nt* 23, 90
swimming trunks badebukse *c* 117
swimsuit badedrakt *c* 117
switch *(electric)* bryter *c* 29
switch on, to sette i gang 119
switchboard operator sentralbordbetjent *c* 26
swollen hoven 139
synagogue synagoge *c* 84
synthetic syntetisk 114
system system *nt* 138

T

table bord *nt* 36; *(list)* tabell *c* 157
tablet *(medical)* tablett *c* 109, 143
tailor's skredder *c* 99
tail pipe eksosrør *nt* 78
take, to ta 18, 25, 60, 73, 76, 102
take away, to *(carry)* ta med seg 62
talcum powder talkum *c* 111
tampon tampong *c* 109
tap *(water)* kran *c* 28
tap beer fatøl *nt* 56
taste, to smake 60
tax skatt *c* 131
tax-free shop tax-free-butikk *c* 19
taxi drosje *c* 18, 19, 21, 31, 67
taxi rank/stand drosjeholdeplass *c* 21
tea te *c* 38, 59, 64
team lag *nt* 89
teashop konditori *nt* 33
teaspoon teskje *c* 107, 143
telegram telegram *nt* 133
telegraph office telesenter *nt* 99, 133
telephone telefon *c* 27, 28, 79, 134
telephone, to *(call)* ringe 134, 136
telephone booth telefonkiosk *c* 134
telephone call (telefon)samtale *c* 136; telefon *c* 136
telephone directory telefonkatalog *c* 134
telephone number (telefon-nummer *nt* 134, 135, 136
telephoto lens teleobjektiv *nt* 125
television TV *c* 23, 28, 119
telex telex *c* 133
telex, to sende telex 130
tell, to si 13, 76, 153
temperature temperatur *c* 142; *(fever)* feber *c* 140
temporary provisorisk 145
ten ti 147
tendon sene *c* 138
tennis tennis *c* 89
tennis court tennisbane *c* 89
tennis match tenniskamp *c* 89
tennis racket (tennis)racket *c* 90
tent telt *nt* 32, 107
tent peg teltplugg *c* 107
tent pole teltstang *c* 107
terrible forferdelig 84
tetanus stivkrampe *c* 140
than enn 14
thank, to takke 10, 95, 96
that den 161; det 11, 100, 161
theatre teater *nt* 82, 86
theft tyveri *nt* 156
their deres 161
then da 15
there der 14
thermometer termometer *nt* 109
these disse 62, 161
they de 162; dem 162
thief tyv *c* 156
thigh lår *nt* 138
thin tynn 113
think, to *(believe)* tro 31, 94
thirsty tørst 13, 35
thirteen tretten 147
thirty tretti 147

this denne 161; dette 11, 100, 161
those dem 62, 120; de 161
thousand tusen 148
thread tråd *c* 27
three tre 147
throat hals *c* 138, 141
throat lozenge halstablett *c* 109
through gjennom 15; til 151
through train gjennomgående tog *nt* 68, 69
thumb tommel *c* 138
thumbtack tegnestift *c* 105
thunder torden *c* 94
thunderstorm tordenvær *nt* 94
Thursday torsdag *c* 150
ticket billett *c* 65, 69, 72, 87, 89
ticket office billettluke *c* 67
tie slips *nt* 117
tie clip slipsklype *c* 122
tie pin slipsnål *c* 122
tight *(close-fitting)* trang 116
tights strømpebukse *c* 117
time tid *c* 80; *(occasion)* gang *c* 95, 148; *(clock)* klokken 153
timetable rutetabell *c* 68
tin *(container)* boks *c* 120
tin opener boksåpner *c* 107
tint hårtoningsmiddel *nt* 111
tinted farget 123
tire dekk *nt* 75
tired trett 13
tissue *(handkerchief)* papirlommetørkle *nt* 111
tissue paper silkepapir *nt* 105
to til 15; å 162
toast ristet brød *nt* 38
tobacco tobakk *c* 126
tobacconist's tobakkshandel *c* 99, 126
today i dag 29, 150, 151
toe tå *c* 138
toilet paper toalettpapir *nt* 111
toiletries bag toalettmappe *c* 111
toiletry toalettartikkel *c* 110
toilets toalett *nt* 27, 32, 67
toilet water eau de toilette *c* 111
tomato tomat *c* 51
tomato juice tomatjuice *c* 43
tomb grav *c* 82
tomorrow i morgen 29, 94, 96, 151
tongue tunge *c* 48, 138
tonic tonic *c* 58
tonight i kveld 29, 86, 87, 88, 96
tonsils mandler *c/pl* 138
too for 15, 19; *(also)* også 15, 75
tool verktøy *nt* 78
too much for mye 15
tooth tann *c* 145
toothache tannpine *c* 145
toothbrush tannbørste *c* 111, 119
toothpaste tannpasta *c* 111
torch *(flashlight)* lommelykt *c* 107
torn avslitt 140
tough *(meat)* seig 60
tour tur *c* 74, 80
tourist office turistkontor *nt* 22, 80
towards mot 15
towel håndkle *nt* 111
tower tårn *nt* 82
town by *c* 19, 88
town hall rådhus *nt* 82
towrope slepetau *nt* 78
tow truck kranbil *c* 78
toy leke *c* 128
toy shop leketøysbutikk *c* 99
track *(railway)* spor *nt* 67, 68, 69
track-and-field meeting friidrettsstevne *nt* 89
tracksuit treningsdrakt *c* 117
traffic trafikk *c* 76
traffic light trafikklys *nt* 77
trailer campingvogn *c* 32
train tog *nt* 66, 67, 68, 69, 70
tram trikk *c* 72
tranquillizer beroligende middel *nt* 143
transfer *(finance)* overføring *c* 131
transformer transformator *c* 119
translate, to oversette 12
translation oversettelse *c* 131
translator oversetter *c* 131
transport transport *c* 74
travel, to reise 93
travel agency reisebyrå *nt* 99
travel guide reisehåndbok *c* 105
traveller's cheque reisesjekk *c* 18, 61, 102, 130
travel sickness reisesyke *c* 108
treatment behandling *c* 143
tree tre *nt* 85
tremendous forskrekkelig 84
trim, to *(a beard)* stusse 31
trip reise *c* 93, 152; tur *c* 74
troll troll *nt* 127
trolley tralle *c* 18, 71
trousers langbukser *c/pl* 117
trout ørret *c* 46; aure *c* 45
try, to forsøke 136; *(sample)* prøve 42, 57
try on, to prøve 115

DICTIONARY

Ordliste

T-shirt T-skjorte *c* 117
tube tube *c* 120
Tuesday tirsdag *c* 150
tumbler drikkeglass *nt* 107
turkey kalkun *c* 50
turn, to *(change direction)* svinge 21
turtleneck høyhalset 117
tweezers pinsett *c* 111
twelve tolv 147
twenty tjue 147
twice to ganger 148
twin beds to senger *c/pl* 23
two to 147
typewriter skrivemaskin *c* 27
typically typisk 127
typing paper skrivemaskinpapir *nt* 105
tyre dekk *nt* 75

U

ugly stygg 14, 84
umbrella paraply *c* 117
uncle onkel *c* 93
unconscious bevisstløs 139
under under 15
underdone *(meat)* råstekt 49; for lite stekt 60
underground *(railway)* T-bane *c* 73
underpants underbukse *c* 117
undershirt trøye *c* 117
understand, to forstå 12, 16
undress, to kle av seg 142
United States USA 146
university universitet *nt* 82
unleaded blyfri 75
until til 15, 150
up opp 15, 155
upper over- 69
upset stomach urolig mage *c* 108
upstairs oppe 15; opp trappen 69
urgent, to be haste 13
urine urin *c* 142
use bruk *c* 17, 109
useful nyttig 15
usual vanlig 143

V

vacancy ledig rom *nt* 23
vacant ledig 14
vacation ferie *c* 16, 151, 152
vaccinate, to vaksinere 140
vacuum flask termosflaske *c* 107
vaginal infection underlivs-betennelse *c* 141
valid gyldig 65
valley dal *c* 85
value verdi *c* 131
value-added tax moms *c* 24, 102
vanilla vanilje *c* 55
VAT *(sales tax)* moms *c* 154
veal kalvekjøtt *nt* 47; kalve- 48
vegetable grønnsak *c* 40, 51
vegetable store grønnsakhandel *c* 99
vegetarian vegetar(isk) 37, 40
vein vene *c* 138; åre *c* 138
venereal disease kjønnssykdom *c* 142
venetian blind persienne *c* 29
venison rådyr *nt* 50
very meget 15
vest trøye *c* 117; *(Am.)* vest *c* 117
veterinarian dyrlege *c* 99
video camera videokamera *nt* 124
video cassette videokassett *c* 119, 124, 127
video recorder videokassett-opptaker *c* 119
view *(panorama)* utsikt *c* 23, 25
viking ship vikingskip *nt* 127
village tettsted *nt* 76
vinegar eddik *c* 37
visit besøk *nt* 92; *(stay)* opphold *nt* 25
visiting hours besøkstid *c* 144
visit, to *(a person)* besøke 95; *(a place)* se 84
vitamin pill vitaminpille *c* 109
voltage strømstyrke *c* 119
vomit, to kaste opp 140

W

waffle vaffel *c* 55
waistcoat vest *c* 117
wait, to vente 108
wait for, to vente på 21, 95
waiter kelner *c* 26; servitør *c* 26
waiting room ventesal *c* 67
waitress serveringsdame *c* 26; servitør *c* 26
wake, to vekke 27, 71
Wales Wales 146
walk, to spasere 74, 85
wall mur *c* 85
wallet lommebok *c* 156
walnut valnøtt *c* 54
want, to *(wish)* ønske 13
warm varm 94
wash, to vaske 29

washbasin vask *c* 28
washcloth ansiktsklut *c* 111
washing powder vaskepulver *nt* 107
watch klokke *c* 121, 122
watchmaker's urmaker *c* 99, 121
watchstrap klokkerem *c* 122
water vann *nt* 23, 28, 32, 38, 75, 91
watercolors *(box of)* malerskrin *nt* 105
waterfall foss *c* 85
water flask feltflaske *c* 107
watermelon vannmelon *c* 54
waterproof vanntett 122
water-ski vannski *c* 91
way vei *c* 76, 77
we vi 162
weak svak 140
weather vær *nt* 94
weather forecast værutsikter *c/pl* 94
wedding ring giftering *c* 122
Wednesday onsdag *c* 150
week uke *c* 16, 20, 24, 80, 151
weekday hverdag *c* 151
weekend helg *c* 24; weekend *c* 20, 151
well bra 10
well brønn *c* 85
well-done *(meat)* godt stekt 49
west vest 77
what hva 11
wheel hjul *nt* 78
when når 11
where hvor 11
which hvilken 11
whipped cream pisket krem *c* 55
white hvit 113
Whit Monday 2. pinsedag *c* 152
who hvem 11
whole hel 49
why hvorfor 11
wick veke *c* 126
wide vid 118
wide-angle lens vidvinkelobjektiv *nt* 125
wife kone *c* 93
wig parykk *c* 111
wild duck villand *c* 50
wind vind *c* 94
window vindu *nt* 28, 36, 100, 112
window seat vindusplass *c* 65, 69
windscreen/shield frontrute *c* 76
windsurfer seilbrett *nt* 91
wine vin *c* 57, 60, 64
wine list vinkart *nt* 57
wine merchant's vinmonopol *nt* 99
winter vinter *c* 149
winter sports vintersport *c* 91
wiper *(car)* vindusvisker *c* 75
wish gratulasjon *c*/ønske *nt* 152
with med 15
withdraw, to *(from account)* ta ut 130
without uten 15
woman kvinne *c* 115, 156
woman's ... dame- 117
wood *(material)* tre *nt* 127
woodcock rugde *c* 50
woodgrouse tiur *c* 50
wool ull *c* 114
word ord *nt* 12, 15, 133
work arbeid *nt* 79
work, to *(function)* fungere 119; virke 28
working day arbeidsdag *c* 151
worse verre 14
wound sår *nt* 139
wrap up, to pakke inn 103
wrapping paper innpakningspapir *nt* 105
wrinkle-free krøllfri 114
wristwatch armbåndsur *nt* 122
write, to skrive 12, 101
writing pad skriveblokk *c* 105
writing paper skrivepapir *nt* 105
wrong feil 14, 135

X

X-ray, to røntgenfotografere 140

Y

year år *nt* 149
yellow gul 113
yes ja 10
yesterday i går 151
yet ennå 15, 16
yoghurt yoghurt *c* 38
you du 162
young ung 14, 149
your din, ditt (*pl* dine) 161
youth hostel vandrerhjem *nt* 22, 32

Z

zero null 147
zip(per) glidelås *c* 117
zoo dyrehage *c* 82
zoology zoologi *c* 83

Norsk register

BERLITZ® Books for travellers

TRAVEL GUIDES • COUNTRY GUIDES

They fit your pocket in both size and price. Modern, up-to-date, Berlitz gets all the information you need into 128 lively pages – 192 or 256 pages for country guides – with colour maps and photos throughout. What to see and do, where to shop, what to eat and drink, how to save.

AFRICA	• Algeria (256 pages) Kenya Morocco South Africa Tunisia
ASIA, MIDDLE EAST	• China (256 pages) Hong Kong • India (256 pages) • Japan (256 pages) Nepal Singapore Sri Lanka Thailand Egypt Jerusalem & Holy Land Saudi Arabia
AUSTRAL-ASIA	• Australia (256 pages) New Zealand
BELGIUM	Brussels
BRITISH ISLES	Channel Islands London Ireland Oxford and Stratford Scotland

FRANCE	Brittany • France (256 pages) French Riviera Loire Valley Normandy Paris NEW: • Paris Address Book
GERMANY	Berlin Munich The Rhine Valley
AUSTRIA, SWITZERLAND	Tyrol Vienna • Switzerland (192 pages)
GREECE, CYPRUS & TURKEY	Athens Corfu Crete Rhodes Greek Islands of Aegean Peloponnese Salonica/North. Greece Cyprus Istanbul/Aegean Coast • Turkey (192 pages)
ITALY and MALTA	Florence Italian Adriatic Italian Riviera • Italy (256 pages) Rome Sicily Venice Malta
NETHER-LANDS and SCANDI-NAVIA	Amsterdam Copenhagen Helsinki Oslo and Bergen Stockholm

PORTUGAL	Algarve Lisbon Madeira
SPAIN	Barcelona/Costa Dorada Canary Islands Costa Blanca Costa Brava Costa del Sol & Andalusia Ibiza and Formentera Madrid Majorca and Minorca
EASTERN EUROPE	Budapest Dubrovnik & S. Dalmatia ● Hungary (192 pages) Istria and Croatian Coast Moscow & Leningrad Prague Split and Dalmatia ● Yugoslavia (256 pages)
NORTH AMERICA	● U.S.A. (256 pages) California Florida Hawaii Miami New York Washington* ● Canada (256 pages) Montreal Toronto
CARIBBEAN, LATIN AMERICA	Puerto Rico Virgin Islands Bahamas Bermuda French West Indies Jamaica Southern Caribbean Mexico City Brazil (Highlights of) Rio de Janeiro
EUROPEAN	Business Travel Guide – Pocket guides: Europe/ Cities of Europe Handbook to Train Travel
CRUISE GUIDES	Caribbean Alaska Handbook to Cruising

DELUXE GUIDES
combine complete travel guide, phrase book and dictionary in one book.
Titles available:
Amsterdam, Barcelona, Budapest, Florence, French Riviera, Madrid, Mexico, Munich, Paris, Rome, Venice.

SKI GUIDES
Top resorts rated, where to ski, colour maps:
Austria
France
Italy
Switzerland

Handbook to
Skiing the Alps

BLUEPRINT GUIDES
Imaginative new large size guide with mapped itineraries special interest checklists, selected restaurant and hotel recommendations, large-scale road atlas, all in full colour.

France, Germany,* Britain, Greece, Hungary, Italy, Spain.

MORE FOR THE $
Over $ 4'000 worth of discount coupons and gift certificates from the finest hotels and restaurants for each country covered: France, Italy.

*in preparation

PHRASE BOOKS

World's bestselling phrase books feature all the expressions and vocabulary you'll need, and pronunciation throughout. 192 pages, 2 colours.

Arabic
Chinese
Danish
Dutch
Finnish
French
German
Greek
Hebrew
Hungarian
Italian
Japanese
Korean
Norwegian
Polish
Portuguese
Russian
Serbo-Croatian
Spanish (Castilian)
Spanish (Lat. Am.)
Swahili
Swedish
Turkish
European Phrase Book
European Menu Reader

All of the above phrase books are available with C60 or C90 cassette and miniscript as a "**cassettepak**".

Cassette and miniscript only are also available in the major languages as a "**phrase cassette**".

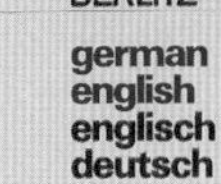

DICTIONARIES

Bilingual with 12,500 concepts each way. Highly practical for travellers, with pronunciation shown plus menu reader, basic expressions and useful information. Over 330 pages.

Danish
Dutch
Finnish
French
German
Italian
Norwegian
Portuguese
Spanish
Swedish

TRAVEL VIDEO

Travel Tips from Berlitz are now part of the informative and colourful videocassette series of over 80 popular destinations produced by Travelview International. Ideal for planning a trip, Travelview videos provide 40 to 60 minutes of valuable destination briefing and a Reference Guide to local hotels and tourist attractions. Available from leading travel agencies and video stores everywhere in the U.S.A. and Canada or call 1-800-325-3108 (Texas, call (713) 975-7077; (403) 248-7170 in Canada; (5) 531-8714 in Mexico City).